Web Performance Engineering in the Age of AI
Mastering Speed and Quality for AI-Generated Applications

Addy Osmani

Web Performance Engineering in the Age of AI

by Addy Osmani

Copyright © 2026 Addy Osmani. All rights reserved.

Published by O'Reilly Media, Inc., 141 Stony Circle, Suite 195, Santa Rosa, CA 95401.

O'Reilly books may be purchased for educational, business, or sales promotional use. Online editions are also available for most titles (*https://oreilly.com*). For more information, contact our corporate/institutional sales department: 800-998-9938 or *corporate@oreilly.com*.

Acquisitions Editor: Louise Corrigan
Development Editor: Sarah Grey
Production Editor: Elizabeth Faerm
Copyeditor: nSight, Inc.
Proofreader: Carol McGillivray

Indexer: nSight, Inc.
Cover Designer: Susan Brown
Cover Illustrator: José Marzan Jr.
Interior Designer: David Futato
Interior Illustrator: Kate Dullea

February 2026: First Edition

Revision History for the First Edition
2026-02-12:   First Release

See *https://oreilly.com/catalog/errata.csp?isbn=9798341660199* for release details.

The O'Reilly logo is a registered trademark of O'Reilly Media, Inc. *Web Performance Engineering in the Age of AI*, the cover image, and related trade dress are trademarks of O'Reilly Media, Inc.

The views expressed in this work are those of the author and do not represent the publisher's views. While the publisher and the author have used good faith efforts to ensure that the information and instructions contained in this work are accurate, the publisher and the author disclaim all responsibility for errors or omissions, including without limitation responsibility for damages resulting from the use of or reliance on this work. Use of the information and instructions contained in this work is at your own risk. If any code samples or other technology this work contains or describes is subject to open source licenses or the intellectual property rights of others, it is your responsibility to ensure that your use thereof complies with such licenses and/or rights.

979-8-341-66019-9

[LSI]

Table of Contents

Preface... xi

Part I.   Performance Is User Experience

1. Why Performance Is User Experience.. 3
    The Cost of Slow: First Impressions and User Satisfaction   5
        The Psychology of Waiting   6
        Evaluating UX Performance: Key Metrics   7
    Performance for All: Ensuring UX Across Devices and Network Conditions   8
    Performance-First Design   10
        The RAIL Model: A User-Centric Performance Framework   10
        Designing for Performance from the Start   11
        Example   12

2. Measuring What Matters: Essential Metrics for User-Centric Performance.......... 13
    Lab Testing and Field Measurements   13
    The CWVs: Key Metrics   14
        Largest Contentful Paint (LCP): Viewing Content Quickly   15
        First Input Delay (FID) and Interaction to Next Paint (INP):
            Ready to React   16
        Cumulative Layout Shift (CLS): Visual Stability   17
        Other Important Metrics   17
    Interpreting and Acting on Reports   18
    Lab Tools   18
        Lighthouse: Performance Auditing   19
        Chrome DevTools Performance Panel:
            Deep Diagnostics with AI Assistance   21

WebPageTest: Realistic Testing and Advanced Analysis	24
Field Tools	27
Capturing CWVs in the Field with web-vitals.js	28
Leveraging CrUX and External Data	31
RUM Beyond Web Vitals	31
Using RUM Data to Drive Improvements	32
Setting Up Performance Budgets and Alerts	33
Case Study: Continuous Monitoring in Practice	34
Conclusion	35

3. AI-Generated Code and the Performance Paradox..................... 37

AI Outputs: Correct but Not Optimal	37
The Hidden Costs of AI-Generated Code	39
Taking Responsibility for Quality and Performance	41
AI-Aided Optimization: The Future?	43
Impact on the Overall Performance Landscape	44
The Human Role in the AI Era	44
A Concluding Thought on AI and Performance	45

Part II. Optimizing Web Performance in the Age of AI

4. Optimizing AI-Generated Frontends............................... 49

CWVs and AI-Generated Code	49
Common Performance Pitfalls in AI-Generated React Components	50
Layout Instability (Poor CLS)	50
Bloated Bundles and Slow Loading (Poor LCP)	52
Main-Thread Bottlenecks and Janky Interactions (Poor INP)	54
Neglected Accessibility and UX Feedback Loops	55
Improving an AI-Generated Component	56
Performance Profiling and the New AI-Assisted DevTools	61
Testing on Real Devices: The Ultimate Validation	64
Embracing AI's Speed While Preserving Quality	65

5. Inside the Browser: How Pages Load and Render...................... 67

Browser Basics	67
Multiprocess Architecture and the Main Thread	68
The Rendering Pipeline	69
The Preload Scanner and Prioritizing Resources	74
Scripts and the Event Loop	75
The RAIL Model	76
Rendering Performance Bottlenecks	77

    Advanced Browser Internals   78
        Chrome's Main-Thread Task Scheduler and Task Priorities   78
        Server-Side Rendering (SSR) and Hydration   80
        The Network Stack and Resource Loading   83
        Putting It Together: A Timeline of an Optimized Load   86
    Conclusion   90

6. Trade-Offs in Performance Optimizations.   **91**
    Balancing Different Performance Metrics   91
    Objective Metrics Versus Subjective Perception   92
    Common Trade-Offs   92
        Bundle Size Versus Network Overheads   92
        Frameworks Versus Vanilla JavaScript   94
        Micro-Optimizations Versus Maintainability   95
    Performance Budgets and Culture   96
    Knowing When to Stop Optimizing   97
    Conclusion   98

Part III. Optimizing JavaScript

7. The Cost of JavaScript.   **101**
    Understanding the Constraints   101
        Device Performance: CPUs, Memory, and the Mobile Gap   101
        Network Constraints: Bandwidth and (Especially) Latency   103
        Browser Architecture: The Main Thread, Parsing, and Execution   104
    The JavaScript Engine   105
        From Interpretation to JIT Compilation: Engine Evolution   106
        Background Compilation, Parsing, and GC   108
        The Limits of Engine Magic   109
    Backend JavaScript Performance   110
        Node.js and the Event Loop   110
        Backend-Specific Optimizations   111
        Monitoring and Observability   113
    Conclusion   113

Part IV. Managing Dependencies and Maintaining Quality

8. Introduction to Third-Party Scripts.   **117**
    Third-Party Code Is Everywhere   118
    Why Third-Party Scripts Affect Performance   119

Measuring Third-Party Scripts' Performance Impact	123
Inventory and Identification: Key Metrics and Indicators	123
Special Considerations for AI-Based Third-Party Scripts	124
Lighthouse and Chrome DevTools	124
WebPageTest (WPT)	125
Principles of Third-Party Optimization	127
Remove, Reduce, Replace	127
Think in Performance Budgets	128
Shifting Left: Involving Everyone	129
The Goal: Fast and Functional	129

9. Loading Third-Party Scripts... 131

Sequencing and Prioritizing	131
Identify Critical Scripts	132
Positioning Script Tags	132
Nonblocking Scripts: async and defer	133
Load Critical Third-Party Scripts Early (but Not Too Early)	134
Preserving Script Order	135
Establish Early Connections with Resource Hints	135
Summarizing Sequencing Best Practices	136
Lazy Loading Third-Party Content	137
Browser-Native Lazy Loading for Iframes	137
Custom Lazy Loading with IntersectionObserver	138
Trade-Offs	140
Example: Lazy Loading an Analytics Script	141
Facades and Click-to-Load Patterns	141
Implementing Click-to-Load	142
Trade-Offs	145
Conditional Loading	145
Device Detection for Performance	146
Network-Aware Loading	147
Trade-Offs	148
Conclusion	149

10. Scheduling and Optimizing Third-Party Scripts (and AI's Role)................... 151

Scheduling Third-Party Scripts	151
The requestIdleCallback API	151
After Onload or First Interaction	152
Idle Until Urgent (IUU) Pattern	153
Breaking Up Long Tasks	153
Using setTimeout as a Fallback or Simpler Option	154
Offloading and Sandboxing Third-Party Scripts	155

Web Workers and Partytown	155
Sandboxing in Iframes	156
Handling Third-Party Logic on the Server Side	157
Framework-Specific Optimizations: Next.js and Beyond	158
The Script Component in Next.js	158
Optimizing in Other Frameworks	161
Optimizing by Site Type	162
Handling Third-Party Scripts in SPAs Versus Multipage Applications (MPAs)	162
Tag Manager Performance Tuning	164
WordPress and Content Management System (CMS) Platforms	164
Ecommerce Sites	166
AI's Role in Third-Party Script Optimization	168

Part V. The Future of Web Performance

11. Building a Performance Culture. 173
Performance as a Feature	173
Educating and Equipping the Team	174
Have a Champion Keep Performance Front of Mind	175
Integrating Performance into Your CI/CD Pipeline and Workflow	176
Leveraging AI for Performance Culture	177
Conclusion	178

12. Web Performance Case Studies and Success Stories. 179
Ecommerce and Retail Performance Wins	182
Rakuten 24: A/B Testing for CWV ROI	182
Vodafone: Faster Landing Page, Higher Sales	183
Shopify's Merchant Stores: Sunday Citizen	184
Shopify's Merchant Stores: Carpe	184
Ray-Ban: Prerendering	185
News and Media: Boosting Engagement with Speed	186
The Telegraph Media Group	186
The Economic Times: Passing CWV at Scale	187
Yahoo! Japan News: Correlating CLS Fixes to Engagement	189
Travel and Hospitality: Speeding Up Booking Experiences	191
redBus: Improving INP for Better Sales	192
Bookaway: Serving a Global Audience with Static Content	193
Finance and Fintech: Building Trust with Speed	194
Financer.com: Speeding Up WordPress for Conversions and SEO	195
AI and Performance: Emerging Success Stories	196

  Vercel: AI-Powered Image Optimization at Scale   196
  Cloudflare: Machine Learning for Performance Prediction   197
  Google Chrome: AI-Assisted Speculation Rules   198
  AI Coding Assistants: A Performance Cautionary Tale   199
  Shopify: AI for Merchant Store Optimization   200
 Key Takeaways   201
 Conclusion   203

13. The Future of Web Performance with AI 205
 The AI Revolution in Web Development   205
 Practical Strategies for the AI Era   206
 Streaming-First AI Interfaces and User Experience:
  A New Performance Paradigm   207
 Streaming Text   209
  Metrics   209
  Performance Budgets   210
  Rendering Tactics   210
  Transport Layer Choices   211
  Perceived Speed Patterns   212
 Streaming UI Components   213
  Streaming UI Metrics   213
  Rendering Tactics for Streaming Components   214
  Failure Modes to Watch   215
 Streaming Content and Media   215
  Lists and Feeds That Grow in Place   215
  Audio and Video Generation or Text to Speech (TTS)   216
  Images That Arrive Progressively   216
 Scheduling and Responsiveness Under Load   217
 Network and Server Pipeline Considerations   218
  Remove Cold-Start Penalties   218
  Implement Backpressure   218
  Cache Smartly   218
  Chunk Thoughtfully   219
 CWV in a Streaming World   219
 Observability and Debugging Streaming Systems   220
  Instrument the Streaming Path with Performance Marks   220
  Build a Stream Trace View   221
  Alert on Stall Patterns   221
 Accessibility   222
 Internationalization   222
 Privacy   222
 Safety   223

Energy and Cost Awareness	223
Design Patterns to Prefer	224
Antipatterns to Avoid	225
A Practical Checklist for Production	226
Conclusion	227

Index... **229**

Preface

On today's web, the difference between a fluid, delightful experience and a frustrating, abandoned one often comes down to milliseconds. Performance is not just a technical metric; it is the bedrock of user satisfaction and business success. At the same time, AI-assisted tools have changed how we design, build, and ship those experiences. We can now generate production-ready frontends or entire apps in minutes, but their performance characteristics still live in the real constraints of browsers, devices, and networks. *Web Performance Engineering in the Age of AI* is a comprehensive guide for engineers and technical leaders who need to deliver fast, responsive, and resilient web experiences in this AI-accelerated era. I'm Addy Osmani, an engineering leader on Google Chrome's web performance team, and in this book I've encapsulated the latest techniques, metrics, browser internals, and AI-aware practices that define modern performance work.

Who Should Read This Book?

This book is for frontend developers, web performance engineers, and technical decision-makers who understand the basics of building websites and are driven to create experiences users *love* by mastering performance optimization. Whether you already lean on tools like Cursor, GitHub Copilot, ChatGPT, Gemini or other LLM-based assistants for day-to-day coding, or are just beginning to bring AI into your workflow, the goal is to help you ship experiences that stay fast and robust regardless of how the code was written. We assume you have some familiarity with HTML, CSS, and JavaScript. From there, we dive deep into the principles and practices required to build and maintain high-performing web applications, including the new realities of AI-generated and AI-augmented code.

What You Will Learn

This book takes a user-experience-first approach, grounding advanced optimization techniques in the fundamental principles of how users perceive and interact with the web. You will learn:

- Why performance *is* user experience, understanding human perception thresholds and the business impact of speed (Part I)
- How to measure and interpret modern performance metrics, particularly the Core Web Vitals (LCP, INP, CLS), and use them to guide optimization efforts (Parts I and II)
- How browsers fetch resources, parse code, render layouts, and paint pixels, providing the foundation needed to optimize each stage (Part II)
- Specific, actionable strategies for optimizing each Core Web Vital, addressing common bottlenecks in loading, interactivity, and layout stability (Part II)
- The inherent costs of JavaScript—network, parsing, compilation, and execution—and modern techniques like code splitting, lazy loading, hydration strategies, and scheduling APIs to mitigate them (Part III)
- How AI-generated code changes the performance landscape: why large language model (LLM) outputs tend to be "correct but not optimal," common pitfalls in AI-generated frontends, and concrete review and optimization techniques you can apply to keep AI-written code fast, accessible, and maintainable (Parts I and II)
- How to work with AI-assisted tooling itself: using Chrome DevTools' AI features, Lighthouse, and the Chrome DevTools Model Context Protocol (MCP) to analyze traces, surface long tasks, and iterate on focused performance fixes while keeping a human in the loop (Part II)
- How to effectively identify, audit, and optimize the performance impact of ubiquitous third-party scripts—including AI-powered widgets and chatbots—using removal, deferral, lazy loading, facades, offloading (web workers and server side), and conditional loading strategies (Part IV)
- How to leverage both laboratory tools (Lighthouse, Chrome DevTools, WebPageTest) and field monitoring (RUM, web-vitals library) to diagnose issues and track improvements continuously (Parts II and IV)
- How performance optimization translates into real-world success through practical case studies across various industries (Part V), including how teams are adapting their practices as AI-generated code and AI-powered experiences become more common

Structure of the Book

The book is structured into five distinct parts, building progressively from foundational concepts to specific challenges and real-world applications:

Part I, "Performance Is User Experience"
Establishes the crucial link between web performance and user satisfaction. We explore human perception of speed, introduce key user-centric metrics like Core Web Vitals, discuss designing for diverse devices and network conditions, and cover the importance of building a performance culture. This part also looks at how AI-assisted development changes engineering workflows, and why the fundamentals of latency, responsiveness, and stability remain nonnegotiable regardless of who—or what—typed the code.

Part II, "Optimizing Web Performance in the Age of AI"
Dives into the technical details. We start with how browsers work under the hood (networking, rendering pipeline, scheduling), and then dedicate chapters to optimizing each Core Web Vital (LCP, INP, CLS) with specific techniques, including advanced browser internals and essential measurement tooling. We then extend these fundamentals to AI-generated frontends and AI-assisted workflows: how to review and harden LLM-written UI code, how to use DevTools' AI analysis and MCP-driven agents responsibly, and how to keep Core Web Vitals as the source of truth when AI is suggesting or modifying code.

Part III, "Optimizing JavaScript"
Focuses specifically on JavaScript, the engine of the interactive web but often a major performance bottleneck. We analyze its costs (CPU, network, memory), explore modern loading and execution strategies (code splitting, SSR/hydration, scheduling APIs), examine JS engine evolution, and discuss the trade-offs involved in optimization. This part also highlights how AI-generated JavaScript tends to amplify existing problems—larger bundles, heavier frameworks, more churn—and offers patterns for keeping that complexity under control.

Part IV, "Managing Dependencies and Maintaining Quality"
Tackles the pervasive challenge of external scripts, including traditional analytics and ads as well as newer AI-backed experiences like chatbots and recommendation widgets. We cover methods for identifying their impact, principles for optimization (removal, deferral, lazy loading, facades), conditional loading strategies for low-end devices and slow networks, offloading techniques (like Web Workers and Partytown), framework-specific solutions (e.g., Next.js's Script component), and building processes for managing them effectively across teams.

Part V, "The Future of Web Performance"
> Presents a collection of recent (2021–2025) real-world case studies. These showcase how companies across different verticals (ecommerce, media, travel, finance) successfully implemented performance optimizations, improved their Core Web Vitals, and achieved significant business results—often while adopting AI tooling and grappling with AI-generated code in production.

Throughout the book, we remain largely framework agnostic when discussing fundamentals, but provide specific examples where relevant to illustrate concepts. Where AI is involved, the emphasis is on using it as an accelerator rather than an autopilot: you will see how to treat AI like a very fast junior developer and how to wrap its output in the same profiling, review, and testing discipline you would apply to any other codebase.

By the end of this book, the goal is that you will not only know *what* to do to optimize web performance but also *why* those techniques work and how to apply them confidently in an environment where AI is writing more of the code and assisting more of the tooling. You will be prepared to evaluate and improve the performance of any web project—human-written, AI-generated, or (most realistically) a mix of both—ensuring your users enjoy the fast, seamless, and reliable experiences they deserve, all achieved through a systematic, metrics-driven approach.

Conventions Used in This Book

The following typographical conventions are used in this book:

Italic
> Indicates new terms, URLs, email addresses, filenames, and file extensions.

`Constant width`
> Used for program listings, as well as within paragraphs to refer to program elements such as variable or function names, databases, data types, environment variables, statements, and keywords.

 This element signifies a tip or suggestion.

O'Reilly Online Learning

For more than 40 years, *O'Reilly Media* has provided technology and business training, knowledge, and insight to help companies succeed.

Our unique network of experts and innovators share their knowledge and expertise through books, articles, and our online learning platform. O'Reilly's online learning platform gives you on-demand access to live training courses, in-depth learning paths, interactive coding environments, and a vast collection of text and video from O'Reilly and 200+ other publishers. For more information, visit *https://oreilly.com*.

How to Contact Us

Please address comments and questions concerning this book to the publisher:

O'Reilly Media, Inc.
141 Stony Circle, Suite 195
Santa Rosa, CA 95401
800-889-8969 (in the United States or Canada)
707-827-7019 (international or local)
707-829-0104 (fax)
support@oreilly.com
https://oreilly.com/about/contact.html

We have a web page for this book, where we list errata and any additional information. You can access this page at *https://oreil.ly/web-performance-engineering*.

For news and information about our books and courses, visit *https://oreilly.com*.

Find us on LinkedIn: *https://linkedin.com/company/oreilly-media*.

Watch us on YouTube: *https://youtube.com/oreillymedia*.

Acknowledgments

This book wouldn't be possible without the collective knowledge of the web performance community. I would like to thank my colleagues on the Chrome team, including Annie Sullivan, who leads Chrome's Speed Metrics team (the group behind Core Web Vitals) and has tirelessly worked to make user-centric performance metrics a cornerstone of web development. I would also like to thank Paul Irish, Elizabeth Sweeny, Victor Porof, and Tze Yi Tan, who have led much of the Chrome Performance Tooling work over time. Thanks to Google web performance advocates like Philip Walton and Jeremy Wagner, who have authored many of the guides referenced in this book and developed the web-vitals library that makes measuring real-user performance simpler.

I am grateful to performance experts outside Google as well. Yoav Weiss's work on resource hints and priority optimizations (and his contributions to standards like Priority Hints (*https://oreil.ly/YP5Cx*)) have influenced the sections on loading optimizations. Thank you to Pat Meenan, the creator of WebPageTest, for pioneering real-world performance testing and providing tools that every webperf engineer uses. I also drew on insights from Tim Kadlec and Tammy Everts, who have long evangelized the business and user experience impact of performance. Barry Pollard's research and writing on optimizing Core Web Vitals (including extensive guides on LCP and CLS) were invaluable, as were contributions from others at web.dev and Chrome Developers. Rick Viscomi's analyses (*https://oreil.ly/nYdtD*) with the HTTP Archive (and the annual Web Almanac) provided important context on how the web is improving over time.

Finally, a special thanks to the developers and readers who push for better performance on the web. Your feedback, questions, and challenges drive the evolution of best practices. I hope this book equips you with the knowledge to tackle your performance goals and contributes in some small way to a faster, better web for everyone.

PART I
Performance Is User Experience

CHAPTER 1
Why Performance Is User Experience

> *You've got to start with the customer experience and work backward to the technology. You can't start with the technology, then try to figure out where to sell it.*
> —Steve Jobs, 1997 (*https://oreil.ly/_HYoc*)

These opening words from Steve Jobs set the stage: great technology begins with a relentless focus on the user's experience. In the world of web development, one of the most critical yet underappreciated aspects of user experience (UX) is *performance*. A site that loads quickly and responds instantaneously feels effortless and satisfying to use, whereas a slow, janky site breeds frustration. As the author of this book and a longtime engineer on the Google Chrome team, I've spent over a decade making the web faster and more user-centric. This includes working on modern challenges like optimizing AI-generated frontends and ensuring that increasingly complex web applications—powered by AI and other cutting-edge technologies—remain fast and responsive. In this solo project, I share insights and lessons learned from my experience leading performance initiatives (like Core Web Vitals [CWVs]) and real-world UX research and audits.

Using an app or site is like walking through a city: if you encounter constant stoplights, detours, or stumbling blocks, the journey becomes unpleasant. Likewise, every delay on a website—an unresponsive button, a long blank screen during load, a jerky scroll—feels like an obstacle in the user's journey, increasing stress and the chance that they'll give up. Users form an impression of a site within seconds, and a slow experience can erode trust in a brand. Studies have found that a significant portion of users won't return to a site if it was painfully slow or buggy on their first visit.

From the moment a user lands on a website or web app, performance begins to shape their opinion. *Speed itself* is a feature—often the very first feature users notice. Research in human-computer interaction (*https://oreil.ly/BE8Zp*) shows that even small delays can interrupt a user's "flow" and increase frustration. A classic rule of thumb from UX research (*https://oreil.ly/yW5Pr*) is that there are certain thresholds in response times that determine user perception: when a system reacts within about 0.1 s, it feels instant; a 1-s response delay keeps the interaction feeling seamless; but anything more than a few seconds starts to feel sluggish and makes the user acutely aware of waiting. Beyond about 10 s, most users become frustrated and may abandon the task altogether.

This book is written for intermediate to advanced software engineers who might be experts in coding or building features but who haven't yet fully embraced performance as a cornerstone of UX. I'll explore the science and principles that connect speed to usability, using a professional yet conversational tone. Along the way, I'll reference both academic research and industry case studies that quantify how much performance affects user satisfaction, engagement, and business success. I'll provide not just metrics and data but a structured narrative about why performance is essential to good UX and how to evaluate it in practice.

I'll start by examining why speed matters to users at a human level. I'll then dive into the metrics and models that help us measure web performance from the user's point of view, including the new Core Web Vitals. I'll discuss designing for a range of devices and network conditions, ensuring even users on low-end hardware or spotty networks get a pleasant experience. I'll look at frameworks like RAIL and tools like Lighthouse and Chrome User Experience Report (CrUX), which can guide our performance audits.

Rather than focusing on low-level optimization techniques, I'll initially stay at the level of principles, metrics, and outcomes—connecting the dots between a faster site and a happier user.

Later sections of this book will build upon this foundation. Part II dives into the technical details of browser rendering and specific techniques for optimizing the Core Web Vitals. Part III takes a deep dive into the performance costs associated with JavaScript and how to manage them effectively. Part IV focuses specifically on the challenges and solutions for optimizing ubiquitous third-party scripts. Finally, Part V reinforces these concepts with real-world case studies showcasing the impact of performance engineering in various industries, as well as advice on building a performance-first culture in your organization.

Throughout, you'll find references to research (by Google and others) that back up my advice, and you'll hear a perspective shaped by my work on Chrome's performance team. By the end, I hope to convince you that performance *is* user experience and that building a fast web is key to delighting customers.

The Cost of Slow: First Impressions and User Satisfaction

Speed is not just a "nice-to-have": it's closely tied to business metrics like bounce rate, conversion, and engagement. Numerous industry studies underline this point. The BBC observed in 2018 (*https://oreil.ly/EP3Dn*) that for every additional second their site took to load, it lost 10% of its users. This kind of loss compounds quickly; a few seconds of delay can nearly halve your audience. Even a one-second delay can cut conversion rates by a notable percentage (Walmart found that for every 1 second improvement (*https://oreil.ly/KWOxQ*) in page load time, conversions increased by 2%, and COOK increased conversions by 7% by reducing page load time by 0.85 s). These real-world numbers make a convincing argument that performance is intrinsically linked to business success and user loyalty.

Because performance is felt immediately, it heavily influences a user's first impression. A fast, smooth experience can convey professionalism and reliability to users, whereas a slow, stuttering experience suggests neglect and can damage credibility. Users' expectations have risen over time—they expect sites to be fast and responsive, often comparing web experiences to native apps. Patience is in short supply: one survey found (*https://oreil.ly/WTn2r*) many users wouldn't wait beyond a few seconds for content, especially on mobile. Delays can also cause anxiety too: "Did my click register, or has the app frozen?"

Internalize that *speed is a pillar of user experience*. Performance improvements aren't just technical tasks for bragging rights—they directly translate into happier users, better engagement, and even positive brand perception. Adopting this mindset prepares you to "work backward to the technology" with the user's needs (fast feedback, minimal waiting) always in focus as the guiding principle.

So what exactly counts as a *fast* experience for users? How slow is *too* slow?

A classic rule, originally noted by researchers like Robert B. Miller (*https://oreil.ly/Pda59*) (who studied response time in 1968) and later popularized by Jakob Nielsen (*https://oreil.ly/lFJWP*), holds that users perceive delays in tiers:

0.1 second or less
    Operations that happen in under a tenth of a second feel instantaneous. This is the threshold where interactions like clicking a button or toggling a UI element feel like there's no delay at all. It maintains the illusion of direct manipulation: the user feels in control because the interface reacts immediately.

Around one second
    A delay around one second is short enough that the user stays in flow, but they do start to notice the lapse. It's the approximate threshold for a seamless continuation of thought since it feels like a natural pause. Any longer, and they might feel the interface is working on something.

Two to nine seconds
> Delays that extend into a few seconds begin to tax the user's patience. Research shows (*https://oreil.ly/Kqfmj*) that user satisfaction drops as wait times increase into this range. People's exact tolerance can vary by context (for instance, a user might wait a bit longer for a video to load than for a search result), but generally, progress indicators or feedback become essential in this range to reassure the user that something is happening.

10 seconds or more
> If they don't see progress after about 10 s, most users will abandon what they're doing and navigate away or try a different approach. Even if they don't leave, their focus is broken: they might switch tasks or get distracted, severely degrading the experience.

The Psychology of Waiting

Let's connect these timing thresholds to cognitive and emotional reactions. Why does a delay of more than a second feel so frustrating? You may be familiar with the idea of *flow* (*https://oreil.ly/D2WA-*): the state of concentration where a user is fully engaged in a task. Interruptions break the user's flow, forcing them to remember what they were doing and resist the urge to divert their attention.

User tolerance can also depend on context: an urgent task like looking up emergency information might make any delay feel unbearable, whereas a casual browsing session might not test a user's patience. Personality plays a role too. There is no single "magic number" of seconds that works for everyone. Instead, you want to be as fast as possible for as many users as possible and certainly stay below the ranges where frustration skyrockets.

Performance issues aren't just minor annoyances—they can fundamentally break the user experience by causing mistakes, double submissions, or navigation to the wrong page. One such phenomenon is "rage clicks"—when a user repeatedly clicks or taps in frustration because the interface isn't responding. An Akamai UX study found (*https://oreil.ly/iPpls*) that rage clicking tends to occur when users try to interact with a page that *looks* ready but isn't actually interactive yet. In fact, many users begin interacting *before* the page is fully interactive; in over 30% of cases studied, pages were still not usable even after the onload event fired, and about 15% of users attempted to click between the moment the page was visually rendered and the moment it became interactive. When the site finally catches up, it might register multiple clicks or unintended actions. For instance, if a buy button lags, a user might tap it twice in frustration, accidentally purchasing two items.

Layout instability can cause errors too: if content shifts suddenly due to slowly loading ads or images, users might click the wrong thing (like a moving link or button), derailing their intended task.

If your app feels slow to respond, users will notice—and many will take action, whether that's hammering the interface, leaving your site, or mentally checking out. This is why you need to measure and improve performance carefully.

Evaluating UX Performance: Key Metrics

No single metric tells the whole story of a page load. The user's experience is a progression of moments, not one instant in time. Historically, developers have looked at metrics like *onload* (the moment when all resources finish loading) or simple stopwatch timings, but these often fail to capture what users actually care about. For example, a page might technically finish loading in 5 s, but if the content is visible and usable in 2 s, the user's *perceived* performance is much better than the onload time would suggest. Conversely, a page might show something at 2 s but remain unresponsive until 10 s due to heavy JavaScript, yielding a bad experience.

This section provides a quick high-level overview of what performance metrics are and why they're important. Chapter 2 will dive deeper into the details of this topic, including defining various metrics that are named briefly here.

Developers used to focus primarily on technical measures of performance, but these didn't always reflect the users' experience. I approach this by looking at four key moments in a loading experience that correspond to users' intuitive questions as the page loads:

Is it happening?
Did the site respond, or is my connection dead? This is the earliest stage. The user has clicked a link or entered a URL and wants confirmation that the page is actually loading. A quick response from the server and some initial paint on screen (even a background color or skeleton UI) can reassure the user that progress is under way.

Relevant metrics:

- First paint (FP)
- Time to first byte from the server

Is it useful?
How soon can the user consume or interact with the primary content? At this stage, it's not enough that something appears; it should be something relevant, like the main text or image on the page.

Relevant metrics:

- First contentful paint (FCP)
- Largest contentful paint (LCP)

Is it usable?
When is the page *ready* for user input without lag? This moment addresses interactivity. A page isn't truly "loaded" from a UX perspective until it's responsive to the user. Users often try to scroll or click as soon as they see content. A page that looks like it has loaded but doesn't respond to input is a tease. This lag often happens because JavaScript is initializing event handlers or hogging the CPU.

Relevant metrics:

- Time to interactive (TTI)
- Interaction to next paint (INP)

Is it delightful?
The final stage is about the smoothness and stability of the experience after the initial load. This includes things like smooth animations, scrolling, and absence of annoying glitches. Once the user starts interacting, the experience should remain consistently good. No one enjoys a site that lags every time you scroll or where pop-ups push content down unexpectedly—it's distracting and frustrating.

Relevant metrics:

- Frame rates
- Cumulative layout shift (CLS)

Performance for All: Ensuring UX Across Devices and Network Conditions

Not all users experience your site in the same environment. Real-world performance is influenced heavily by the user's device and network. A site that feels snappy on a developer's high-end laptop with fiber internet could be unbearably slow on a budget Android phone on a 3G network. To truly prioritize UX, you need to consider performance equity: delivering a usable, if not delightful, experience to as many users as possible, not just those with the latest hardware.

Let's start by comparing the capabilities of mobile devices and desktops. Mobile devices (especially low- to midrange ones) have different chips, significantly less CPU power, and often less memory than desktop computers. They also might be doing more, like background tasks or battery-saving throttling. This means heavy web pages tax them more. The majority of the world isn't using the latest iPhone: more than 60% of smartphones shipped globally (*https://oreil.ly/h9GxP*) in 2019 were midrange or low-end devices, not flagship iPhones or Samsungs. Many users will experience your site under constrained conditions.

Suppose your web app loads 2 MB of JavaScript. On a newer desktop with a cable connection from this decade, that might take 2 s to download and maybe 200 ms to execute, so perhaps 2.2 s total. On a midrange mobile on a 3G or spotty 4G or 5G network, that same 2 MB might take 8 to 10 s to download and 2 or more seconds to execute. Now we're looking at 12 s or more before it's interactive—a completely different experience. Devices can literally overheat or have their CPUs drop frequency during such loads, making things even worse over time. The user's context dramatically changes the performance envelope (the range of conditions under which your site must perform acceptably).

Think of the *tail* of your users. Maybe a 90th-percentile user (one of the slower cases) is on a five-year-old phone with a poor connection. Even if the "average" user is OK, if *this* user has to wait 10 or more seconds, that's a UX failure for a sizable chunk of the audience. I recommend setting performance budgets with these tail scenarios in mind (I'll expand on this in Part II of the book).

Mobile networks often have high latency (hundreds of milliseconds round-trip), which can severely slow down resource loading, especially if the site requires many sequential requests, which can be critical for things like handshakes or if resources aren't optimized. Bandwidth caps the throughput; large images or videos can be particularly slow on limited bandwidth.

According to some mobile UX research, mobile users *appear* slightly more patient: one source suggests (*https://oreil.ly/uV_8W*) many mobile users will wait 6 to 10 s before abandoning a page, possibly because they're used to things being slower on mobile. However, that doesn't mean you should aim for 6 s; it's more of a last-resort tolerance. In fact, Google's mobile benchmarks (*https://oreil.ly/Y2sFE*) say 53% of mobile site visits are abandoned if a page takes more than 3 s to load. Patience varies, but the safest course is to be as fast as possible on mobile too.

In some countries, data is costly, and most users in developing countries access the web primarily on low-end mobile devices. A slow site that forces multiple reloads or downloads can have a financial cost to the user. For these users, a 5 MB site or a heavy web app might be practically unusable. Respecting your users means considering these factors as well. True UX excellence means serving *all* your users well, not just those with the newest gear. Set performance budgets and expectations with mobile and global users in mind. Performance is relative, depending on where and how a user is accessing your site—and good engineers and UX practitioners account for that variability.

Performance-First Design

This section introduces some high-level principles for designing and building with performance in mind from the start. The advice here is more about mindset and guidelines than specific optimizations. It's about baking performance considerations into the design and architecture phases, not just tweaking at the end.

The RAIL Model: A User-Centric Performance Framework

Before we discuss Google's Core Web Vitals in Chapter 2, I want to introduce you to its predecessor. RAIL (*https://oreil.ly/XCHts*) is a slightly older model to guide UX performance thinking, also developed by Google's Chrome team. RAIL stands for the four steps of a web app's lifecycle and their corresponding performance goals: response, animation, idle, and load. The strength of RAIL is that it ties performance goals to what users perceive in different scenarios. Let's look at each component:

Response
> When the user initiates an action (tapping a button, starting an animation), the site should respond to that input quickly. RAIL's guideline is to process events within about 50 ms and update the UI by about 100 ms, so that the user feels it's instantaneous. I advise designers to avoid doing heavy work directly on input events that would delay feedback. If the user is working on something like a form submission, at least acknowledge the click immediately (visual feedback) and perhaps show a spinner to communicate that the action is in progress. If you can't respond fully within 100 ms, at least acknowledge within that time, then do the rest in the background.

Animation
> For things like scrolling, animations, or transitions, the goal is to keep them smooth—ideally 60 frames per second. This means each frame must be produced in 16 ms or less. Choppy animations and janky UI transitions degrade the experience of an otherwise fast app. RAIL reminds us to consider the postload interactions too.

Idle
> Use idle time wisely. This part of RAIL is about doing background work when the user isn't actively interacting, so as not to interfere with responsiveness. For example, after the main load, if the user is reading an article, the app might quietly preload the next page or do other low-priority work in small chunks, so that if the user suddenly interacts, the app can stop the background work and respond. Don't hog the thread with continuous work; break tasks up so the app remains responsive. Users value apps that *continue* to feel snappy.

Load
> Aim to deliver useful content quickly. RAIL suggested about one second for a mobile load; in practice, for complex sites, one second on mobile is hard, but the principle is to load and render core content as soon as possible. Within 2 to 5 s, the content should be fully interactive (depending on context). These are goals to strive for; every extra second hurts.

Table 1-1 shows RAIL's key performance goals.

Table 1-1. Key RAIL performance goals

RAIL component	Performance goal	Research basis
Response	<100 ms to respond to user input	Based on Jakob Nielsen's guidelines (*https://oreil.ly/ATq-z*) on perceived instantaneousness
Animation	60 fps (16 ms per frame)	Based on human visual system's ability to track motion smoothly
Idle	Use idle periods in ≤50 ms chunks	Allows the browser to remain responsive to user input
Load	<1 s to useful content on average device	Based on Robert Miller's research (*https://oreil.ly/ON8KJ*) on maintaining user flow and attention

Each goal is backed by user research on how delays affect perception and the overall user experience.

RAIL provides a mental model that helps engineers, developers, and designers focus on the user when thinking about performance.

Designing for Performance from the Start

It's a good design principle to set a *performance budget*: that is, limiting how "heavy" a page or app is allowed to be, so that it meets your performance goals. This might look something like "Our home page should be no more than 150 KB of critical JavaScript/CSS and 100 KB of images on initial load." The exact numbers aren't important here, but the practice is. You'll use your metrics (covered in Chapter 2) to derive this budget. If a certain script or feature will push you over budget and slow things down, that's a signal to reconsider or find another approach. Treat performance as a design constraint, not an afterthought: much like you wouldn't design a UI that doesn't fit on common screen sizes, don't design one that only works on top-tier devices or connections.

Progressive enhancement and *graceful degradation* are strategies to deliver acceptable performance universally. *Progressive enhancement* means to serve a simple layout and functionality to older browsers or very slow clients, then enhance it if the client can handle more. *Graceful degradation* is the complementary approach: you design for modern, capable browsers first but ensure the experience degrades gracefully (remains functional, if less feature-rich) on older or less capable devices. This way, everyone gets something rather than some getting nothing (or a terribly slow experience). From a UX perspective, it's better to have a simplified but fast experience than a flashy but unusable one.

Example

Imagine you're designing a travel booking site's search results page. A performance-first approach would mean only loading the first few results immediately (enough to show quickly). You'd defer loading images until they are needed or in view, and you'd show placeholders for things like maps rather than loading them up front. Think about what the user needs *first* and deliver that fast, then load any additional bells and whistles.

You can also use design reviews to talk about performance. When reviewing a new feature, ask how it will impact load time or interactivity. If a proposed feature would add 1 MB of script, consider alternatives: could it be done server side or after initial load? This is about culture as much as technique: making performance a criterion in decision making at all levels. (For more on performance culture, see Chapter 11.)

With these guiding principles and mental models to help you approach building fast experiences, I want you to feel equipped not just to measure and diagnose but to proactively design for speed. Performance isn't a technical afterthought; it's a design philosophy. If you start with that philosophy, you'll make smarter decisions from the get-go.

CHAPTER 2
Measuring What Matters: Essential Metrics for User-Centric Performance

In 2020, Google introduced a landmark effort to distill web performance into a few key metrics that everyone should focus on: Core Web Vitals (CWVs). This chapter takes an in-depth look at each of the CWVs and why they matter. As someone who worked on this effort, I provide a behind-the-scenes perspective on how we defined these metrics and the reasoning for their specific goals.

I'll structure this chapter by discussing each metric in turn, including what it measures, how to interpret it, and what the recommended targets (ranges for good, needs improvement, and poor) are. Importantly, I tie each metric to the UX outcome it represents and present some of the research ("the science behind Web Vitals") that validates its importance. This chapter offers a basic rundown of key metrics but doesn't go into great detail: for specifics on optimizing these metrics, see Chapter 6.

The three initial CWVs were largest contentful paint (LCP), first input delay (FID), and cumulative layout shift (CLS). FID was later replaced with interaction to next paint (INP). Each metric addresses one aspect of the page experience: loading speed, interactivity, and visual stability, respectively.

Lab Testing and Field Measurements

There are two fundamental approaches (*https://oreil.ly/eHJ86*): lab data (synthetic testing) and field data (real user data). Both are valuable, and they complement each other.

Lab testing is when you test a site's performance in a controlled environment: for example, running it through a tool like Lighthouse (see "Lab Tools" on page 18), which can simulate different devices and networks. Lab tests are great for reproducibility and debugging, because they eliminate the variability of real-world conditions. You can run a Lighthouse audit on your site and get a consistent performance score and metrics. Using lab tests during development is a great way to catch problems early and to set a baseline for improvements.

Field monitoring is about gathering data from real users in the wild. The Chrome User Experience Report (CrUX) (*https://oreil.ly/T8K8u*) is a public dataset of real user metrics that provides aggregated performance stats for real Chrome users on your site. It's accessible via tools like PageSpeed Insights or BigQuery. CrUX gives you monthly aggregated stats for LCP, INP, and CLS for your site's users (if it has enough traffic). This is useful to benchmark where you stand. If, say, only 50% of your users have good LCP, you know half your users are having a subpar experience, which is motivation to improve.

You can also run your own analytics via the Web Vitals JavaScript library (*https://oreil.ly/fsPRT*) (covered later in this chapter) or another real user monitoring (RUM) solution to capture metrics from actual visitors. RUM refers to the practice of collecting performance data from actual users as they interact with your site in production, giving you insights into how the site performs across different devices, networks, and locations. Other great tools include WebPageTest (*https://webpagetest.org*) for deeper analysis (like filmstrips and CPU profiles) and the DevTools Performance panel (*https://oreil.ly/BkjWZ*) for profiling runtime performance.

Field data is the true measure of what users experience, capturing the full range of devices, networks, and user behaviors. It might differ from lab results: for example, your Lighthouse (lab) LCP might be 2.0 s (great), but your field data could show many users at 4 s, perhaps because a lot of your users are on slower phones than the lab tool assumes. The lab provides ideal (or at least standardized) conditions, while the field is reality, with all the variability that implies.

Savvy performance engineers use lab tools for diagnostics and field tools for validation. Set up some way to collect these metrics continuously, so you can see if, for example, a new deployment causes LCP to spike for users or a certain region is slower.

The CWVs: Key Metrics

Google's analysis of millions of page impressions found that achieving good scores on all three CWVs led to 24% less abandonment on average, with similar improvements across different site categories, like news and ecommerce sites. The three CWV metrics weren't chosen arbitrarily; they correspond to real improvements in user behavior and satisfaction. When we defined these metrics at Google, we reviewed the existing literature and did our own user studies.

These metrics are field measurable in browsers, meaning they can be collected from real users, not just lab simulations. At the time, this marked a huge shift in how we judge performance: it's about real UX, not just theoretical load times. Modern browsers (Chrome in particular) expose APIs to measure these metrics, so developers can track them in production. CrUX also gathers anonymized data (*https://oreil.ly/nT7b2*) on these metrics across the web, and Google has even made page experience a factor in rankings (*https://oreil.ly/wI4BI*) (in case you need further incentive to care about CWVs). Let's look at each one in more detail.

Largest Contentful Paint (LCP): Viewing Content Quickly

Goal: Aim for an LCP of under 2.5 s (at the 75th percentile of users).

LCP measures loading speed from the *user's* point of view. More specifically, it marks the moment when the largest piece of content (likely the main article text, image, or feature element in the viewport) has rendered on the screen. Why the largest? Because usually that's the thing users are waiting for: the big image or the main headline and block of text. A fast LCP means the page appears useful reassuringly quickly; the user can see the primary content without undue delay. It's about delivering on that "Is it useful?" moment promptly.

Sharp-eyed readers may have noticed that I've also mentioned *first contentful paint* (FCP). The difference between these two metrics is that FCP might trigger as soon as a tiny header or spinner appears, whereas LCP waits for the actual substantive content. Users care about when the page *feels* loaded, not just about when something flickers onto the screen.

An LCP of under 2.5 s is the "good" threshold defined by CWVs, after careful analysis. This goal is ambitious enough to ensure a good UX but achievable for a reasonable number of sites with current technology.

In lab tests, if the LCP is high, check the waterfall to find the resource or CPU task delaying it. If the LCP is OK in lab tests (around 2 s) but field tests show it as high, maybe your lab tests didn't capture a worst-case scenario, like a slower network or device.

To make it concrete, let's say you click a headline leading to a news article. A good LCP would mean that within 2.5 s, the headline and perhaps the lead paragraph or main image are visible.

First Input Delay (FID) and Interaction to Next Paint (INP): Ready to React

Goal: Keep at least 75% of interactions below 200 ms.

In the first incarnation of CWVs, the FID metric provided an early look at responsiveness. FID measures the time from a user's *first* interaction with a site (like clicking a link or tapping a button) to when the browser actually responds. However, we found that focusing only on the *first* interaction missed important aspects of ongoing usability—after all, users keep interacting well beyond that point.

That's where INP comes in. INP is a newer metric that replaced FID as one of the CWVs. It's designed to capture *overall* responsiveness, not just the initial click. It measures the time from a user's interaction (tap, click, or keyboard event) until the next frame is painted—essentially tracking how quickly the page can visually respond to each interaction. A low INP score is good, indicating that the site consistently feels snappy across *all* user actions. A high INP score suggests that the site occasionally lags or locks up, creating frustrating moments.

The recommended target for INP is to keep the majority (75th percentile) of interactions below 200 ms, based on research indicating (*https://oreil.ly/VfSN6*) that beyond about 100 to 200 ms, the interface starts feeling sluggish. When pages are busy parsing large JavaScript bundles or handling long tasks on the main thread, interactions can queue up, leading to higher INP. By measuring INP, developers can see how often these slowdowns occur and prioritize fixing them. Measuring and lowering INP ensures the site feels consistently responsive, letting users flow seamlessly through tasks.

If INP shows a high value, it likely measured one of your event handlers taking a long time or an input being delayed. But in lab tests, by default, there aren't many interactions—so Lighthouse might synthesize an interaction after load on the first contentful element to estimate INP. If it's high, treat it like total blocking time (discussed below) keeping the main thread busy.

In practice, INP builds on lessons learned from FID—highlighting where main-thread bloat, large scripts, and other factors disrupt responsiveness. But whereas FID ends after that initial interaction, INP shines a light on every interaction that follows, giving teams a more complete picture of real-world user experience. By keeping INP low, you reduce the risk of sudden UI stalls at any point, helping your site truly "stay ready to react."

Cumulative Layout Shift (CLS): Visual Stability

Goal: Achieve a CLS score of less than 0.1 for 75% of page loads.

CLS is the newest of these three concepts for many developers, as it addresses a type of UX issue that historically wasn't captured by load time or speed metrics. It measures how much the page's layout moves around unexpectedly during the load (or even later). It's a score that accumulates every time things jump on screen. Layout instability can cause serious frustration and even accidental clicks on the wrong element.

CLS is calculated simply: it looks at the portion of the screen that shifted and how far it moved, and tallies a score. Small movements or shifts of off-screen elements barely count, but big, visible jumps yield a higher score. The goal is to have a CLS score of less than 0.1 for 75% of page loads. In practice, that means almost no noticeable unexpected shifts. If you meet this goal, your page is likely very stable and user-friendly in terms of visual consistency. If it's more than 0.1, look at the elements to find and fix the cause. Does Lighthouse list the top shifting elements? Does the DevTools timeline or WebPageTest's session filmstrip show any janky animation?

The CWVs distill Google's advice on the most critical UX aspects of performance. Understanding them will help you prioritize what to fix or optimize.

Other Important Metrics

Other important metrics that aren't part of the CWVs include:

Total blocking time (TBT)
A lab-only metric summing how long tasks >50 ms run between FCP and TTI. It's a proxy for how busy the main thread is. If it's high, INP might also be an issue. You can lower TBT by optimizing JavaScript (see Chapter 7). For example, if your TBT is 600 ms, you probably have a big chunk of script blocking the main thread.

Speed index (SI)
This somewhat arcane metric measures how quickly content is visually populated (using a filmstrip tool). It's not a Core Web Vital, but is part of the Lighthouse score. If LCP is fine, usually SI is fine too. If SI is high, you likely have a progressive rendering issue (the content starts appearing late).

Time to interactive (TTI)
This measures the time until the page is idle enough to reliably respond. If you optimize TBT and JavaScript, TTI will drop. TTI sometimes overshoots LCP if you have a lot of postload JavaScript. If TTI is much after LCP, it means the user sees the content but can't interact fully with it until later—which might correlate with heavy JavaScript tying things up.

Interpreting and Acting on Reports

If Lighthouse says your site's interactivity is high (say, eight seconds), that likely means users see content but can't use it for another eight seconds: an obvious UX issue. If CLS is flagged as "needs improvement," hunt down which elements are causing layout jumps. If your tool doesn't tell you, maybe it's an image without dimensions or an ad slot.

Consider each metric and consider it from the user's point of view. Do the measurements you're getting align with feedback or session recordings, if available? "I clicked but nothing happened" is a clue indicating interactivity problems; "the page jumps around" tells you to look into CLS issues.

Consider closing the loop: measure, find issues, fix them, then measure again. Performance work is iterative. One team set up a performance budget and discovered they had exceeded it when marketing added a huge third-party script. Thanks to monitoring, they caught it and worked with marketing to load it differently, with no regression in UX metrics. By making performance metrics as much a part of your monitoring as error logs or uptime, your team can keep UX at the forefront. On the Chrome team and other teams at Google, we treat certain performance metrics as key success criteria. At Chrome itself, we constantly track how fast pages load and respond, because any regression could hurt our billions of users.

In summary, measure what you treasure. Performance is crucial; you now know how to keep an eye on it in your day-to-day development and in production. By combining lab and field results and integrating performance checks into your regular workflow, you can make performance sustainable and actionable.

The rest of this chapter takes a closer look at how to use specific lab and field measurement tools.

Lab Tools

Lab tests are reproducible and let you test changes quickly. They complement field data by allowing deeper debugging. The goal of this section is to show you how to use these tools to catch regressions and verify improvements. Each tool has its nuances. All of the tools covered here can emulate mobile devices and apply network throttling to approximate real user conditions. Your results might vary from run to run, especially LCP (due to variability in network timing) and TBT (due to simulation). Always run a tool a few times, or do three runs and report the median scores. Your environment can also cause variation. DevTools and Lighthouse use your machine, but they might throttle it; PageSpeed Insights uses a datacenter.

Let's dive into how to make the most of each.

Lighthouse: Performance Auditing

Lighthouse (*https://oreil.ly/hRTaK*) is a popular open source tool for performance auditing, developed by the Google Chrome team. Lighthouse loads your page in a controlled environment according to the constraints of the device and network you specify, and collects performance metrics. It then gives a performance score on a scale of 0 to 100 (higher is better), which is a weighted composite of these metrics. Lighthouse focuses primarily on *page load* performance.

To use Lighthouse effectively, run it on critical pages and examine the opportunities for improvement it lists, like "reduce unused JS" or "enable text compression." These are valuable hints about what might be slowing the load. Lighthouse can guide you to where the big problems lie, like large images, slow server response, or heavy scripting. It also flags your CWVs in lab form. It is integrated into Chrome DevTools (go to Audits or the "Lighthouse" panel) and is also available via the command-line interface (lhci or lighthouse via the Node Package Manager, a tool for installing JavaScript packages and tools) or the PageSpeed Insights web UI (*https://oreil.ly/i8t2W*).

Lighthouse metrics include:

- FCP
- SI (visual progress metric)
- LCP
- TTI
- TBT
- CLS
- INP[1]

To run a Lighthouse audit, open the page you want to audit in DevTools, then select "Perform an audit." Note that Lighthouse performs an automated page load without simulating many user interactions, so metrics like INP are synthesized. For instance, Lighthouse will attempt a click on an interactive element after page load to generate an INP measurement, but this may not capture all the interaction patterns real users experience. Choose Performance (and other metrics, if you want). It will reload the page in a controlled way, throttling CPU and network. It will then output:

- A performance score
- A list of metrics and their values (including your CWVs)
- A "filmstrip" (a series of screenshots) showing how the page rendered over time
- Diagnostics alerting you to problems, like "Main thread was busy for X ms" or "DOM size is Y"

---

[1] INP reporting was added in Lighthouse 10, and as of Lighthouse 11, it is included in the performance-score calculation as part of the CWV, replacing FID.

- "Opportunities" or ways to improve the page's score, like "Eliminate render-blocking resources" or "Reduce unused JavaScript," along with the estimated savings of each improvement
- Specific items like the LCP element, what its load time was, and which resource caused it

Use Lighthouse primarily to see your metric values and to catch obvious problems. Don't obsess over the single score. Trying to optimize for a perfect 100 can lead to diminishing returns or unnatural patterns. For instance, Lighthouse might say that you "reduced unused CSS," which is good, but splitting the Cascading Style Sheets (CSS) too much might actually hurt real users by causing extra requests.

Running Lighthouse before and after making changes is a good way to verify that your changes achieved the expected improvements. Say you decide to optimize your page's images by compressing them and adding dimensions. If you run Lighthouse before the changes and then afterward, you might expect to see results like the following:

- CLS should drop to around 0 if images were the cause. Lighthouse might drop the "Image elements have no explicit width/height" warning.
- LCP might improve if images are loading faster due to compression.
- TBT or INP might not change unless you also remove heavy JavaScript. In that case, TBT should go down.

Lighthouse also has a tool to integrate in your organization's CI/CD pipeline. It can alert you if a performance score or specific metric regresses beyond a certain threshold. You might set it up to run on a representative page after each commit. It has also added user flows, so you can script what a user might do and then let it play out.

In summary, Lighthouse is your quick audit tool to get a broad sense of page performance and some guidance on what to fix. It's often the first thing you'll run on a new site.

Chrome DevTools Performance Panel: Deep Diagnostics with AI Assistance

Once you have an app running, the best way to uncover performance problems is to profile it with real tools. Chrome DevTools is the workhorse for this. Using the Performance panel, you can record a session of your site running, capturing all the JavaScript execution, rendering, layout calculations, and network activity that occur. This is incredibly valuable for pinpointing issues. You might discover, for instance, that a single function (maybe an AI-generated data-processing loop) is taking 200 ms of CPU time and causing a visible stall, or that a layout thrash is happening (where multiple style recalculations are triggered unnecessarily).

The Performance panel is a diagnostic tool; it does not give you a score. It's where you spend time analyzing a performance recording and say, "Ah, that 300 ms pause is our third-party script," or "Layout took too long here, maybe due to a huge DOM."

Traditionally, analyzing these performance profiles required significant expertise. You'd look at the flame graphs and stack traces to deduce what's slowing things down. However, we now have AI assistance in DevTools itself (*https://oreil.ly/_-wcg*). Chrome has integrated an "Ask AI" feature, powered by Google's Gemini model, directly into various panels, including Performance (Figure 2-1). This means you can ask the browser to interpret the performance profile for you. For example, after recording a performance profile, you can right-click on a long task in the performance flame chart and click "Ask AI," and the AI will provide an analysis of that call stack or a summary of what might be causing a slowdown. It's like having a performance expert looking over your shoulder, pointing out the obvious (and sometimes nonobvious) culprits.

In addition to the Performance panel, Chrome's DevTools AI integration extends to other areas useful for quality: the Sources panel (you can ask about code and even get suggestions for fixes or explanations of errors), the Network panel (you can inquire why a certain request failed or why it's slow), and even a Console AI, which can explain console errors and warnings in plain language. For instance, if your AI-generated code throws a warning like "[Deprecation] Some API is deprecated," the console's "Explain" feature can use AI to tell you what that means and how to update it. This is a huge boon when dealing with unfamiliar output from an AI: sometimes AI uses an outdated approach it saw in its training data, and DevTools might warn about it, so you know to modernize that bit of code.

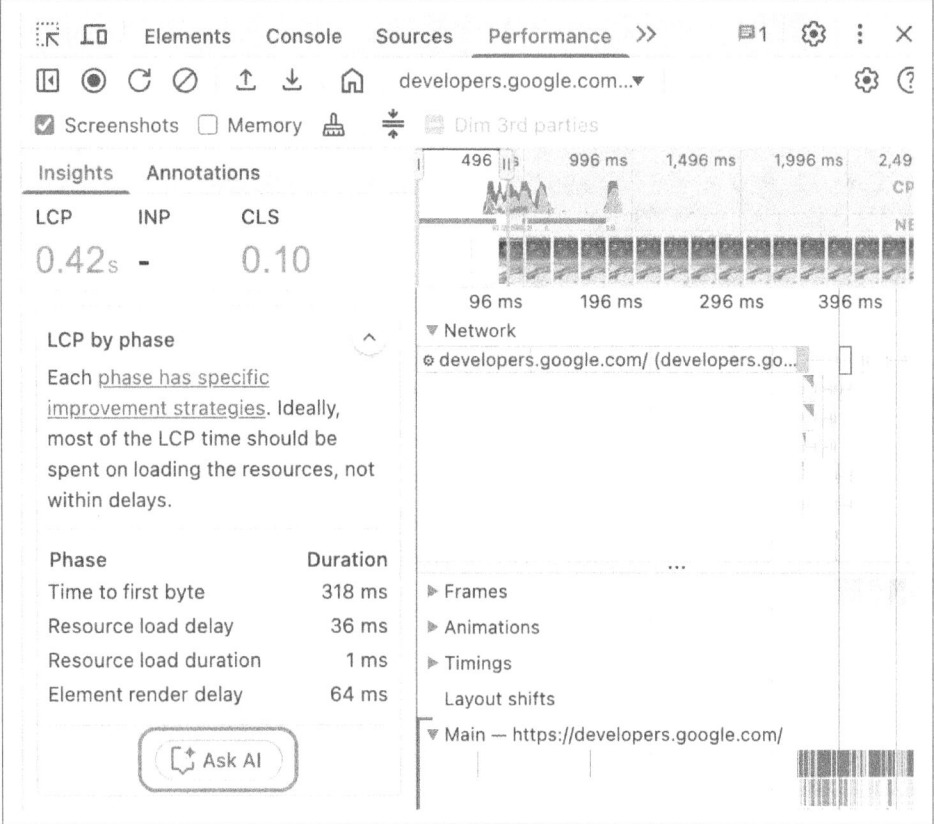

Figure 2-1. The Chrome DevTools Performance panel now includes an AI assistant (Gemini) that can analyze a recorded profile

To use these features, ensure you're on a recent version of Chrome, or at least a Chrome DevTools version that includes Gemini (Chrome 111+ started introducing these AI tools in preview). For performance, the workflow is:

1. Open the DevTools Performance panel.
2. Hit "Record."
3. Interact with your site (load it, click around).
4. Stop recording.
5. Examine the call tree or summary.

You can then ask questions like "What caused the largest layout shift?" or "Why is the page load slow?" This helps find the exact places in code that need optimization—which might very well be the ones the AI wrote in a suboptimal way. If you check "Enable web vitals," it will show LCP markers and CLS occurrences on the timeline.

The Performance panel's interface displays a wealth of information, and while it can initially seem overwhelming, understanding its key components will help you quickly identify performance issues:

- The summary bars at the top provide FPS, CPU, and NET charts and show statistics, like if the frame rate went below 60 frames per second.
- Below that is a network-request waterfall (similar to the Network panel but aligned in the timeline).
- Main-thread activity is shown as a long horizontal bar, with colored segments showing script execution (yellow), style/layout (purple), paint (green), and so on. You can zoom in to see each function call if source maps are available.
- The Bottom-up and Call Tree tabs show aggregated time per function and per activity type. These are good for finding what took the most time on the main thread.

When you record a page load, you'll see:

- A green triangle marking FCP and a bigger one for LCP. You can hover over the LCP marker and see the element and time.
- Long yellow blocks show script executions. If you identify one that took 200 ms, clicking it should show the call stack, pinpointing the JavaScript file and function. This is a great way to find things like a heavy evaluation from a library that might be slowing things down.
- Purple blocks represent layout and style calculations. You might see one large purple block after an image loads, for example. Clicking on it might reveal that the browser recalculated styles for 5,000 elements. This could indicate either a very large Document Object Model (DOM) tree that needs recalculation or style thrashing—a performance problem where the browser is forced to recalculate styles multiple times unnecessarily, often caused by JavaScript that alternately reads layout properties and modifies the DOM.
- If layout shift events occurred, you might see red triangle markers. The Summary view also lists "Layout shift events: X occurred (score Y)." If you click on a layout shift event in the timeline, the Details side panel will highlight which DOM element moved and by how much. This is extremely useful, as you can then target that element.
- A network request waterfall lets you see if any gaps in CPU correspond to network waits and vice versa. Perhaps the main thread was idle while waiting for CSS or was busy executing JavaScript while some requests got delayed.

- An Insights panel highlights significant issues automatically, with the "Ask AI" button at the bottom. This is like an on-the-fly audit, specialized for the trace. It's handy for catching big things without hunting manually.

The JavaScript Profiler is another tool in DevTools that provides detailed information on code coverage, showing which JavaScript was executed and which unused, memory usage, and function-level performance data. However, for most web performance work, the Performance panel provides sufficient detail without requiring a separate profiling step, since it shows you function call stacks and timing information. The dedicated Profiler is most useful when you need to drill down into specific function-level performance characteristics or track memory-consumption patterns over time. For general web performance analysis, the Performance panel's timeline view is typically sufficient to pinpoint which scripts are consuming too much CPU time, making the separate Profiler tool necessary only for specialized debugging scenarios.

DevTools can throttle the network to mimic various networks and CPU performance levels. The throttling drop-down menu offers preset options like Fast 3G and Slow 4G for network emulation. When I refer to a "midrange device," I typically mean a device with moderate CPU performance—not the latest flagship phone, but not the cheapest budget device either. A midrange device in 2025 might have a CPU that's four to six times slower than the CPU of a high-end desktop. The DevTools CPU-throttling options (such as 4x slowdown) can help simulate these conditions. For consistency, do multiple runs or use a consistent throttle.

Overall, the DevTools Performance panel is one of the most powerful and comprehensive tools available for web performance analysis, offering deep insights into every aspect of page behavior. It requires some practice to read, but once you get used to it, you can fairly quickly diagnose if the bottleneck is CPU or network and find the specific resource or script.

WebPageTest: Realistic Testing and Advanced Analysis

WebPageTest (WPT) (*http://webpagetest.org*) is a web-based tool for testing performance on real browsers (*https://oreil.ly/1hg_r*). It was originally developed by AOL's Pat Meenan in 2010 and is now part of Catchpoint. It offers plenty of configuration (device profiles, network throttling, multiple runs) and provides waterfalls, filmstrips, Web Vitals, and even some suggestions. WPT is great for more "realistic" testing, like simulating a slow mobile on 4G, and for generating videos or filmstrips to visualize what a user would see at each second of load. The Web Vitals overlay and connection usage breakdown let you highlight element by element. The result it returns include:

- A waterfall chart showing resource loading
- A filmstrip and video recording of the page load

- Metrics like start render, SI, LCP, CLS, and INP
- A Web Vitals section
- A *visual performance score*: a composite metric representing how quickly the visible page content is displayed to the user (taking into account multiple factors like start render, SI, and visual completeness)
- A detailed load-time breakdown

WPT has a public instance (*http://webpagetest.org*), and you can self-host as well. There's also an API and a new WPT UI with some paid features.

WPT and Lighthouse complement each other well, but WPT offers some distinct advantages:

- WPT uses an actual browser without artificial throttling (unless you set it). You can test on high-end or low-end devices by choosing an agent or adding throttle. For multiple runs, it gives you information about the median and variability.
- WPT shows the network details much more clearly than Lighthouse does. The waterfall is very detailed: you see each request, when DNS, connect, Secure Sockets Layer (SSL), time to first byte (TTFB), content download, etc. You also see HTTP headers and bytes, which help you find big responses or see if compression is working.
- WPT can capture things like above-the-fold render progress (SI). The filmstrips are especially helpful if you're presenting to stakeholders: "See, it's blank for three seconds, then shows content."
- WPT's interface also calls out issues like long blocking requests. It may even show an optimization checklist (like Lighthouse, but network-focused).
- You can test different scenarios easily: with auth, with a slow connection, on different devices, and so forth.

WPT also can simulate user flows via scripting, similar to Lighthouse flows. This is particularly useful for testing authenticated pages or multistep interactions. Here is an example script that demonstrates logging in and then navigating to a dashboard:

```
navigate https://example.com/login
setValue name=username user1
setValue name=password secret
submitForm id=loginForm
waitForComplete
navigate https://example.com/dashboard
```

This script logs in to a site using form credentials, waits for the login to complete, then navigates to the dashboard page and times its load. This capability is particularly valuable for testing authenticated flows or multistep user journeys that the Lighthouse CLI can't easily handle without additional scripting infrastructure.

PageSpeed Insights (*https://pagespeed.web.dev*) is easier to use than WPT, combining Lighthouse (lab) data with CrUX (*https://oreil.ly/IP0aD*) (field) data. WPT is more detailed but requires you to do more interpretation. Often I use PageSpeed Insights first to get a quick Lighthouse score, then WPT to verify those findings in detail.

The HTTP Archive (run by Rick Viscomi and team) collects WPT data for thousands of sites monthly. Tools like the Web Almanac use that data (*https://oreil.ly/3t3wh*) to report trends, like median LCP. It's not a tool you'd use for single-site testing, but it's interesting for benchmarking.

To use these tools together, your lab-testing workflow might look something like this:

- Use Lighthouse to get a quick sense of what's going on and a list of issues.
- Use DevTools Performance to pinpoint the root causes of those issues.
- Use WPT to confirm real-world improvements under realistic network conditions to generate visual proof for stakeholders and to catch things Lighthouse might not.

> ### Third-Party Tools and Integrations
>
> Beyond free tools like WPT, Chrome DevTools, and Lighthouse, there are commercial and hosted services that build on similar engines and add dashboards, alerts, collaboration features, and long-term history:
>
> *SpeedCurve and Calibre*
> > SpeedCurve (*https://oreil.ly/fa6jF*) and Calibre (*https://calibreapp.com*) are full web performance platforms that combine synthetic lab testing with RUM, so you see both controlled test runs and how real users experience your site in production. They run tests from multiple regions using real browsers, track CWVs, and often blend in CrUX data to show how you compare to origin and competitor benchmarks. On top of that, they provide dashboards, performance budgets, alerts, and trends aimed at whole teams, turning one-off Lighthouse or WPT runs into an ongoing monitoring and governance workflow.
>
> *DebugBear and YellowLabTools*
> > DebugBear (*https://oreil.ly/gE1IZ*) is a hosted monitoring service that runs scheduled Lighthouse audits and other synthetic tests, storing every run so you get historical charts, diff views, and alerts when scores or CWVs regress. It also pulls in field data such as CrUX and optional RUM, helping you tie changes in metrics back to specific deployments, URLs, or code paths instead of treating each Lighthouse report in isolation. YellowLabTools (*https://yellowlab.tools*), by contrast, is a free, open source

analyzer that focuses on frontend code quality, scanning for problems like oversized DOM trees, heavy JavaScript, complex CSS, and other patterns that typically hurt performance before a page even renders.

Puppeteer and the Chrome DevTools Protocol
Puppeteer (*https://oreil.ly/-QzfY*) is a Node.js library that controls Chrome or Chromium via the Chrome DevTools Protocol (CDP), giving you scriptable access to a real browser in both headless and headed modes. You can script key user journeys, capture performance traces and metrics, and export Chrome trace files for deeper analysis in DevTools or Perfetto, which makes it useful for building custom performance checks that go beyond what Lighthouse provides out of the box. One pattern is to wire Puppeteer together with the Lighthouse Node module or DevTools Performance APIs in your continuous integration (CI) pipeline so every pull request or release runs repeatable, browser-level performance tests against critical flows.

Keep in mind that Chrome DevTools itself can impact performance results: running a profile or Lighthouse (*https://oreil.ly/Z-Tku*) inside the DevTools interface keeps the tab visible, consumes extra memory, and slightly changes how work is scheduled. Lighthouse in PageSpeed Insights, Lighthouse CI, and most third-party platforms instead run tests in headless Chrome with fixed settings, and services built on WPT or similar lab tooling execute in controlled environments for more repeatable numbers. Expect small differences between Lighthouse in DevTools, PageSpeed Insights, and hosted monitors; use DevTools for local debugging, but treat scripted, headless runs in CI and your monitoring dashboards as the canonical source for budgets and regressions.

Moving forward, the best practice is to combine synthetic monitoring and RUM rather than choosing one or the other. Synthetic tests give deterministic baselines, run even when traffic is low, and are ideal for guarding critical flows in staging or production with alerts. RUM captures what real people see across devices, networks, and regions, making it better for prioritizing work that actually moves CWVs and business metrics; most modern platforms let you run both side by side so you can detect regressions early and still validate their real-world impact.

By mastering lab tools, you can optimize a site as much as possible in development. But lab tests alone aren't enough; the real proof is in production with real users. That's where we turn to RUM and continuous monitoring.

Field Tools

While lab tools provide controlled and reproducible testing environments, field tools capture the reality of how your site performs for actual users, measuring real user experiences in production environments.

RUM involves measuring performance metrics from users' devices as they use your site. It captures the wild variety of device speeds, network conditions, and user behaviors that lab tests can only approximate. Google's CWVs are specifically defined in terms of RUM data. In fact, to know if you pass the CWVs threshold for SEO or UX goals, just look at your 75th percentile field metrics, as collected by CrUX or your own RUM tool.

In this section, I'll show you how to use Google's web-vitals.js library to capture Web Vitals in JavaScript and send them to an analytics endpoint. I'll mention some other approaches, too, like using the PerformanceObserver API directly if you need custom logic. I'll cover integration via sending metrics to Google Analytics or your own server, and possibly tagging them with metadata. And I'll look a bit closer at CrUX and how tools like PageSpeed Insights and Search Console use it.

To finish the chapter, I'll discuss setting up performance budgets and alerting, other metrics you might want to track, and data-privacy compliance considerations.

Capturing CWVs in the Field with web-vitals.js

Google provides an open source web-vitals library (*https://oreil.ly/fsPRT*) that abstracts the browser APIs to get metrics, including LCP, CLS, INP, FID, FCP, and TTFB (if needed). The library is available on npm or as a script.

Internally, it uses PerformanceObserver to get LCP, CLS, and INP, including waiting for the *page hide event* (a browser event that fires when the page is being unloaded, such as when the user navigates away, closes the tab, or switches to another application) to capture final metric values before the page session ends. It applies any necessary polyfills or fixes, like for INP support in browsers that might not have it natively yet, and it provides a simple callback with the metric value and some metadata.

To use web-vitals, run the following script:

```
<script src="https://unpkg.com/web-vitals@3/dist/web-vitals.iife.js"></script>

<script>

  webVitals.getCLS(console.log);

  webVitals.getLCP(console.log);

  webVitals.getINP(console.log);

</script>
```

This logs the metrics to console. To send them to a server, run the following:

```
function sendToAnalytics(metric) {
  const body = JSON.stringify(metric);
  // Use navigator.sendBeacon for efficient async send that doesn't block unload
  navigator.sendBeacon('/analytics', body);
}

webVitals.getCLS(sendToAnalytics);
webVitals.getLCP(sendToAnalytics);
webVitals.getINP(sendToAnalytics);
```

Each `metric` object has properties like `name` ("CLS"), `value` (0.07), `entries` (any related `PerformanceEntry` instances), and maybe `id` (an ID for the metric instance).

It's important to wait for the metrics to finalize. LCP is typically determined at or just after load, but if the user backgrounds the page and comes back, it can update. The library handles this and will call your callback when the value is final (or on page hide). CLS accumulates until the page is unloaded or hidden (or after a max session gap). The library reports it at page unload or when it's stable after input. INP is reported at page unload, or after five seconds of no input events. The INP value that `web-vitals` provides should generally align with what CrUX computes, as both follow the same methodology. However, CrUX aggregates data across many users and reports the 75th percentile, while `web-vitals` gives you individual session values. The calculation methodology is consistent, but you'll need to aggregate your own RUM data to compare directly with CrUX percentiles.

Once you've captured the metrics, you need to send them somewhere for analysis. Common approaches include:

- A custom endpoint on your server (like `/analytics` in the last code example). From there, you can store it in a database or forward it to a monitoring system.
- Directly to Google Analytics (GA4) as a custom metric, such as `event("web_vital", { name: 'LCP', value: 2500 })`. Google has some guides (*https://oreil.ly/WJnmg*) on measuring CWVs in Google Analytics. The `web-vitals` docs also give examples of integration.
- A dedicated RUM analytics service, like SpeedCurve's LUX, Akamai mPulse, NewRelic Browser, or Datadog RUM. Many offer Web Vitals tracking out of the box. If you already use one of these services for other RUM (like JS error logging), see if it can track CWVs.

For dimensioning and context, it's often useful to tag each metric with the following:

- The page route or template (such as `Home` or `ProductPage`).
- The user's device or OS (you can use `userAgent` or Network Information API for effective type, though support varies).
- Whether the visitor is new or returning can be valuable context for analysis. First-time visitors typically load all resources from the network, which often results in slower load times, while returning users benefit from browser caching. This distinction helps you understand whether performance issues affect all users or primarily first-time visitors. You can track this by setting a cookie or using `localStorage` to identify repeat visits.
- The user's connection type: use `navigator.connection.effectiveType` (to get "4g," "5g," and so on) and `saveData`.

This data can help you later do segmented analysis—for example, analyzing LCP differences on mobile versus desktop. Be mindful of not sending excessive data—just what's needed to analyze.

TTFB is mostly relevant if you want to correlate it with backend slowness or measure it to monitor your server. web-vitals captures TTFB with `getTTFB`, but CrUX doesn't include it. If you prefer not to use a library, you can use PerformanceObserver directly by setting up something like the following:

```
const po = new PerformanceObserver(list => {
  for (const entry of list.getEntries()) {
    if (entry.entryType === 'largest-contentful-paint') {
      // record entry.renderTime or entry.loadTime
    }
  }
});

po.observe({type: 'largest-contentful-paint', buffered: true});
```

The code is similar for layout shift, with the `entry.value` of each shift. The web-vitals library handles a lot of edge cases, like capturing CLS correctly after multiple shifts and grouping them or waiting for page lifecycle events. Thus, using it saves time and ensures alignment with how Google calculates things.

The Event Timing API (which powers INP measurement) is widely supported in modern versions of Chrome (version 109 and later) and other Chromium-based browsers. The web-vitals library handles browser differences gracefully and provides polyfills where needed. Since CWVs primarily reflect Chrome user experience data through CrUX, Chrome's support is most critical for production monitoring.

Leveraging CrUX and External Data

You've learned that CrUX is a public dataset of real user experience metrics for millions of origins, collected from Chrome users who have opted into syncing their browsing histories and not setting up certain privacy restrictions. It's aggregated by origin and also by "experience type" (like mobile versus desktop). It's accessible via BigQuery (for advanced SQL users), the PageSpeed Insights API, and the PageSpeed Insights UI and Search Console. Search Console's CWVs report (*https://oreil.ly/ sH9Kh*) is basically a view of CrUX for your verified site, highlighting if 75th percentiles pass or not.

CrUX data is great for seeing the big picture. Your insights might look like this one from the Web Almanac (*https://oreil.ly/cB_1M*): "In the last 28 days, 68% of our mobile users had good LCP (<2.5s), 23% needs improvement, 9% poor." It might also break down the percentile values: p75 LCP = 2.8 s (so a failing score). CrUX also shows if that's an improvement or decline from previous measurements (Search Console tracks this history with red, yellow, and green counts).

You can also use CrUX to benchmark your site against competitors, since its data is public for all origins above a traffic threshold. Tools like HTTP Archive's CWVs dashboard and the web.dev Compare tool allow you to compare two sites' CrUX scores.

If you don't have your own RUM in place yet, start with CrUX to identify issues. However, be aware of its limitations: CrUX is only for Chrome and doesn't give granular insight into causes. Additionally, CrUX only covers core metrics, nothing custom. And if your site is low traffic or its traffic is mostly non-Chrome, it might not have data.

RUM Beyond Web Vitals

While CWVs are the primary focus, RUM can also include:

Custom metrics
   For instance, you might measure the time for search results to appear after the user triggers a search, which could be as important as LCP for that feature.

Span metrics
   These measure how long a user stays on the page until they can complete a key task.

Page resource-load stats
> You might log bytes or number of requests for each user to see variance (though Google Analytics can track that via hits as well).

Long task monitoring
> You can use the Long Tasks API in RUM to record tasks that exceed, say, 250 ms on a user's device. That could feed your analytics to help you know how often users suffer janky episodes. Some RUM services do this, reporting a "UI thread busy" percentage.

Memory
> Memory usage is harder to quantify than loading or interaction metrics, but there are now a few browser-level options you can use from script. In Chromium-based browsers, `performance.memory` exposes a legacy, nonstandard view of the JavaScript heap size and related values; this can help with local diagnostics, but it is not cross browser and may change or be removed. For production-facing measurements, prefer the newer `performance.measureUserAgentSpecificMemory()` method (part of the User Agent Specific Memory API), which aggregates the memory usage of the page, its iframes, and workers into a single report suitable for tracking leaks and regressions over a session. This API is implemented in modern versions of Chrome, Microsoft Edge, and Opera.

Focus RUM on metrics that tie to user experience, including CWVs. If your site has huge traffic, you don't need to analyze every single user's data—you can sample (like 1% of sessions) to reduce data volume. If you're using Google Analytics, it can handle a lot, but it's still best not to overcollect if you don't need to.

Using RUM Data to Drive Improvements

Once you have RUM data, share it within your team. You might even make it a key performance indicator alongside other product metrics: you could have a dashboard that correlates CWVs with conversion rates. Often, faster sites equal better engagement. For example, if after a performance fix, your LCP improves and you notice that the bounce rate has decreased, trumpet that! It builds a case that performance work is worth it.

Use your RUM data to identify outlier pages or user segments. If a particular page template has worse LCP (maybe due to heavy images), target it for optimization. If certain geographies have poor TTFB, consider deploying a content delivery network (CDN) point of presence (PoP) in those regions to reduce latency. If your RUM shows that most users have good INP but a small percent have terrible INP, investigate the cause. If it's due to old devices, consider dropping heavy effects for those devices, if possible.

Don't forget to feed the findings back into your lab testing. If RUM says that your p75 LCP is 3 s but your lab test always shows 1.5 s, maybe your lab conditions are too optimistic. Adjust them to better match real conditions, perhaps increasing throttle or testing on slower CPUs. Then you can better reproduce those real-world issues in the lab.

Setting Up Performance Budgets and Alerts

Once you have your RUM data flowing, establish your thresholds to aim for and create alerts for any regressions:

Your CWVs budget
    Perhaps your CWV performance budget looks like this: "Our goals are: p75 LCP < 2.5 s on mobile, p75 INP < 200 ms, p75 CLS < 0.1." You can set Search Console to alert you if any of these metrics go worse than the budgeted values so you can take action. For instance, if many URLs drop to "Poor," it will flag an issue.

Resource budgets
    Many teams enforce budgets outside the CWVs, such as that no page should ship more than X KB of JavaScript or CSS, or no image larger than Y. Use `webpack-bundle-analyzer` to check bundle sizes, and the Lighthouse CI can check "total bytes of JavaScript" (there's also a Lighthouse audit for that).

CI blocking
    As mentioned, integrate performance tests in CI. For example, run Lighthouse on a key page as part of the build. If the score or specific metric regresses by more than 10% compared to the last build, fail the tests, issue a warning, or use the bundle size check in CI.

Monitoring
    If using a RUM service or Google Analytics, set up an alert to tell you if the average or p90 Web Vitals degrade beyond the threshold for a day. For example, NewRelic can track custom events: you send LCP as an event and set an alert if median LCP is more than a certain value X for more than Y minutes.

Continuous improvement
    Performance is an ongoing effort, and things tend to slow down over time as features are added. Continuous tracking helps catch when you need to allocate time to optimize again. Let's say that in Q3 you see LCP creeping up, perhaps due to accumulated minor additions—that means it's time to refactor or optimize assets again.

Watch out for particular regressions after deployments. For instance, if you deploy a third-party chat widget and the next day RUM shows a spike in CLS, alerting can help you catch that quickly. Then you can determine the cause (maybe the widget injected an element that caused layout shift) and can roll back the deployment or fix the issue.

Case Study: Continuous Monitoring in Practice

To illustrate how these concepts work in practice, let's consider a fictional ecommerce site.

The site's team implements the web-vitals library on every page, sending measurements to Google Analytics for aggregation and analysis. Using Google Analytics, the team computes monthly 75th-percentile values for LCP, INP, and CLS across different page types—home pages, category pages, and product pages.

Through this analysis, the team discovers that the product pages have a 75th-percentile LCP of 3.2 s on mobile, which falls into the "needs improvement" category. Investigation reveals that the slow performance is primarily due to large, unoptimized images and multiple third-party scripts that block rendering. Armed with this data, the team allocates a sprint to address the issues: the team implements an image CDN to serve optimized images, configure lazy loading for below-the-fold content, and defer noncritical third-party scripts so they don't block initial page rendering (all techniques I'll cover in detail in Parts II through IV of this book).

After deployment, the team members watch Google Analytics for the next week and find that the p75 LCP drops to 2.4 s, which is "good." Success! The team also notices that conversion on product pages upticks slightly, which could be related.

To make sure this success continues, the team sets up a Lighthouse CI job on the product page to ensure that no one accidentally reintroduces huge images or heavy scripts that break the budget. The team also schedules monthly team performance-review meetings to look at RUM trends and make sure it's on track, or plan new improvements if needed (like adopting HTTP/3 or new compression).

The team agrees that when adding a new feature (say, a 360° viewer on product image), it will test its impact using lab tools and monitor RUM after release for any negative changes (maybe it added some layout shifts or interactivity delays).

The team also commits to keeping its Search Console CWVs green (which helps SEO).

The loop of measure—improve—measure is continuous.

By embedding performance in its monitoring and dev pipeline, the team ensures that it remains a priority and that the gains don't regress over time as the site evolves.

Conclusion

You have now journeyed through the browser's rendering pipeline and explored a comprehensive set of techniques for optimizing the CWVs: LCP, INP, and CLS. You've also seen the importance of measuring these improvements using both lab tools and RUM. By understanding browser internals (see Chapter 5) and applying targeted optimizations—from resource-loading strategies to efficient rendering and interaction handling (see Chapter 6)—you can significantly enhance the user experience.

In Chapter 3, I'll finish Part I by looking at how the rise of AI-generated code is influencing performance.

CHAPTER 3

AI-Generated Code and the Performance Paradox

AI-assisted code generation has rapidly moved from a novelty to an everyday tool in modern development. Large language models (LLMs) and AI coding assistants can produce web application code in seconds, offering solutions that *appear* to work in the browser. This speed and convenience, however, come with a paradox: These tools currently optimize for *correctness* (satisfying the prompt's intent) and perhaps style—not for performance. The training data they learn from is a mix of code from the web, which includes both good and bad practices. So an AI might regurgitate a solution that works but isn't optimal, efficient, accessible, or user-friendly. In practice, many developers are discovering that AI-generated apps function adequately but exhibit serious performance and quality issues when held to real-world standards.

This chapter looks at the problem at a high level and evaluates how human developers' role is evolving. The chapters that follow will then offer some concrete techniques for optimizing AI-generated code.

AI Outputs: Correct but Not Optimal

LLMs have essentially ingested the world's open source code and learned common patterns. This means the code they generate tends to follow the *average* practices found online. Unfortunately, "average" web code is often far from ideal in terms of performance. For instance, many web tutorials use simplistic approaches for clarity (like using for…in loops in ways that aren't optimal, or constructing DOM with string concatenation). AI might consider those "normal" and replicate them, even if better methods exist today.

AI models prioritize producing functionally correct code that meets the prompt's requirements. If the majority of examples for a pattern were not performance-optimized, the AI's baseline suggestion won't be either. AI models do not inherently consider nonfunctional requirements like performance optimizations, accessibility labels, or polished user experience details unless explicitly asked. They don't have an inherent sense of what is efficient, unless efficiency correlates with some signal in the training data (like popularity or upvotes—and popularity doesn't always equal performance).

The result is that an AI will happily generate a React component or an HTML page that renders and passes basic tests, yet the implementation may be riddled with inefficiencies. For example, an AI might choose a brute-force approach or pull in a heavy library for a task where a lightweight, optimized solution exists—simply because the brute-force method was common in its training data. The code *works*, and it's even idiomatic at first glance, but it can be slow or resource-intensive to execute.

Thus, developers should continue to rely on profiling and testing tools. If an AI wrote a chunk of code, profile it under realistic conditions. If it's fine, great. If not, treat it as you would any problematic code: iterate and optimize it until it meets your standards.

Equally concerning, AI-generated code often lacks accessibility and UX considerations. An AI is unlikely to add proper ARIA roles, alt text for images, or keyboard navigation support unless prompted, as those details are often omitted in the code it learned from. It may also ignore UX niceties like responsive design, error handling, or loading states. The outcome is code that *runs*, but it delivers a subpar experience to users—especially users on slow devices or those relying on assistive technologies. In short, AI tends to give you a 70% solution; the last 30%—which includes critical aspects like performance tuning and accessibility—is left to the developer to figure out.

Recent evidence suggests we should be cautious about assuming net wins from AI assistance. A randomized controlled trial (*https://oreil.ly/S1HEa*) of experienced developers in 2025 found they completed tasks 19% slower with AI tools than without, even though they *believed* they were working faster. Performance engineering inherits that same paradox: "more code faster" is not the same as "faster code for users." Our job is to keep outcomes tied to the Core Web Vitals and real devices, not perceived velocity.

The Hidden Costs of AI-Generated Code

That "last 30%" of polish and optimization is not optional. Poor performance and quality can undermine the benefits of rapid AI-assisted development. It's increasingly clear that AI-generated code can harbor hidden costs that negate its productivity gains if left unaddressed. Recent research and case studies are shining a light on just how significant these issues can be:

Performance pitfalls
While LLMs excel at producing working code, they struggle with producing efficient code. One extensive experiment (*https://oreil.ly/ztIoT*) by an AI tooling company, published in 2025, found that a shocking 90% of the code optimizations suggested by leading LLMs either changed the code's behavior incorrectly or failed to improve performance at all. In other words, when asked to make code faster, the majority of AI's suggestions were useless or even harmful. This isn't entirely surprising—optimization is a complex task requiring runtime insight and benchmarking, which LLMs lack. They operate in a vacuum of static patterns. An AI will typically implement the first approach that meets the requirements, not necessarily the fastest or most scalable approach. If you then ask it to "optimize" that code, it often performs superficial tweaks that sound plausible but don't actually move the needle (or, worse, break something in the process). The consequence is that if a developer relies on AI output without a manual performance review, they may be shipping code that uses far more CPU, memory, or network resources than necessary. The impact appears in users' browsers as slower load times, janky interactions, and low frame rates.

Accessibility issues
Accessibility is often an afterthought in much of the code found in public repositories, and LLMs reflect that gap. Empirical evaluations have highlighted that AI-generated UIs tend to have significant accessibility violations. In one 2024 study (*https://oreil.ly/wOXJH*), 88 developers prompted ChatGPT to build websites and then checked them with automated accessibility tools. The results showed that a large majority (84%) of ChatGPT-generated websites contained *multiple accessibility problems.*

Common issues included missing alternative text on images, lack of semantic HTML structure for screen readers, insufficient color contrast, and missing keyboard navigation support. The study's authors had to iterate with increasingly specific prompts to fix these problems—something only a knowledgeable developer would know to do. The clear takeaway was that *you cannot rely on a chatbot to produce production-ready accessible code.* An AI may, for instance, create a visually appealing button but forget the ARIA label needed for screen readers, or lay out content in a way that makes sense visually but is incoherent when linearized for a blind user. These oversights can alienate a segment of your users and even pose legal risks in regions with strict accessibility laws.

Poor UX and polish

Beyond raw metrics and accessibility compliance, there are myriad subtle UX aspects that AIs often overlook. For example, an AI-generated form might not include client-side validation or helpful error messages, frustrating users. Or it might not implement responsive design properly, causing a layout to break on mobile devices.

Another example is the lack of performance-oriented UX considerations: an AI might fetch a large dataset and render it all at once in a single list, without any loading spinners or progressive loading. Users facing a blank screen might think the app is frozen, whereas a human developer would likely implement a loading indicator or skeleton UI for better perceived performance. Similarly, an AI might not consider using content placeholders to reserve space (preventing layout shifts) or splitting a long task into smaller chunks to avoid freezing the interface. These are the kinds of UX refinements that come from developer intuition and experience—something an AI won't inherently have.

Code bloat and unused features

Code generation can lead to code bloat if you're not careful. AI might suggest using a large library or include polyfills, extra logging, or support for scenarios you don't need, simply because it has seen those patterns frequently. This results in more JavaScript to send to users and potentially more features than necessary being loaded. It's a bit like a junior developer overengineering a solution. For example, the AI might see a pattern and think, "Oh, use `lodash.debounce` here," and add an import—whereas you might have achieved the same result with a few lines of native JavaScript. If taken at face value, this could bloat your bundle with a new dependency.

As the human in the loop, you should question: *do we really need that library, or can it be done in vanilla JS?* If a dependency is truly helpful and already used elsewhere, fine—but be mindful of unnecessary additions.

AI copying outdated or inefficient patterns

The AI might output code that was common a decade ago but has since been superseded by better approaches (like using modern APIs that are faster or more secure). For instance, it might use `document.write()` or an old-school `XMLHttpRequest` instead of modern `Fetch` or `async/await` patterns, depending on what it saw during training. Those might still work, but they could be suboptimal or have known issues. An engineer needs to ensure that all AI code aligns with current best practices.

All these hidden costs of AI-generated code are starting to surface as real pain points in teams that enthusiastically adopted AI assistants. A survey by Harness in late 2024 (*https://oreil.ly/0WFo8*), for instance, reported that 52% of engineering leaders observed performance problems in their software as a direct result of increased AI-generated code usage. In other words, over half of the tech leaders noticed that after integrating tools like GitHub Copilot, the resulting code was hurting their app's speed or efficiency. This is a stark reminder that the speed of development doesn't equal the speed of the delivered application.

Why do these problems occur so frequently? Fundamentally, LLMs lack the contextual awareness and foresight that performance engineering demands. Performance optimization often requires understanding how code interacts with real browsers, devices, networks, and users—contexts that an offline code generator simply doesn't have. An AI doesn't run your code; it can't *feel* that a certain loop is slow or that a certain image is loading too sluggishly. It has no concept of network latency or how a layout looks on a phone versus a desktop. It also doesn't inherently know the significance of metrics like time to first byte or first contentful paint unless told. In short, LLMs have a performance blind spot: they prioritize the path of least resistance (getting a working answer) and lack the ability to verify or benchmark the efficiency of their output in a runtime environment.

For example, suppose you ask an AI to "filter out duplicates from an array of objects by a key." It might produce a solution using a double nested loop, which works but is $O(n^2)$—fine for 100 items, disastrous for 100,000 items. A performance-conscious human dev might instead use a set or a dictionary to track seen keys in $O(n)$ time. The AI doesn't *know* your performance requirements; it just gives a plausible solution from typical patterns. If you don't review it carefully, you might introduce a significant slowness.

Another example, say you want to manipulate the DOM in a certain way. The AI might generate code that queries the DOM repeatedly inside a loop, which can be much slower than caching a reference. Or it might not batch DOM updates, leading to layout thrashing. A seasoned developer would catch that and adjust it, but an AI likely wouldn't unless specifically instructed.

The first point is clear: *AI-generated code is not inherently optimized.*

Taking Responsibility for Quality and Performance

Given these limitations, it becomes evident that *developers must take responsibility for the quality of AI-generated code.* In an AI-assisted engineering workflow, the human developer's role is more critical than ever—not as a code typist but as a reviewer, tester, and performance engineer. The mantra to adopt is: *treat AI-generated code as you would code written by a junior developer.* That means rigorous code review, profiling, auditing, and optimizing before that code ever reaches production users. The AI may get you started, but it's the developer's job to ask: *Is this code doing anything wasteful? Is it following best practices for performance and accessibility? What can I improve here?* Embracing that mindset is essential to reaping AI's benefits without falling victim to its blind spots.

In practical terms, taking responsibility starts with a thorough code review and audit. Just as you wouldn't merge a new developer's code without reading it, you should carefully read and understand AI-generated code before trusting it. Look out for obvious inefficiencies: N+1 database queries, unbounded loops, lack of caching, heavy libraries imported for trivial tasks, etc. Even for frontend code, examine the DOM structure or React component tree that the AI produces—is it nesting too many elements? Using any outdated patterns? Perhaps generating inline styles or causing lots of unnecessary rerenders? These are things an experienced developer can often spot on sight.

After an initial audit, the next step is profiling and testing the code under realistic conditions. It's crucial to run the application (or component) and use performance profiling tools to see how it behaves. Measure how long it takes to load, how large the JavaScript bundle is, and how it performs under load. Many performance issues don't become apparent until you simulate a real user scenario. For example, an AI might produce a perfectly correct function to render a list of items, but if that list is 10,000 items long, only by profiling it will you notice that the rendering locks up the main thread for several seconds. It's the developer's responsibility to catch that and then refactor the code (perhaps implementing virtualization or pagination, in this scenario).

Moreover, developers must close the loop by *optimizing* the AI output. Where the AI stops, the engineer's work begins: adding missing accessibility attributes, refactoring for better performance, and enhancing the UX. Fortunately, the same developer who uses AI to get a jump-start can also use modern tools (and even AI *within* those tools) to guide their optimization. You've already begun to explore some concrete techniques for pinpointing issues, from using Chrome's performance panel and Lighthouse audits to leveraging new AI-powered features in DevTools. The key point is that *AI assistance does not absolve developers from thinking*. On the contrary, it should shift your thinking to a higher level: you spend less time writing boilerplate and more time scrutinizing and fine-tuning the results.

It's worth noting that these performance and quality concerns aren't limited to frontend code. While our focus here is on web apps, AI-generated backend code can also be problematic. Server-side AI-generated code might introduce inefficient algorithms or security vulnerabilities. I've seen cases of AI-generated SQL queries that miss needed indexes, or chatbot-written API code that makes serial requests where batching is needed. All of these can hurt performance and scalability on the backend. The common theme is that AI models are not (yet) experts in optimization or architecture—the AI provides a raw solution, and the human must refine it. For web developers, this means *owning* your app's performance and quality from end to end, regardless of which parts were AI-generated.

AI-assisted engineering offers incredible gains in developer productivity, but it also changes the developer's job description. We become more like performance coaches and quality assurance guardians for the code that AIs generate. By approaching AI-generated code with a critical eye and the right techniques, developers can harness the speed of AI *without* sacrificing the performance and user experience that users ultimately care about.

Code Volume, Churn, and Bundle Cost

New 2025 data (*https://oreil.ly/MTSNk*) shows a rise in cloned code blocks and short-term churn in AI-assisted repositories. That pattern tends to increase bundle size and parse/execute time unless teams aggressively dedupe and enforce size budgets. Treat "generated volume" as a cost center you must manage.

AI-Aided Optimization: The Future?

Could AI help identify or fix performance issues? Possibly, yes—but in practice, this is still in its early days. In the future, we might see smarter AI tools that can analyze a codebase and suggest performance improvements ("This function is called often and could be memoized," or "These network requests could be parallelized"). This is a topic of active research. As of 2025, however, most AI coding tools are generative (creating code from descriptions) rather than analytical on runtime performance metrics.

One area AI *can* help with today is writing tedious optimization boilerplate *when you know what you want*. For example, if you need to set up a web worker to offload a heavy computation, an AI can scaffold that. If you know you need a more efficient algorithm but you forget the exact implementation details, the AI can produce that quickly. It's like having a very fast reference manual that can produce code.

However, *you* have to know what to ask for. AI won't automatically decide to optimize a working solution unless you explicitly prompt it that way. If you prompt it to "improve the performance of this function," it might attempt something, maybe unrolling a loop or using a different data structure. But the AI's fixes are only as good as its understanding of what *performance* means in context—which is tricky without actual profiling data. As you saw earlier, many AI-suggested "optimizations" don't pan out.

Agents are also beginning to optimize with runtime context. When connected to DevTools through the new MCP server (*https://oreil.ly/qv7_V*), an agent can record a trace, identify the top long tasks affecting INP, and propose focused refactors. This is promising for "find the hot path and suggest a fix," but in 2025, it still requires human review and verification with Lighthouse or RUM to avoid overfitting or regressions.

Impact on the Overall Performance Landscape

Because it's so easy to generate code with AI, AI assistance could lead to *more* code being produced overall, inadvertently making apps heavier. If you don't carefully prune your AI outputs, you could end up with a lot of extra code. For example, an AI might implement edge cases or add configuration options you didn't ask for explicitly, simply because its training examples often did so. That could mean delivering more JavaScript or CSS to users.

On the other hand, AI might also produce more consistent code patterns, which could make it easier for humans to follow up with manual optimizations. If AI tends to output a common structure for certain tasks, browser engines or tools might eventually optimize for those patterns (this is speculative but possible).

For now, the pragmatic approach is to *treat AI-generated code like code from a junior teammate: it needs thorough code review and testing.* Check its performance implications. If you integrate AI-written code, run Lighthouse or WebPageTest on your app and see if any metrics regressed or if bundle size jumped. It's also wise to incorporate linting and analysis tools in your workflow when using AI. For example, run ESLint (perhaps with performance-focused rules) or a bundle size analyzer after adding AI-written code. These can catch obvious issues, like including a huge library or using a very inefficient DOM method.

It's worth noting that industry surveys confirm these cautionary perspectives. Over half of developers (and engineering leaders) report (*https://oreil.ly/GZRwP*) that increased AI-generated code has led to more performance problems in their applications. So while AI can accelerate coding, it doesn't absolve us from our performance engineering responsibilities.

The Human Role in the AI Era

AI can accelerate coding, but the human developer's role shifts more toward verification, integration, and making higher-level decisions. When it comes to performance, *humans still need to set the goals and judge the outcomes.* AI might one day autonomously optimize algorithms (there's research, for example, on AI optimizing compiler output or finding micro-optimizations in code), but in typical app development, we're not there yet.

In a sense, AI is just another tool—like a more advanced Stack Overflow. And just as you wouldn't copy-paste an answer from Stack Overflow without understanding it (one hopes!), you shouldn't blindly trust AI answers. The advantage with AI is that you can iteratively prompt it ("now make it faster," "now use a binary search," etc.), which can be educational for the developer and can yield better code after a few rounds. But it's a dialogue, not a one-shot solution.

A Concluding Thought on AI and Performance

As AI becomes a more prevalent part of writing frontend code, you can adapt by including performance criteria in your AI usage. For example, if using Copilot or ChatGPT, occasionally stop and ask: "Is there a more efficient approach here?" You can even prompt the AI for it: "Can we do this with less time complexity or memory usage?" Sometimes it will respond with a better solution.

In summary, AI-generated code can impact performance positively or negatively depending on how it's used. It's not a replacement for performance expertise. If misused or unvetted, it could lull teams into shipping heavier or slower code under the false sense of security that "the AI wrote it, so it must be fine." Use AI to handle the boilerplate and mundane parts of your code, while you focus on critical thinking about resource usage and user experience.

The key is to maintain a performance-review mindset. Automated and AI assistance don't absolve us from profiling and testing our applications. We must continue to measure outcomes and enforce standards. The end user doesn't care if code was written by an AI or a human—they only care how fast and smooth the experience is. It's our job to ensure that AI is a help, not a hindrance, to that end goal.

Now that Part I of this book has given you a high-level overview of what's at play in web performance in the AI age, Part II gets into the specifics of optimization.

PART II
Optimizing Web Performance in the Age of AI

CHAPTER 4
Optimizing AI-Generated Frontends

Speed and responsiveness are core to user satisfaction in web applications. When working with AI-generated frontend code, performance engineering becomes a deliberate exercise. In this chapter, we explore how to ensure that applications created with LLM assistance meet the high bar for web performance and quality. We'll use Core Web Vitals (CWVs) as a framework to understand key aspects of performance, identify common pitfalls in AI-generated React code, and walk through practical examples of diagnosing and fixing issues. We'll also see how modern tools—from Chrome DevTools (now augmented with an AI "Ask Gemini" assistant) to Google Lighthouse—can assist in this optimization process. The goal is to empower you, the developer, to turn an AI-generated baseline into a finely tuned, user-centric web application.

CWVs and AI-Generated Code

As covered in Chapter 2, Google's CWVs—largest contentful paint (LCP), interaction to next paint (INP), and cumulative layout shift (CLS)—provide a framework for measuring user experience in terms of performance. These metrics zero in on what users feel most: *Does it load quickly? Is it responsive? Is it stable?*

When working with AI-generated code, these metrics take on special significance. AI-generated apps often inadvertently create performance issues that directly impact CWVs:

LCP issues
  An AI might unknowingly make choices that bloat loading performance, such as not compressing images, loading too much data up front, or failing to prioritize critical CSS and JavaScript.

INP issues

> AI-generated code doing heavy work on the main thread can make the app unresponsive. For instance, a common issue is an AI writing a slow JavaScript loop or a big JSON parse that blocks the thread, so when the user clicks a button, nothing happens for a second. Ensuring snappy interactivity often means breaking up long tasks, using web workers for heavy computations, or deferring noncritical work—strategies that typically require human intervention to implement.

CLS issues

> AI-generated code often overlooks the nuances that prevent layout shifts. For example, an AI might insert an `<img>` without specifying its width and height or including a placeholder space, meaning that when the image loads, it suddenly pushes text around. Or it might fetch data and inject a list of items above existing content, causing everything to reflow.

When reviewing AI-generated apps, you should immediately ask: *How will this affect LCP? Could it hurt interactivity with any heavy computations or large synchronous tasks? Will it introduce layout shifts due to dynamic Document Object Model (DOM) changes without precautions?* By keeping these questions in mind, you can systematically find and fix issues.

As you've seen from Chapter 2, modern tooling like Google Lighthouse can simulate a page load and give you LCP, CLS, INP, and other scores, often flagging specific problem areas. Running a Lighthouse audit on your AI-generated page is a great starting point to see where it stands. In essence, the CWVs act as a quantitative lens through which to view the quality of AI-generated code. Next, I'll discuss typical problem patterns that cause poor scores and how to address them.

Common Performance Pitfalls in AI-Generated React Components

React is a popular target for AI code generation. Many developers ask LLMs to generate React components, hooks, or even entire apps. React apps, however, are not magically free from performance issues. In fact, there are well-known pitfalls in React that can lead to poor performance or UX, and an AI might stumble into many of them if not guided. This section breaks down a few common CWV-related issues that arise when AI generates React frontend code.

Layout Instability (Poor CLS)

One frequent oversight is that AI-generated React components may not ensure a stable layout. For example, consider an AI-generated image gallery component. The AI might produce code like the following, which I've simplified for illustration:

```
function Gallery({ images }) {
  return (
    <div className="gallery">
      {images.map((img) => (
        <img src={img.src} alt={img.altText} />
      ))}
    </div>
  );
}
```

At first glance, this is a valid React component that will display a list of images. However, it has no consideration for preventing layout shifts. The images are rendered as they load, and if each image is a different size (or if the network delivers them at different times), the surrounding content will shift as each image appears. Users will see the gallery content jumping around—a classic high-CLS scenario. A human developer with experience in web performance would know to add something like width and height attributes (or CSS aspect-ratio boxes) for each image or to use a placeholder that reserves space, to ensure the layout is stable as images load. The AI, unless prompted specifically about this, doesn't have that intuition.

Another layout issue can occur with how AI injects content. Suppose AI-generated code fetches some data on mount and then renders it:

```
useEffect(() => {
  fetchData().then((newItems) => setItems(newItems));
}, []);
//...
return (
  <div>
    <Header /> {/* static header */}
    {items.map((item) => (
      <ItemCard data={item} />
    ))}
  </div>
);
```

This looks normal: it shows a header and, once the data is fetched, a list of item cards. But consider the visual behavior. If the <Header> is fixed at the top and the list appears below it, what happens when the data arrives? If initially the list was empty and then suddenly dozens of <ItemCard> elements populate the DOM, the sudden expansion can push other content (or the page footer) downward, causing a layout shift. If the AI didn't include any loading indicator or placeholder of fixed height, the user might experience a jarring jump.

The timing of state updates in React can also produce jank if not handled carefully. For example, setting state multiple times in quick succession can lead to multiple rerenders. In short, AI-generated React code often doesn't handle the visual stability aspects needed to prevent CLS.

So how do we address this issue? Developers should explicitly enforce stable layouts in AI-generated components. That means manually adding image dimensions or CSS aspect ratios, setting min-heights for containers that will be dynamically populated, and using techniques like skeleton screens or loading spinners for content that arrives later. Also, be wary of AI code that directly manipulates the DOM outside React (like via `document.querySelector` in an effect): such code can bypass React's virtual DOM diffing and cause unexpected layout changes (most AI-generated React code sticks to React paradigms, but layout shifts can still occur). The key is to reserve space for content and avoid sudden DOM injections that shift existing elements.

Bloated Bundles and Slow Loading (Poor LCP)

Another common pitfall is that AI-generated code might inadvertently create a large JavaScript bundle or load excessive resources, hurting the LCP. For instance, if you ask an AI to implement a certain UI component, it might import a heavy library for a small functionality. I've seen cases where an AI, in an attempt to create a date picker or chart, pulled in an *entire* library like Moment.js or D3 because it "knew" that would be one way to solve the problem. The result was adding hundreds of kilobytes of JavaScript, increasing download and parse times and delaying the rendering of the largest element. An experienced developer might have solved the same problem with a lighter approach or by code splitting the heavy component to load only when needed. An AI likely won't do that unless prompted.

Another example is not deferring noncritical work. An AI might put a data fetch or an expensive computation right in a component's initialization or top-level effect, without considering delaying it. If that code executes immediately on page load, it could delay the rendering of the main content. Also, AI might not add performance optimizations like `<link rel="preload">` for critical assets or `async/defer` on noncritical scripts in an HTML document it generates, which a skilled performance engineer would use to improve load times.

To combat slow loads in AI-generated apps, profile the network and bundle. Use tools like Webpack bundle analyzers to see if the AI included something unexpectedly large. Check the Network panel in Chrome DevTools to observe how many requests are being made and their sizes. It's not uncommon to find that an AI solution is making multiple sequential API calls where one batched request would do, or loading an image at full resolution where a thumbnail would suffice. By catching these, you can refactor. You might split the code, using React's `lazy()` and `<Suspense>` to load heavy components or libraries only when needed; remove or replace heavy libraries with lighter alternatives; and compress or resize images appropriately.

Running a Lighthouse audit will also call out issues like enormous network payloads or unused JavaScript, which often directly point to AI-induced bloat. If your

AI-generated page has a poor LCP, those audits will give clues—perhaps a large script is blocking rendering or a big image wasn't optimized.

Modern build tools and module bundlers (Webpack, Rollup, Parcel, etc.) allow us to split our JavaScript into smaller chunks. Instead of one monolithic bundle that includes everything (which increases initial download and parse cost), you can create multiple bundles and load some of them on demand. The simplest example is *route-based splitting*: for a single-page application, the code for each route (page) can be split and only loaded when the user navigates to that route. If your home page and dashboard have entirely separate code, why burden the home page with dashboard code that may never be used in that session?

Code splitting can drastically reduce the amount of JavaScript needed at initial page load. As a rule of thumb, performance experts often suggest (*https://oreil.ly/hD0k7*) that if your bundle exceeds ~50–100 KB (compressed), it's worth splitting. With HTTP/2 and HTTP/3, the overhead of multiple small files is reduced (thanks to multiplexing and header compression), so the old fear of "too many files" is less acute. The emphasis is on loading "just enough" code to render what the user needs first. The team that runs Chrome's V8 JavaScript engine puts it plainly (*https://oreil.ly/Q-Hyx*): "Avoid having just a single large bundle; if a bundle exceeds ~50–100 kB, split it up into separate smaller bundles." On mobile, the threshold is even lower due to slower networks and parse times.

How do you implement code splitting? You do it practically, often by using dynamic `import()` in JavaScript or lazy loading facilities in frameworks. For example, in React, you might use `React.lazy` or a library like React Loadable to split components. In Webpack, write `import('./Chart.JavaScript')` to split off a separate chunk. When the user actually needs that code (that is, when they navigate to the section with the chart), the app triggers loading that chunk.

Another useful pattern is Import on Interaction (*https://oreil.ly/XCOXg*), as Patterns.dev names it. Suppose you have an expensive component (say, a rich-text editor or a large third-party widget) that the user only sees after clicking a button. You can design your app so that the code for that component doesn't load until the user clicks that button. This way, users who never use that feature never pay the cost for it. To quote Patterns.dev, "loading resources eagerly can block the main thread if they are costly, pushing out how soon a user can interact…Instead, load them at a more opportune moment, such as when the user clicks to interact or when the browser is idle." By deferring noncritical code in this manner, you improve interactivity metrics, because less JavaScript is occupying the main thread early on.

A complementary approach is Import on Visibility (*https://oreil.ly/Xb82H*). This is like interaction-based loading, but it's triggered by scrolling: if a component or section of the page (like a "comments" widget at the bottom of an article) isn't in the viewport initially, the browser won't load its JavaScript until the user scrolls it into view. Using the `IntersectionObserver` API, you can detect when an element becomes visible and then import the necessary module. This way, content "below the fold" doesn't slow down the initial rendering of content above the fold.

Main-Thread Bottlenecks and Janky Interactions (Poor INP)

LLMs do not understand the concept of the browser's main thread or the event loop; they'll happily write code that monopolizes the CPU if it solves the problem. In React, an AI might generate a computationally heavy operation inside a component or as part of state updates. For example, suppose you ask for a component that filters a list of items based on user input, and the AI integrates that logic:

```
function FilteredList({ items, query }) {
  const filteredItems = items.filter((item) => matchesQuery(item, query));
  // ... then maps filteredItems to JSX ...
}
```

This looks straightforward, but if `items` is large and this component rerenders frequently (say `query` is bound to a text input where the user types), it could become a performance nightmare. With every keystroke, the entire list (maybe thousands of items) is filtered on the main thread. This could cause noticeable input lag or even freeze if the list is big enough. A human developer might immediately think to debounce the filtering or move heavy computation to a web worker, but the AI-provided code won't do that unless explicitly told. Similarly, an AI might sort data in the render path, perform deep copies of large objects, or update state in a loop—all patterns that can lead to long tasks that block the UI.

The result of such patterns is often a high total blocking time (TBT) in lab tests and poor interaction to next paint (INP) in the field. Users experience this as the UI stuttering or being unresponsive to clicks and keypresses. In extreme cases, the browser might even throw a "Page Unresponsive" warning if a JavaScript function runs for too long uninterrupted. Watch out for any AI-generated code that performs heavy synchronous work on the main thread.

Profiling the runtime performance is key here. Use the Chrome DevTools Performance panel to record a timeline while you interact with your page. The flame chart will show you if there are long tasks, like a 300-ms or 500-ms JavaScript function blocking the main thread. If you see a big chunk of activity corresponding to an AI-generated function, that's a red flag.

So how do we address this issue? Optimize by splitting that work, using techniques like `requestAnimationFrame` to chunk it across multiple frames, or offloading it, perhaps using web workers for heavy computations or employing memoization to avoid repeating expensive calculations unnecessarily.

In React specifically, look for places to use `React.memo` or `useMemo/useCallback`. An AI might not add these performance optimizations on its own. For instance, if the AI created a component that rerenders frequently even though its props haven't changed, wrapping it in `React.memo` can prevent needless recalculations and DOM updates. Similarly, if the AI calculates derived data on every render, you can wrap that in a `useMemo` to only redo it when the inputs change. This kind of tuning requires understanding which parts of the UI are truly dynamic and static—context that comes from *you*, not the AI.

Neglected Accessibility and UX Feedback Loops

While not CWVs, accessibility and good UX often intersect with performance. A classic example is focus management. If a user clicks a button that opens an AI-coded modal, did the AI ensure that keyboard focus moves into the modal for screen-reader users? Possibly not. That could leave some users "stuck," not knowing that new content has appeared.

Performance-wise, if the AI's code doesn't include ARIA live regions or other cues, a screen reader might not even announce that dynamic content is loading or has loaded—effectively "hiding" slow loads from users. This ties into perceived performance: even if your app is a bit slow, a good UX will reassure the user with spinners, progress bars, and ARIA announcements like "Loading…" so they know the app hasn't frozen. AI tends to skip those niceties unless asked.

AI-generated code also might not handle error states or edge cases. If a network request fails, the AI code might simply `console.log` it and do nothing, meaning the user could be staring at a spinner forever with no message. A human would likely add a timeout or an error message like "Failed to load data, please try again." While this is more about robustness, it impacts perceived performance and user trust—the app *feels* unresponsive or broken if there's no feedback.

In summary, AI-generated React code often covers the "happy path"—the simplest scenario, where everything loads and nothing goes wrong—but omits these critical UX contingencies. Developers need to fill in these gaps to deliver a truly polished product. That means adding loading indicators, focus management, ARIA attributes, error handling, and other UX enhancements to ensure that *all* users (including those with assistive tech or poor network conditions) get a smooth experience.

Having enumerated these pitfalls, let's shift to a more concrete view—improving an actual AI-generated component. This will illustrate the process and mindset a developer should apply.

Improving an AI-Generated Component

Let's say you ask an LLM:

> Create a React component that displays a list of articles with a title, image, and summary. It should fetch the list from an API and include a search filter to find articles by title.

This is a realistic prompt for a simple content feed page. The AI might produce something like this:

```
// AI-generated ArticleList component (simplified)
function ArticleList() {
  const [articles, setArticles] = useState([]);
  const [search, setSearch] = useState("");

  useEffect(() => {
    fetch("/api/articles")
      .then((res) => res.json())
      .then((data) => setArticles(data));
  }, []);

  const filtered = articles.filter((article) =>
    article.title.toLowerCase().includes(search.toLowerCase())
  );

  return (
    <div>
      <h1>Articles</h1>
      <input
        type="text"
        placeholder="Search..."
        value={search}
        onChange={(e) => setSearch(e.target.value)}
      />
      <div>
        {filtered.map((article) => (
          <div className="article-card" key={article.id}>
            <img src={article.imageUrl} alt={article.title} />
            <h2>{article.title}</h2>
            <p>{article.summary}</p>
          </div>
        ))}
      </div>
    </div>
  );
}
```

At a glance, this code is quite reasonable: it fetches data on mount, allows searching by title, and displays a list of article cards with an image, title, and summary. Many developers might even accept this as is if it appears to work. But as a performance engineer, I see multiple issues:

No loading state
> During the fetch, this component renders nothing but the heading until the data arrives. If the API is slow, the user sees a blank area under the "Articles" header, with no indication that content is loading. When the data finally arrives, the entire list of articles pops into the DOM at once, potentially causing a layout shift if the page was initially shorter. There is no feedback to the user that something is happening in the background or that they should wait.

Potential layout shift from images
> The images in each article card are rendered directly from `article.imageUrl` without width and height attributes or placeholders. Unless all images coincidentally have the same dimensions or load instantly, this can cause CLSs as each image loads. The `<h2>` and `<p>` text might move down or around when the image above them appears, which is exactly the kind of CLS issue we discussed.

Main-thread blocking filter
> The filtering logic `articles.filter(...)` runs on every keystroke in the search input. If there are a thousand articles, every character typed will cause a refiltering of all articles. In React, updating the search state on every keypress triggers a rerender and recomputation. This could become sluggish as the list grows. Also, the filter comparison uses `toLowerCase()` on each title for each keystroke. That much string manipulation is fine for small lists, but across hundreds or thousands of items, it can add up, scaling linearly to make typing feel laggy.

No code-splitting or heavy-library concerns
> In this particular example, the AI didn't use any large external library, which is good. But what if the summary needed Markdown rendering and the AI pulled in a hefty Markdown parser library? That's not the case here, but it's always something to watch for in AI-generated code. Here, the bundle size might be OK, but it's worth checking if any polyfills (like for `fetch`) might be needed for older browsers. That's a minor point in this example.

Now, how can you improve this code? Let's walk through some optimizations step by step:

Add a loading state to improve UX and avoid layout jank
> You can introduce a piece of state like `isLoading` and set it to `true` before the fetch and `false` after data arrives. While loading, instead of rendering nothing, it will render a placeholder—maybe some skeleton cards or at least a spinner, so users aren't left guessing. It also reserves space for the content, preventing a big

shift when the real articles load. Also, what if the API call fails? You should handle that by perhaps setting an error state and displaying a message or a retry button. The AI did none of that.

Prevent uncontrolled rerendering during filtering

You can debounce the filter input to avoid filtering on every single keystroke. For instance, you can use a useRef or a small debounce hook so it only filters after the user has paused typing for, say, 300 ms. Alternatively, if you expect a huge list, consider moving the filtering to a web worker (this is probably overkill unless the dataset is very large).

Another easy optimization is to memoize the filtered results, so that if search changes quickly or toggles back and forth, it's not recomputing everything from scratch each time. You could use useMemo for the filtered list:

```
import React, { useMemo } from 'react';

// ...inside your component
const filteredArticles = useMemo(() => {
  // Return all articles if the search is empty
  if (!search) {
    return articles;
  }

  // Otherwise, return filtered articles
  return articles.filter(article =>
    article.title.toLowerCase().includes(search.toLowerCase())
  );
}, [articles, search]);
```

In this case, debouncing is usually more effective than memoization for rapid typing. The key point is that the filtering logic doesn't make the UI sluggish.

Optimize the images for CLS and performance

Set explicit widths and heights (or CSS aspect ratios, via styles) on the <img> elements. If the API provides image dimensions, use them. If not, at least set a fixed size for thumbnails. Additionally, add loading="lazy" to defer loading images that might be below the fold. Lazy loading images can dramatically improve LCP if many images are present, because the browser then only fetches the ones needed for the initial viewport. Also, consider using srcset for responsive images or a low-quality placeholder technique. This is beyond the initial AI's scope, but a human can layer it on.

Consider splitting out large content or heavy computations

If the list of articles is very long, an advanced optimization would be to use windowing or virtualization libraries so only the visible items are in the DOM, rather than rendering all of them at once. An AI is very unlikely to implement list virtualization by itself. It's an enhancement you might add if profiling shows that rendering a thousand <div>s is too slow or memory-intensive.

After implementing some of these changes, your improved component might look like this:

```
import React, { useState, useEffect, useMemo } from 'react';

const SkeletonCard = () => (
  <div className="skeleton-card">
    <div className="skeleton-img"></div>
    <div className="skeleton-text"></div>
    <div className="skeleton-text short"></div>
  </div>
);

function ArticleList() {
  const [articles, setArticles] = useState([]);
  const [search, setSearch] = useState("");
  const [isLoading, setIsLoading] = useState(false);
  const [error, setError] = useState(null);

  useEffect(() => {
    setIsLoading(true);
    fetch("/api/articles")
      .then(res => res.json())
      .then(data => {
        setArticles(data);
        setIsLoading(false);
      })
      .catch(err => {
        console.error(err);
        setError("Failed to load articles");
        setIsLoading(false);
      });
  }, []);

  // Debounce the search input value
  const [debouncedSearch, setDebouncedSearch] = useState("");
  useEffect(() => {
    const handler = setTimeout(() => setDebouncedSearch(search), 300);
    return () => clearTimeout(handler);
  }, [search]);

  const filtered = useMemo(() => {
    if (!debouncedSearch) return articles;
    return articles.filter(article =>
      article.title.toLowerCase().includes(debouncedSearch.toLowerCase())
    );
  }, [articles, debouncedSearch]);

  return (
```

```
    <div>
      <h1>Articles</h1>
      <input
        type="text"
        placeholder="Search..."
        value={search}
        onChange={e => setSearch(e.target.value)}
      />

      {/* 3. Removed all backslashes '\' from JSX tags and expressions */}
      {error && <p className="error">{error}</p>}

      {isLoading ? (
        <div className="skeleton-list">
          {/* Skeleton UI indicating loading state */}
          <SkeletonCard />
          <SkeletonCard />
          <SkeletonCard />
        </div>
      ) : (
        <div className="article-list">
          {/* 4. Corrected '=\>' to '=>' in the map function */}
          {filtered.map(article => (
            <div className="article-card" key={article.id}>
              {/* Reserve space for images with width/height attrs */}
              <img
                src={article.imageUrl}
                alt={article.title}
                width="150"
                height="100"
                loading="lazy"
              />
              <h2>{article.title}</h2>
              <p>{article.summary}</p>
            </div>
          ))}
        </div>
      )}
    </div>
  );
}
```

While this code example is a bit more verbose, it addresses the issues:

- The page now informs the user when content is loading.
- It uses a <SkeletonCard> component to show placeholder cards that mimic the shape of an article card, reserving space and avoiding a big layout jump when real content arrives.
- It handles errors gracefully by showing an error message if the fetch fails.

- You debounced the search input to avoid heavy refiltering on every keystroke, and used `useMemo` to avoid filtering more than necessary. The filtering now happens after the user stops typing for 300 ms, reducing work—and the heavy lifting is only done when the debounced search term changes.
- Adding explicit widths and heights to the `<img>` makes the browser allocate space for it immediately, preventing layout shift when it loads. You also marked images as `loading="lazy"` to defer those not immediately in view. In a real app, you'd choose appropriate sizes and perhaps use responsive `srcset` for different screen sizes, but the idea stands.

These improvements would translate to better CWVs:

- LCP improves because things aren't blocking the main thread as much. The fetch still happens but shows a skeleton almost immediately, so the user perceives progress. Lazy loading images makes the initial render lighter.
- INP improves because typing in the search box no longer does tons of work on each letter—the debounce means if the user types quickly, we only filter after they pause, plus the heavy computation is reduced via memoization.
- CLS improves dramatically because the skeleton ensures that when real content replaces it, the layout is similar (no big jumps), and the images have reserved space so their loading doesn't push text around.
- Accessibility and general UX are also better—for instance, adding a live region announcement ("Loading articles…") when starting to fetch means that now users get feedback on what's happening or if something went wrong.

This example encapsulates a general principle: *AI can generate a baseline implementation, but it's typically up to the developer to refine that implementation with performance and quality in mind*. Each fix applied here is a known best practice that an experienced engineer would carry out almost by reflex. The AI, however, lacks those instincts. It doesn't feel the pain of a slow site. We do (or at least our users do), which is why we must be proactive.

Performance Profiling and the New AI-Assisted DevTools

Once you have an AI-generated app (or any app) running, the best way to uncover performance problems is to profile it with real tools. Chrome DevTools is the workhorse for this. By using the Performance panel in Chrome, you can record a session of your site running—capturing all the JavaScript execution, rendering, layout calculations, and network activity that occur. This is incredibly valuable for pinpointing issues. You might discover, for instance, that a single function (maybe an AI-generated data-processing loop) is taking 200 ms of CPU time and causing a visible stall, or that a layout thrash is happening (multiple style recalculations triggered unnecessarily).

Before AI, analyzing these performance profiles required significant expertise. You'd look at the flame graphs and stack traces to deduce what's slowing things down. However, DevTools itself now offers AI assistance (*https://oreil.ly/6lKU-*) by integrating an "Ask AI" feature, powered by Google's Gemini model, directly into various panels, including Performance. You can literally ask the browser to interpret the performance profile for you. For example, after recording a performance timeline, you can right-click on a long task in the flame chart and click "Debug with AI" (exact text may differ), and the AI will provide an analysis of that call stack or a summary of what might be causing a slowdown, as shown in Figure 4-1.

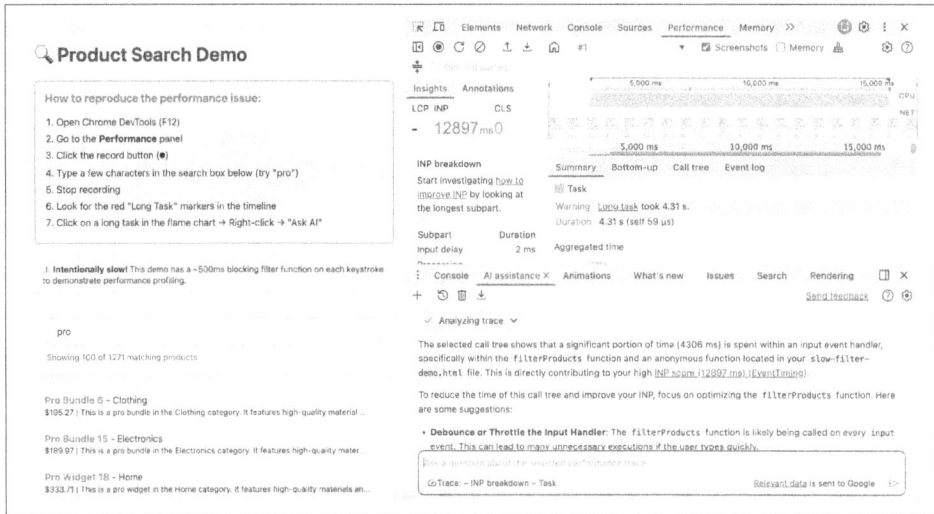

Figure 4-1. The Chrome DevTools Performance panel with an AI analysis highlighting something like "This long task is a data-filtering function that runs on each keystroke, which is causing input delay, `filterProducts` is the root cause"—confirming our suspicion about the filter

Chrome's DevTools AI integration extends beyond the Performance panel to other useful areas. In the Sources panel, you can ask about specific code ("Why is this function slow?" or even "Suggest a fix for this deprecated API usage"), and it can provide suggestions or explanations. The Network panel's AI can explain why a certain request failed or is slow ("This request is not cached and is 5 MB"). There's even a Console AI that can explain console errors and warnings in more depth. For instance, if your AI-generated code triggers a warning like "[Deprecation] Some API is deprecated," the console's "Explain" feature can use AI to tell you what that means and how to update it. This is a huge boon when dealing with unfamiliar AI-generated code. If the AI uses an outdated approach it saw in training data, the DevTools AI assistant might warn you about it and guide you to modernize that bit of code.

To use these features, you need a recent version of Chrome. Once enabled, you'll typically see an "AI" icon or an "Ask AI" (text may differ) context menu in various parts of DevTools. For performance, the workflow is: open DevTools Performance panel, hit Record, interact with your site (e.g., load it, click around, type in inputs), stop recording, then examine the call tree or summary. You can then ask questions like "What caused the largest layout shift?" or "Why is the page load slow?" and get answers. In the context of AI-generated apps, this is fantastic because it helps find the exact places in code that need optimization—which might very well be the ones the AI wrote in a suboptimal way. For example, the AI analysis might reveal that "Layout shift was caused by an image element added to the DOM without dimensions"—confirming our earlier suspicion and guiding the fix.

While DevTools is great for an in-depth analysis in your local environment, don't forget automated tools and external testing, as covered in Chapter 2.

Coding agents generate code without seeing how it behaves in a live browser. The new Chrome DevTools Model Context Protocol (MCP) server (*https://oreil.ly/u89da*) removes that blindfold. Through the MCP, your agent can drive a real Chrome browser; record traces and inspect the DOM, network, and performance; and then propose targeted fixes. In practice, this lets you pair an agent with the exact same telemetry you would use in DevTools, closing the loop between generation and runtime evidence.

The MCP server (*https://oreil.ly/922t5*) exposes DevTools capabilities to agents such as Gemini, Claude, Cursor, or Copilot. Agents can start or attach to a tab, run Lighthouse, capture a Performance trace, query layout and network waterfalls, and iteratively apply changes while measuring their effect.

Here's a pragmatic workflow for the MCP server that you can adopt today:

1. Stand up the DevTools MCP server locally, with your app running.
2. Prompt the agent to record a performance trace during a realistic user action, then summarize long tasks and probable causes for INP and LCP.
3. Have it draft candidate diffs that reduce long tasks or CLS sources.
4. Retrace then compare before-and-after metrics.

You can gate-check this by integrating performance-regression detection into your continuous integration pipeline: set up automated Lighthouse audits and scripted MCP traces that run on every pull request or commit, and configure your CI to fail the build if CWV metrics (LCP, INP, CLS) regress beyond acceptable thresholds. Many teams use tools like Lighthouse CI, which provides a command-line interface and CI for running Lighthouse audits and comparing results. You can also script the MCP server to capture specific user flows and validate that critical interactions remain fast. The key is to make performance a first-class concern in your development workflow—treating performance budgets as seriously as functional tests.

The MCP server does not replace expert analysis. It accelerates the "find and iterate" loop and gives you a reproducible, measurable path from suspected problem to verified improvement.

Testing on Real Devices: The Ultimate Validation

Even after all this profiling and tooling, one fundamental truth remains: the best way to know if your app performs well is to test it on a real device under real conditions. Lab measurements and AI analyses are immensely helpful for pinpointing and fixing issues, but they must be corroborated in the real world. Especially for performance, differences in device speed, network quality, and user behavior can reveal issues that synthetic tests don't.

If your AI-generated app is meant to run on a variety of devices, be sure to try it on a typical low-end smartphone, possibly on a throttled network connection (DevTools can simulate slow 3G, but an actual budget phone on a spotty network often gives a fuller picture). See how the app *feels*. Does it take too long to load? Is scrolling smooth? Does tapping buttons give instant feedback? Also, check for any obvious accessibility flows. Try using it with a screen reader or only a keyboard to navigate, to catch things the AI might have missed (like focus not moving into a modal, or missing form labels).

Why emphasize this when we have so many fancy tools? Because users don't use DevTools—they use the actual website. Sometimes an AI "optimization" might look good in theory but not yield the expected benefit on a real device. Conversely, certain issues (like a subtle layout shift or microstutter) might not get flagged strongly by metrics but can be very noticeable to users. By testing the app yourself (and better yet, getting some colleagues or beta users to try it), you complete the quality loop. You might discover, for example, that an AI-chosen image format isn't supported on some browsers or that overall memory usage is high and causing crashes on older phones—things you'd only catch by actively using the app in a real environment.

Using tools to gather performance data from actual users (often you can track CWVs through analytics or services like Google's CrUX will tell you if your optimizations are truly hitting the mark in production. If you have real user monitoring set up, pay close attention to those metrics after deploying any AI-generated features. Are users experiencing slower load times or interactions? If so, roll back or continue optimizing. In the AI era, a developer's role includes being the guardian of user experience postrelease, not just during development.

Embracing AI's Speed While Preserving Quality

This chapter focused on concrete strategies to bridge the gap between AI-generated code and high-performance, high-quality web apps. It's a lot to take in: you've considered CWVs as a guiding compass, dissected typical issues in AI-generated React code, optimized an example component, and leveraged both human expertise and AI-enhanced tools to improve outcomes.

The overarching message is one of balance. Embrace the productivity boost of AI—the ability to scaffold an app or feature in minutes—but counterbalance it with the due diligence of performance engineering and quality assurance.

The encouraging news is that the ecosystem is evolving alongside AI. Just as AI can generate code, it can also help *audit* code. I can imagine a not-so-distant future where your IDE or CI pipeline has an AI checker that flags in the following way: "Hey, that code you got from Copilot is making a blocking call on the main thread—consider refactoring it." In fact, tools and browser extensions are already cropping up to analyze code for performance antipatterns. Until those become more mature, the best approach is a combination of traditional best practices and new AI-powered assistive tools.

In conclusion, *AI-assisted development doesn't remove the need for skilled engineers—it amplifies the need for our skill in areas that AI isn't good at.* Performance, accessibility, security, and overall polish remain squarely in the human court—for now. Applications generated by large language models can be a fantastic starting point, but they achieve their full potential only when a developer guides them to the finish line.

When you build with AI, *you* are still the architect and the quality controller. By profiling, auditing, and iterating on AI-generated output, you ensure that the end result meets the rigorous standards of modern web performance engineering. The users get fast, smooth, and accessible experiences—and they won't know (or care) that an AI was involved in creating it, because you ensured that the final product was worth delivering.

CHAPTER 5
Inside the Browser: How Pages Load and Render

So far in this book, you've learned *why* web performance is crucial for user experience and business success, and you've gotten familiar with key metrics like the Core Web Vitals. In this chapter, I turn to the technical foundations. To effectively optimize loading speed, interactivity, and visual stability, you first need a solid understanding of *how browsers work*. This chapter dives into the journey that browsers like Chrome take when they transform code and resources into a fully rendered, interactive page. This knowledge will lay the groundwork for the specific optimization strategies discussed in the chapters that follow.

Browser Basics

Modern web browsers are incredibly sophisticated. They parse HTML; load resources like scripts, styles, and images; execute JavaScript; compute styles and layouts; and paint pixels to the screen—all while responding to user input and trying to keep animations smooth. To optimize performance, it's critical to understand the steps the browser goes through and how to speed or block those steps. This chapter demystifies the browser's rendering pipeline, as well as how browser schedules work on the CPU, with a focus on Chrome (Blink engine). While Chrome is my primary focus here, the fundamental concepts apply broadly across modern browsers—though the specific implementation details may vary. Chrome's dominance in market share and its well-documented architecture make it an ideal case study, and understanding Chrome helps you reason about performance across all browsers you need to support.

I'll start by following the lifecycle of a page load: from navigation start, through loading and parsing, to rendering and interactivity. Then I'll give you a peek into Chrome's architecture, including some more advanced concepts like the main thread, the compositor thread, the network stack, and how tasks are prioritized.

Multiprocess Architecture and the Main Thread

A *thread* is a basic unit of execution within a program—think of it as a sequence of instructions that the CPU can execute independently. Multiple threads can run concurrently within a single process, allowing a program to do several things at once, like parsing HTML while handling user input.

Chrome and other modern browsers use a *multiprocess architecture* for stability and security. This means the browser runs multiple separate processes (isolated programs in memory), each with its own threads. If one process crashes (say, due to a buggy website), it doesn't bring down the entire browser—only that tab might fail. When you navigate to a new site, Chrome typically spins up a new renderer process (isolated from others) to handle that page. The *renderer process* is where Blink, the rendering engine, runs. It contains threads, including:

- The *main thread*, which runs JavaScript and most of the Document Object Model (DOM) manipulations
- A *compositor thread*, which helps with handling graphics layers and smooth scrolling
- *Raster threads* for painting pixels
- *Worker threads*, if your site uses web workers or service workers

The main thread is the orchestrator of the browser's activity. It executes JavaScript, parses HTML into a DOM, computes CSS styles and layouts, and processes user events. The main thread can become a bottleneck: for instance, if it's busy running a large script, it can't simultaneously respond to user input or render updates. This is why many performance techniques focus on moving work off the main thread.

Chrome's architecture means that the network runs in a separate process (the browser process or a dedicated network service process), so *network events* (like responses arriving) are delivered to the renderer asynchronously. The renderer's main thread has to coordinate, parse, and execute network data, like HTML and XML HTTP requests (XHRs).

It's also important to understand *incremental rendering*: browsers try to display content as soon as possible. They don't wait for everything to be done. This means a page might paint some content (perhaps a header and spinner) after receiving a bit of HTML and CSS, even while the rest of the page is still loading. The largest contentful paint (LCP) metric often corresponds to one of these early renderings (ideally the first meaningful one).

The Rendering Pipeline

In a renderer process, the pipeline for loading a page goes roughly as shown in Figure 5-1.

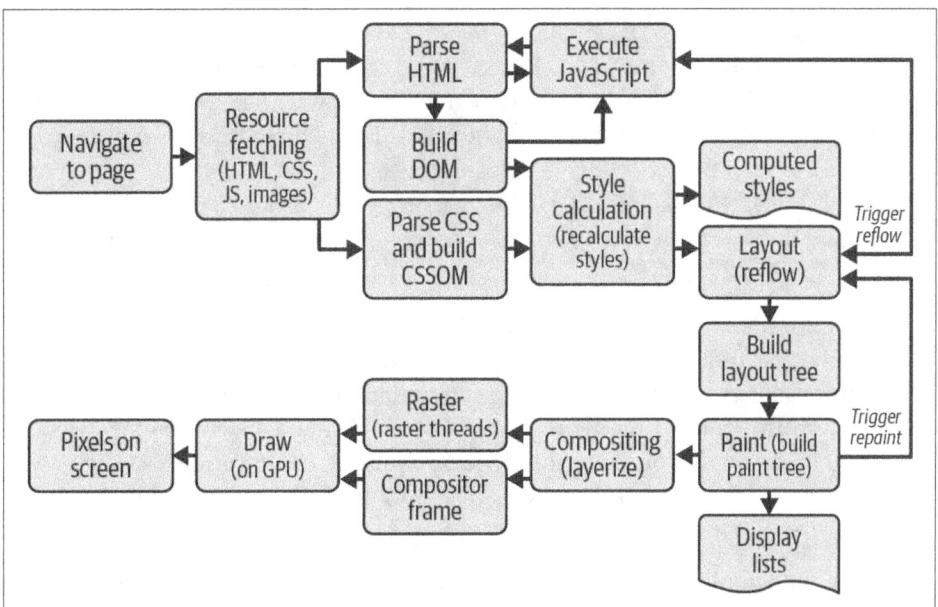

Figure 5-1. The Chrome rendering pipeline, from HTML to pixels: navigation/resource fetching, parsing, styling, layout, painting, and compositing

This breaks down into six steps:

Step 1. Navigation and resource fetching

When you click a link or type a URL, the browser kicks off a navigation process. It performs a DNS lookup, establishes a connection (TCP or QUIC), and sends an HTTP request. Meanwhile, it gets a renderer process ready.

For a new connection, establishing TCP involves a three-way handshake (SYN, SYN-ACK, ACK), which takes one round trip. For HTTPS, there's an additional TLS handshake to set up encryption. (In TLS 1.2, this required another round trip or two, but TLS 1.3 reduced it to one extra round trip.) These handshakes contribute directly to TTFB. Additionally, TCP uses *slow start*: it begins transmitting data at a conservative rate and ramps up over time. This means the first few kilobytes of data may arrive more slowly than later chunks, which is why reducing the size of critical resources (like initial HTML) and using protocols like HTTP/3 with the QUIC protocol (which combines connection setup and encryption into fewer round trips) can be so beneficial.

When the server responds to the HTTP request, data starts streaming in. The first piece is often the HTML of the page. This initial document response is critical; the time until the first byte arrives (TTFB) contributes to LCP, and if it's slow, everything is delayed.

Step 2: HTML parsing and DOM construction

The renderer's main thread receives the bytes of HTML and begins to parse them into the DOM tree. Parsing is incremental: the browser parses and renders progressively rather than waiting for all of the HTML to download. As it parses tags, it creates DOM nodes. If it encounters a `<script>` tag (without special attributes), it will pause the HTML parsing to fetch and execute that script, because the script might `document.write` more HTML. This can block progress.

Step 3: CSS parsing and style calculation

Alongside the DOM, the browser builds the CSS Object Model (CSSOM) by parsing CSS files, which it might discover from `<link>` tags or @import rules. Now it can perform *style calculation*, computing the styles for each DOM node—which in this context means resolving CSS rules into actual styles for each element. It can do this once both the CSSOM and the DOM (or at least the part of the DOM that's parsed) are ready. In DevTools this is called "Recalculate Style."

Step 4: Layout (reflow)

Using the DOM and the computed styles, the browser can determine the page's geometry of each element—how big it is and where it goes on the page. This gives the page its layout. The browser generates a *layout tree*, which is mostly the DOM but with coordinates.

Layout depends on the screen's size and on the page's content and styles. For example, say the browser figures out that your header is 80 px tall and spans the full width, and that the image is 600 px wide and 400 px tall and located at (X,Y) position. A `<div>` with a width of 50% needs to know the parent width before it can compute its own pixel width.

Step 5: Painting

After layout, the browser knows what each node should look like: its styles, dimensions, and so on. The next step is *painting*, or drawing out the pixels for each node. This could involve drawing text glyphs, filling backgrounds, and drawing images, borders, and shadows, among other things. Painting is often broken into drawing commands, like "draw a red rectangle here, then draw this text…"

Step 6: Compositing

Compositing involves combining layers and handling any 3D transforms (CSS properties like `transform: translateZ()` or `transform: rotate3d()`) or transparency between them. Modern browsers often break the page into multiple layers. For example, if the page has a fixed-position element or one with a CSS transform, it might be on its own layer. The compositor thread takes these painted layers (which might be rasterized by raster threads, often on the GPU) and composites them together into the final image that is displayed. The output is a bitmap for each frame, handed off to the GPU to display on screen.

Crucially, many of these steps happen iteratively and can overlap. For example, while the HTML is being parsed, if the parser encounters an <img> tag, it will start an image network request *in parallel* (*https://oreil.ly/gZr5b*), thanks to the preload scanner, which scans ahead for resources. The CPU (which does the parsing) and network (which fetches the images, scripts, and so on) work concurrently. However, certain things *block* others. For instance:

- A <script> without defer/async blocks the HTML parser; rendering is blocked until the script is executed.
- A <link rel="stylesheet"> blocks the content below it from rendering. The browser will delay drawing content that comes after the CSS in the DOM until the CSS is loaded and processed, to avoid showing unstyled content.
- A large JavaScript execution on the main thread (from any source, like a big React hydration routine) can block user input handling and delay things like layout or painting updates.

Throughout this pipeline, the browser is constrained by the critical path for loading: it can't render anything to the screen until it has at least parsed some HTML and the CSS for those elements. That's why optimizing the critical rendering path (such as by inlining critical CSS and deferring scripts) is so important for LCP, as you saw in Chapter 4.

Example

Let's break down an example to illustrate these stages. Suppose your HTML starts as follows:

```
<html>

  <head>

    <link rel="stylesheet" href="style.css">

    <script src="app.js"></script>

  </head>

  <body>

    <h1>Welcome</h1>
```

```
        <p>Hello world.</p>

        <img src="hero.jpg" alt="Hero image">

        ...

    </body>

</html>
```

When the browser starts loading this page, it parses the `<head>` and sees a stylesheet link. It sends a request for `style.css` and will block rendering until this CSS is loaded and processed, because anything in the body might depend on it.

It also sees a script tag for `app.js` without `defer/async`. This will block the HTML parser until the script is downloaded and executed (the parser will stop at this point in the HTML). If `app.js` is large, this could be a significant pause. (If it were `defer` or at the bottom of the body, it wouldn't block parsing, but that's a topic for Chapter 6.)

Once the script is executed, the parser continues down to `<body>`. It encounters `<h1>`, `<p>`, and so on, and builds DOM nodes for them. When it encounters `<img src="hero.jpg">`, it triggers a network request for the image, then continues parsing.

Assuming `style.css` has arrived by now, the browser builds the CSSOM. Now it can calculate styles. Let's say `style.css` defines the `<h1>` color and maybe sets the `<img>` width to 100%: the browser applies those styles. Now it has enough to do the first layout: it knows the `<h1>` text and probably the font, so it can measure that. (If it's a web font that hasn't yet loaded, the browser might use a fallback font first.) If the `<p>` and `<img>` have an intrinsic or specified size, it knows that too. It computes layout, positioning the `<h1>` at the top, then `<p>` below it, and so on.

Next, the browser paints those elements it has. If the image hasn't loaded yet but the browser knows its dimensions from HTML or CSS, the browser may just reserve an area for it and paint nothing or use a placeholder. (If it doesn't know the image's dimensions, this would cause a layout shift issue, as I discussed in Chapter 4.)

On a slow network, this initial paint might happen at, say, 1.5 s after navigation. At that point the user sees the heading "Welcome" and the paragraph text, and maybe an empty image frame. If the `<h1>` is the largest element, that would be an *initial contentful paint*. But when the image `hero.jpg` finally loads at 2.0 s, it is larger, so it becomes the LCP. At the moment it fully renders, the LCP timestamp is recorded.

Meanwhile, if `app.js` attached any event handlers for interactivity during its execution, those are ready. But if `app.js` also did something heavy (like rendering a big interactive widget or performing data processing), that would have taken time on the main thread, potentially delaying the layout and/or paint.

After the initial load, the user might scroll or click. Chrome's main thread will handle those events. If nothing heavy is blocking, it can respond immediately. But if `app.js` schedules some long-running task (like parsing a huge JSON file) right after load, that could interfere with the page's responsiveness. This is exactly what the interaction to next paint (INP) metric catches: if the user tries to click during that busy time, they'll experience a delay.

So the pipeline is: Networking → Parsing → (blocking on CSS/JS) → Style → Layout → Paint → Composite. This happens once initially, and then again and again for each frame update or user interaction that changes the page.

After the initial load, any changes to the DOM or style will trigger parts of this pipeline again. For example:

- Changing an element's classes or styles triggers style recalculation (and likely layout and paint).
- Adding or removing DOM nodes triggers layout updates and paints.
- Animating properties might go through layout: if you animate `height`, for example, that triggers layout every frame. Or they can be handled by the compositor: if you animate `transform` or `opacity`, those can often be done purely by the compositor on the GPU, without redoing the layout for each frame. Animations that avoid layout or paint work are much more efficient for keeping to a rate of 60 fps.
- Scrolling can be handled by the compositor for a smooth scroll, but if new content comes into view, like images loading as you scroll, that might trigger layout and paint.

RenderingNG

While the RenderingNG project shipped several years ago (2021–2022), its architectural improvements remain the foundation of Chrome's current rendering performance, making it still relevant to understand. Chrome's rendering engine (Blink) underwent a major overhaul to improve performance and reliability by rearchitecting how layout, painting, and compositing work—and these improvements are what you're working with today when optimizing for Chrome.

Chrome's layout module was rewritten as Layout Next Generation (LayoutNG). This rewrite made the engine more robust and often faster with complex layouts like tables, flexboxes, and grids. Essentially, LayoutNG is a cleaner, more modular codebase that can handle edge cases better and compute layouts more efficiently. For example, it can better isolate layout work to specific subtrees of the DOM rather than recalculating the entire page. Its performance still depends on the DOM size and changes, though. Layout is usually $O(n)$ with respect to the number of elements that need layout. If you dirty the whole DOM, layout cost is proportional to DOM size. LayoutNG tries to scope layout to subtrees where possible.

As part of the improvements to painting and the compositor, Chrome splits rendering into layers. Some elements get their own layers, like video elements and elements with a fixed position or with certain CSS (like `will-change`). These layers can be rasterized independently. Chrome breaks large layers into tiles and rasterizes them in parallel threads. CSS, once fetched, is parsed on a separate thread as well, so parsing it doesn't block the main thread except when it needs to execute JavaScript.

The *compositor thread* coordinates these layers. It can scroll and move them: for example, a fixed header stays put by the compositor and does not need the main thread. The actual drawing of bitmaps from vector instructions happens on *raster threads* (tile workers), often leveraging the GPU via the Skia graphics library. When you have a complex image or large CSS blur effect, it can be processed off the main thread on a parallel thread. Compositor thread then takes the rasterized layers and composites them into the final image, typically applying transforms every frame for animations. This is efficient if the main thread doesn't need to recalculate the layout or style. If you animate transforms or opacity, those animations run on the compositor thread only; the main thread can be idle or doing other stuff. This means they typically stay smooth even if the main thread is busy.

Partial paint is now an option as well: instead of repainting the whole screen on each change, Chrome tracks damage regions and only repaints invalidated regions.

Forcing a layer (via `will-change: transform` or `translateZ(0)` hack historically) can help isolate an element so its changes don't trigger relayouts of other elements. But since each layer is a surface, overusing layers can take a toll on memory. Use them judiciously.

The Preload Scanner and Prioritizing Resources

While the HTML parser is parsing, Chrome employs a clever mechanism called the *preload scanner*. This is essentially a secondary parser that scans ahead in the incoming HTML for resource references, like `<img src>` or `<link href>` or `<script src>`. As soon as it finds one, it initiates the network request for that resource *without waiting for the main parser to reach that point*. For example, even if a script tag is at the bottom of the HTML, the preload scanner can start fetching that script early, so that by the time the main parser actually gets there, the script might already be downloaded, speeding up the execution. The preload scanner is one reason why putting CSS at top and scripts at bottom works well: the CSS gets discovered and downloaded early, blocking the render but at least getting started ASAP. Scripts (with defer) get downloaded early, too, but are executed later.

Browsers also prioritize resources. For example, the browser might assign the CSS and JS needed for the initial render a high priority, while giving images below the fold a lower priority until needed. Chrome has an internal prioritization scheme for network requests. For instance, images might start at low priority, but if they are likely to be in viewport or are discovered early, their priority can be raised. One new development is that Chrome now gives developers influence over priority via the Priority Hints API (using the `fetchpriority` attribute), which I'll discuss in "Common Trade-Offs" on page 92.

Scripts and the Event Loop

JavaScript execution in the browser happens within the main thread's event loop. The *event loop* processes tasks in a queue (actually multiple queues of differing priority in modern browsers). When a script is downloaded and a task is queued to execute it, it runs to completion before the browser can do other work on that thread, like rendering or handling input. This "run-to-completion" model (*https://oreil.ly/AfEmf*) means a long-running script can block the thread for its entire duration. After the script executes, control returns to the browser's rendering pipeline, which applies any changes.

The browser's event loop intermixes different kinds of tasks: user input events, script timeouts, network callbacks, rendering tasks, etc. Browsers like Chrome implement sophisticated scheduling so that high-priority tasks (like user input handlers or animation frames) are handled before less urgent tasks (like background timers). Later in this chapter I will discuss Chrome's scheduler (*https://oreil.ly/tbCS6*) and new APIs like `scheduler.postTask()`, which allow you to post tasks with designated priority queues (such as `user-blocking`, `user-visible`, or `background`). For now, just be aware that not all tasks are equal and that the browser tries to keep the page responsive by juggling tasks appropriately.

Another concept is *microtasks*, like promise continuations, versus *macrotasks*, like regular events and timers. An *event loop tick* refers to one iteration of the event loop—the browser picks a task from the queue, runs it to completion, then processes all queued microtasks. Finally, it may render an update before starting the next tick with another task.

Microtasks run immediately after the current task, before the browser can do other work like rerendering. This is why if you continuously schedule work using `.then()` or use `async/await` in a tight loop, you can starve the event loop and block the UI, because the browser must finish the entire queue of microtasks before it can render a single frame. They can starve the event loop if a microtask keeps queuing another microtask (like a recursive Promise chain).

For example, this code will freeze the UI:

```
function recursiveMicrotask() {

  Promise.resolve().then(() => {

    // Do some work
```

```
      recursiveMicrotask(); // Immediately queue another microtask
  });
}

recursiveMicrotask(); // This will block the browser indefinitely
```

Since each microtask queues another before the tick completes, the browser never gets a chance to render or handle user input. To avoid this, break work into macrotasks using `setTimeout` or the scheduler API to yield control back to the browser periodically. The scheduler API's priorities mainly apply to macrotasks. Microtasks always run immediately next unless you break out of them, so avoid unbounded microtask loops.

The RAIL Model

You met RAIL (response, animation, idle, load) in Chapter 1. Here, you will just use it as a lens for how microtasks and scheduled work affect the main thread.

Response and animation are where long microtask chains can really hurt you. Work that runs in microtasks after an input event still counts against the same response window, and microtasks scheduled inside `requestAnimationFrame` run before paint. So keep per-interaction work small (to help stay within the INP budget) and avoid piling heavy microtasks into frames that need to render.

Idle is where you can safely move nonurgent work that would otherwise block inputs or animation. The `requestIdleCallback` API lets you schedule this kind of work so it only runs when the main thread has time:

```
const workQueue = [];

function processWork(deadline) {

  // deadline.timeRemaining() tells you how much time you have

  while (deadline.timeRemaining() > 0 && workQueue.length > 0) {

    const task = workQueue.shift();

    processTask(task);

  }

  // If more work remains, schedule another callback

  if (workQueue.length > 0) {

    requestIdleCallback(processWork);
```

```
        }
    }
    requestIdleCallback(processWork);
```

Even then, break larger jobs into small chunks and yield regularly so that new input and rendering work can run in between idle slices.

Load is mostly about keeping startup work (including microtasks) from delaying the moment when primary content appears and becomes interactive. Use RAIL as a checklist: anything that is not critical to initial response, animation, or load can usually be pushed into idle time.

Rendering Performance Bottlenecks

If you know the pipeline, you can anticipate where performance issues are likely to arise. Some key trouble spots are:

Network latency or bandwidth
> A slow server response or large resources (images, videos, big JavaScript files) can increase loading time. If the HTML is slow to arrive (a high TTFB), everything is delayed, affecting LCP. If critical CSS or JavaScript is slow, it can block rendering or interaction readiness.

Parsing and script execution
> Large JavaScript bundles take time to download, parse, and execute. If the main thread is busy executing a script when the user interacts, that interaction will be delayed, affecting INP. If scripts block the parser for too long, they will delay when content appears, affecting LCP.

Layout and paint complexity
> Deeply nested styles or very complex layouts with thousands of DOM nodes can slow down style calculation and layout, which can cause janky interactions or slow rendering. This affects INP and potentially cumulative layout shift (CLS), if things shift slowly. Large repaints, like redrawing a big canvas or reflowing a giant table, can also slow down frame rendering.

Layout thrashing
> If JavaScript repeatedly forces layout calculations in a loop (for example, reading DOM size, then modifying DOM, then reading again), the browser may do multiple style and layout passes where one would suffice. This can massively degrade performance.

Unscheduled background work
> Scripts like those for analytics or ads often do their work on timers or after load. If these run without care, they can steal precious main-thread time. For example, an analytics script doing heavy computation right as the page is becoming interactive could interfere with the user's first interaction.

Visual stability issues
> If content is inserted dynamically without reserving space, the user experiences layout shifts (poor CLS). This might not slow down the CPU, but it harms UX. Some layout shifts, like loading ads or images without dimensions, can also trigger additional layout calculations.

Chrome's engine is heavily optimized: the RenderingNG project revamped its layout, paint, and compositing systems to handle complex pages more efficiently. However, even with these optimizations, poorly designed content can still overload the main thread. No matter how optimized the engine, web content that does too much will still be slow. A performance engineer's job is often to simplify and shorten the work the browser has to do—or defer it until it's less critical.

Now that you have a high-level understanding of what the browser is doing, we can look at some of its more advanced internals.

Advanced Browser Internals

This section is a dedicated deep dive into Chrome's internal architecture and how it relates to performance. I'll explore how Chrome prioritizes and schedules tasks on the main thread, examine the trade-offs of SSR and hydration strategies, and investigate the network stack's role in resource loading—giving you a complete picture of the browser's internal machinery. It explores how Chrome's scheduler prioritizes tasks and how the network stack handles resource loading and prioritization. By understanding these internals, you can better reason about performance trade-offs and align your decisions with the browser's behavior. This knowledge is not strictly required to optimize a site (which is why earlier chapters focused on direct tips), but it provides a foundation for truly expert-level performance engineering. It helps in diagnosing weird edge cases and understanding why certain optimizations have the effect they do.

Chrome's Main-Thread Task Scheduler and Task Priorities

The browser's main thread faces competing demands, including executing JavaScript, responding to user input, and updating the screen with layout and paint. Chrome's main-thread scheduler uses multiple task queues with different priorities to ensure that high-priority work, like handling input and animation, isn't starved by low-priority tasks. This system is often referred to as the Blink scheduler, since Blink is Chrome's rendering engine.

Chrome categorizes tasks internally. While the exact details are proprietary, generally, user input and event-handling tasks go into a high-priority queue, so that the scheduler will run them before other tasks if possible. Animation and rendering tasks also get a high priority; for example, the tasks that run for requestAnimationFrame callbacks are prioritized to keep animations smooth. In Figure 5-2, we can see the spectrum of task priorities from high end to low end.

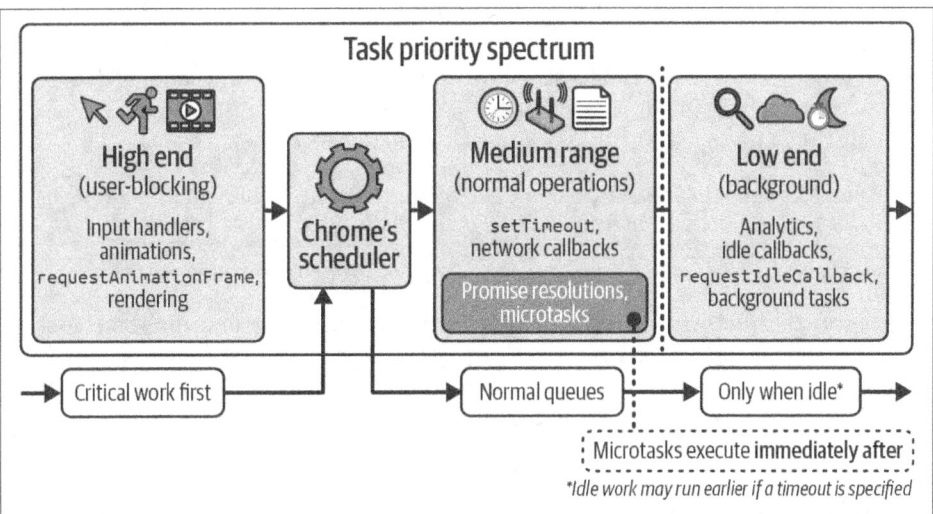

Figure 5-2. Task priority spectrum

You can visualize task priorities on a spectrum: at the *high* end are user-blocking tasks (input handlers, animations), in the *medium* range are normal operations (setTimeout, network callbacks), and at the *low* end are background tasks (analytics, idle callbacks). Chrome's scheduler uses this priority hierarchy to ensure the most critical work happens first.

Normal tasks that get a medium priority include setTimeout. Note that promise resolutions execute as microtasks, not macrotasks—they run immediately after the current task completes, before any other macrotasks. However, when promises trigger callbacks that schedule new work (like fetching data), those new tasks go into the normal priority queues. Microtasks, as previously noted, happen immediately after each task, but tasks triggered by microtasks also go into queues. Networking tasks like fetch callbacks are usually normal priority as well, but if they trigger UI, they become part of a user workflow.

A low priority is assigned to idle tasks, such as those scheduled via `requestIdleCall
back` or marked as background by the scheduler API. These should run only when
nothing urgent is happening.

In earlier Chrome versions, tasks were mostly "first in, first out" (FIFO), which meant
that a big chunk of script could delay input handling until it finished. That's where the
RAIL model applies to scheduling: ensuring that response and animation tasks are
timely. For example, if an input happens while JavaScript is running, Chrome can't
truly preempt the JavaScript: it's single-threaded and can't be interrupted except at
awaits or yields. Instead, at the next opportunity (the end of task or an await),
Chrome can prioritize the input handling task before resuming other work. This is
why yielding helps: it gives the scheduler a chance to intervene and pick a more
important task next. Thus, the scheduler's power is mostly in ordering tasks, not
breaking into running tasks, though new research may change that in the future.

The `scheduler.postTask` API gives developers a hook (*https://oreil.ly/9RoP7*) into
these priorities:

```
scheduler.postTask(myFunc, { priority: 'user-blocking' });
```

When you call this API, it posts `myFunc` to the queue designated for user-blocking
tasks, which has the highest priority. This is effectively similar to running `myFunc` as if
it were an input handler or critical task. Use this for things that affect UX immediately. Conversely, if you used `priority: 'background'`, it would go into a low-
priority queue.

As a rule of thumb, use `'user-blocking'` for work that must complete before the
user can interact, `'user-visible'` (the default) for work that affects what's on screen,
and `'background'` for analytics, prefetching, or other noncritical tasks. If a user input
comes along, Chrome can run that input's tasks first (if input tasks are user-blocking)
and only run the background when idle. Using `scheduler.yield()` gives even finer
control: you can yield with a specific priority hint for resuming.

This scheduler is only for the main thread. Web workers have their own thread and
message queue. They can't directly mess with the DOM, but they're great for heavy
work. Using workers effectively means putting fewer heavy tasks on the main thread,
which implicitly improves its ability to handle input.

Server-Side Rendering (SSR) and Hydration

While careful task scheduling helps manage main-thread load, another powerful
approach is to reduce the amount of client-side work required in the first place—
which is where SSR comes in.

Loading less JavaScript is one side of the coin; rendering sooner is the other. One of
the most effective ways to improve the *perceived* performance of a web app is to do

work on the server so that the user sees meaningful content faster. This is the idea behind SSR: you run your UI generation logic on the server to produce HTML and send that to the browser, so it can display content without waiting for all the JavaScript to load. For JavaScript-heavy apps, SSR can dramatically improve metrics like LCP because the server can usually render the basic HTML faster than the browser can download, parse, and execute JavaScript to do the same work.

However, SSR comes with a follow-up cost: hydration. *Hydration* is the process where the client-side JavaScript takes over a server-rendered page, attaches event listeners, and makes the page interactive. Essentially, after the HTML loads and displays, the app's JavaScript bundles run and "hydrate" the static HTML by binding it to the framework's runtime (converting it into a live app). Hydration often involves rerunning the component-rendering logic on the client to attach events and restore any dynamic state. It's called "hydration" because it's like adding water to dehydrated (static) content to make it live.

Hydration itself is additional JavaScript work that happens on page load. In an ideal world, the server would render the content and the client would just handle interactions after that. In practice, most frameworks need to re-run or do a reconciliation to wire up the page. This means SSR will likely save time on *rendering* (the user sees content faster), but the JavaScript bundle still needs to hydrate, and during hydration the page might not respond to input. It's not uncommon to see fast LCP but slow time to interactive (TTI) if hydration is heavy.

Some experts have pointed out that hydration can be very inefficient. Miško Hevery, the creator of Angular and Qwik, has provocatively said (*https://oreil.ly/iuqjm*) that "hydration is pure overhead," essentially redoing work that the server already did. When you hydrate, you typically download the same component code that rendered on the server, then execute it to recover event handlers and state in the browser. This can be CPU intensive and duplicates logic. As Hevery puts it, hydration is a "horrible workaround because web frameworks don't embrace how browsers actually work." These strong words reflect that hydration doesn't add new user value—it just makes the page interactive in a roundabout way.

So what can you do? There are a few approaches:

Partial hydration/islands architecture
    This modern architectural pattern is gaining traction and is used by frameworks like Astro, Marko, Qwik, Fresh, and Eleventy (with is:land). The idea is to only hydrate the parts of the page that truly need JavaScript, possibly doing so independently. Instead of one giant app booting on the client, you think of your page as composed of "islands" of interactivity within a static shell. For example, on a news article page, the header navigation drop-downs and comments section might be interactive, but the article text is static. You could serve all of the HTML but then *only hydrate the nav and comments components*, leaving the rest static.

This significantly reduces the JavaScript cost because you're not hydrating components that don't need it.

Progressive hydration
Some frameworks perform hydration in chunks or during idle time, and they also hydrate the least critical parts of the page last. One technique is to use `requestIdleCallback` to hydrate components when the browser is idle. However, be cautious: delaying hydration too much can leave interactive elements unresponsive if the user tries to interact before hydration completes. The key is to prioritize hydrating visible, interactive components first and defer only truly noncritical elements. Jason Miller, creator of Preact, suggests an *incremental hydration* approach, where you let the main thread handle user-critical tasks first and then hydrate in the background when free. This ensures that hydration tasks don't block first input. In practice, few frameworks automatically do this yet, but it's a pattern developers can implement.

Resumability
Hevery's framework Qwik takes a radical approach: eliminate hydration entirely by designing the framework to resume exactly where the server left off. Qwik serializes the state of the app into the HTML (as `JavaScriptON` or a script), so the client side does not need to rerun components to know what the state is. It also can attach event listeners in a lazy way: rather than adding all event handlers on load, Qwik attaches a single global handler that, when an element is clicked, can fetch the code for that specific listener on the fly. The result is that a Qwik app can be interactive without running any JavaScript at startup, only downloading and executing code in response to user interactions. This fulfills Hevery's vision of no-overhead hydration: resumability focuses on transferring all state to the client, allowing the client to reason about the app without downloading the code eagerly. Only a user interaction forces the client to download code for that specific interaction—there's no duplicate work as in hydration, thus no overhead.

In essence, the app is instantly interactive up to the first user interaction, at which point it pulls in just the needed code. This is a fairly new approach and requires a framework built for it (Qwik is one of the first). It shows a direction: frameworks trying to minimize or eliminate the cost of hydration to truly deliver on the promise of SSR without the usual downsides. If you're using a more traditional framework like React, consider frameworks like Next.js or Remix, which implement SSR and can do some selective hydration for you. Vue and Svelte both support SSR as well.

At a minimum, be aware that hydration costs exist. Measure it with tools like Chrome's DevTools Performance Profiler, which will show you what big rerender or script-execution chunks will happen during hydration. If they're large, you might need to simplify your app's initial load or split up that hydration work.

SSR is a powerful technique, but it shifts some burden to the client in the form of hydration. The goal of many modern approaches is to reduce that burden: *partial hydration* ensures you only hydrate what's needed, and *resumability* aims to skip hydration altogether. For our purposes, the key takeaway is: render on the server when you can; in the client, do as little work as possible to go interactive. A page that shows up fast and then spends five seconds "hydrating" isn't a win if the user can't do anything in those five seconds. You want pages that show up fast *and* respond fast.

Combining SSR with code splitting (so that hydration scripts themselves are split by component) can help. React 18 introduced selective hydration (*https://oreil.ly/YC3R_*) as part of its concurrent rendering features, allowing React to prioritize hydrating components that the user is interacting with, which significantly improves perceived interactivity during the hydration phase.

The Network Stack and Resource Loading

Chrome's network architecture plays a crucial role in how quickly resources load and how efficiently the browser handles multiple concurrent requests. Understanding the network stack helps you reason about connection pooling and HTTP/2 and HTTP/3 prioritization, and how to influence resource loading through hints and optimization techniques. The network interacts closely with parsing: while the network service downloads data on a separate thread, the main thread remains responsible for parsing that data. This means a busy main thread can create bottlenecks even when network speed is adequate.

Network Service architecture

Chrome's network stack runs in a separate process called the Network Service. Prior to approximately 2019, network operations ran in the browser process, but the current architecture isolates networking into its own service process. This separation improves security and stability—if network code encounters an issue, it won't directly crash the rendering engine.

When the renderer process needs a resource, it sends a request to the Network Service, which manages the actual network operations: socket management, DNS resolution, TLS negotiation, and data transmission. The Network Service handles protocol details transparently, whether using HTTP/1.1, HTTP/2, or HTTP/3.

Chrome's multiprocess architecture also affects how cross-origin resources are loaded, with separate processes handling different origins for security isolation. Within the renderer itself, beyond the main thread, the compositor and raster threads handle graphics operations. You can exploit this architecture by offloading heavy canvas rendering to a worker with `OffscreenCanvas`, which allows raster threads to do the work without blocking the main thread.

HTTP/2, HTTP/3, and request multiplexing

Modern protocols significantly impact loading performance. With HTTP/2, a single TCP connection can carry multiple requests concurrently through multiplexing—combining multiple signals or streams into a single shared communication channel to improve efficiency and reduce costs, eliminating the need for multiple connections per domain. However, HTTP/2's prioritization mechanism (using weights and dependencies) has historically been problematic. Many servers didn't implement it well, and network conditions like packet loss could undermine it. Chrome compensated with its own simpler internal scheduling, limiting in-flight requests and prioritizing high-importance resources first.

HTTP/3, built on QUIC, takes multiplexing to the transport level, eliminating head-of-line blocking that plagued HTTP/2 over TCP. When one packet is lost in HTTP/2, it can block all streams on that connection; HTTP/3 avoids this because QUIC handles streams independently. HTTP/3 introduces a new priority scheme (*https://oreil.ly/bLj5m*) where clients send Priority headers to indicate relative urgency of requests. Chrome's `fetchpriority` attribute translates directly to these protocol-level hints in both HTTP/2 and HTTP/3. The spec also mentions "Priority update frames" in HTTP/3, which Chrome uses to dynamically adjust priorities during the connection lifetime.

Many top sites now use HTTP/3. QUIC's 0-RTT connection resumption integrates the TLS handshake with connection setup, so TTFB on subsequent connections can be significantly lower. While HTTP/3 is still relatively new, it continues to improve and gain adoption.

Note that Chrome has removed support for HTTP/2 Server Push due to complexity and underuse. Early Hints (discussed later on) are now the recommended alternative for pushing critical resources.

Connection setup and resource hints

Before fetching resources, the browser must establish connections, which involves DNS lookup and TCP/TLS handshaking. This is where resource hints like `<link rel="preconnect">` and `<link rel="dns-prefetch">` become valuable. These hints allow the Network Service to perform DNS resolution and optionally establish TCP/TLS connections to a host in advance, so when the actual resource request comes, the connection is ready, saving round trips.

Similarly, Early Hints (HTTP 103 status code) enable servers to send preliminary link headers before the main response. Chrome's network stack treats these as preload instructions and initiates fetches immediately, merging them with any duplicate requests that come later. This allows critical resources like CSS and fonts to start loading even before the HTML fully arrives.

Request prioritization and scheduling

Chrome assigns internal priorities to different resource types to ensure critical resources load first. HTML typically gets the highest priority, CSS and JavaScript get high priority, and images receive medium or low priority, depending on heuristics. For above-the-fold images, Chrome might assign higher priority—likely because the preload scanner flags images in the immediate viewport if their dimensions are known. The `fetchpriority` attribute gives developers explicit control over these priorities, and `<link rel="preload">` resources are treated as high priority by default.

For resource scheduling, Chrome limits concurrent requests on HTTP/1.1 connections (typically around six per domain), but on HTTP/2 it can send many requests concurrently. Still, Chrome maintains internal bandwidth-allocation logic to prevent lower-priority resources from starving critical ones. In practice, HTTP/2 prioritization has been a known problem area—it can be undermined by packet loss, and many servers haven't implemented it well.

When using script tags, `async` and `defer` attributes tell Chrome that scripts can load in parallel without blocking rendering. The preload scanner won't treat them with the same highest priority as CSS. Chrome actually deprioritizes `defer` scripts somewhat compared to CSS or images needed for LCP. If you notice resource contention clogging the pipeline, ensure that the `as` attribute on preload links matches the resource type to get correct prioritization.

Caching and service workers

Chrome's HTTP cache, stored on disk (or in memory for small items), is keyed by URL and relevant headers. When navigating or reloading, Chrome may reuse cached resources or validate them with the server via `304 Not Modified` responses. Effective caching dramatically improves loading metrics like LCP, since cached resources require no network wait or minimal validation time.

If a service worker controls the page, requests are intercepted and routed through it first. This adds slight overhead, especially if the service worker isn't already running and must be started. However, service workers can serve resources directly from cache, often making responses significantly faster than network requests. As a performance engineer, ensure your service worker is optimized and consider using `navigationPreload` to allow network requests to start in parallel with service worker startup.

Network stack and main-thread interaction

While the Network Service runs on a separate thread—ensuring downloads don't block the main thread—parsing the received data happens on the main thread. HTML, CSS, JSON, and other formats all require main-thread parsing. Large JSON payloads can block the main thread during parsing, potentially causing jank. You can mitigate this by using the Streams API (`response.body`) to parse data in chunks or by parsing in a web worker to keep the main thread free.

Client hints and adaptive loading

The network stack can expose Client Hints such as the device's downlink speed and effective connection type, allowing you to adapt resource loading to network conditions. Chrome previously sent a `Save-Data:` on header when users enabled Lite mode (though Lite mode has since been removed from newer Chrome versions). If you receive `Save-Data` hints from browsers that support them, you might opt to serve smaller images or defer noncritical resources to respect users' data constraints.

Speculative loading and prerendering

Chrome supports advanced speculative loading techniques. The Speculation Rules API and the new `<link rel="prerender">` allow Chrome to prerender likely next pages in a hidden context. When the user navigates, the prerendered page can display instantly. This is called Prerender2, an evolution of the original prerendering feature, and it can dramatically improve multipage navigation performance. While not yet widely adopted by developers directly, search engines like Google are already using Speculation Rules to prerender search results. As the browser support and tooling mature, this technique is likely to grow in importance for multipage applications.

Putting It Together: A Timeline of an Optimized Load

Now that we've explored Chrome's architecture, rendering pipeline, task scheduler, and network stack in detail, let's walk through a complete, optimized page load from start to finish. This narrative demonstrates how all the concepts we've discussed—task scheduling, resource prioritization, efficient rendering, and careful JavaScript execution—work together to create a fast, responsive user experience.

Navigation start and service worker check

When the user clicks a link or enters a URL, Chrome's browser process immediately checks whether a service worker controls the target origin. If a service worker is registered and active, it gets the first opportunity to handle the navigation request. An optimized service worker responds quickly—either serving cached content instantly or allowing the request to pass through to the network without introducing delay. To avoid service worker startup latency blocking the network request, you've implemented `navigationPreload`, which allows the network fetch to begin in parallel with service worker initialization, ensuring you get the best of both worlds: cache control and fast network fallback.

Network connection and early hints

With the navigation request proceeding, Chrome's Network Service begins DNS lookup for the target domain. Because you've included a `<link rel="preconnect">` hint for the origin in the referring page (or the user has visited recently), the DNS is likely already resolved and a connection may already be open. The connection uses HTTP/3 with 0-RTT resumption, combining connection setup and TLS handshake into a single round trip, minimizing TTFB.

As the server receives the request, it immediately sends an HTTP 103 Early Hints response containing Link headers for critical resources—the main CSS file and hero image. Chrome's network stack treats these as preload instructions and initiates fetches for both resources right away, even before the HTML response begins streaming. This parallel loading saves precious milliseconds on the critical rendering path.

HTML arrival and parsing

The HTML response begins streaming to the renderer process. The main thread, which may have just finished tidying up the previous page's unload events, switches context to the new document and begins parsing the HTML bytes into a DOM tree. Meanwhile, Chrome's preload scanner runs on a secondary thread, racing ahead of the main parser to discover resource references like stylesheets, scripts, and images.

The preload scanner quickly identifies the same CSS file and hero image that Early Hints already referenced. Chrome's network stack recognizes these as duplicates and doesn't create redundant requests—the Early Hints fetches are already in flight. The scanner also discovers a `defer` script at the bottom of the document and initiates its download, though this script won't block parsing or rendering.

The CSS arrives from the network shortly after HTML parsing begins. CSS parsing happens on a worker thread, not blocking the main thread. However, the main thread must wait for the CSS to be processed before rendering content that depends on it—Chrome won't paint the body of the page until it knows how to style it, preventing a flash of unstyled content.

Main-thread scheduling and script execution

Our HTML includes a small analytics initialization script in the head with an `async` attribute. As soon as this script is fetched, Chrome queues a task to execute it. The task scheduler assigns it normal priority: it's not user-blocking, so if critical work like parsing or initial layout were competing, those would go first. However, during initial page load, user input is unlikely, so the script executes without much contention. The script itself is small and completes quickly (under 50 ms), so it doesn't significantly delay parsing or rendering.

Because you've used `defer` for your main application JavaScript bundle, it won't execute until after the DOM is fully parsed—this keeps it from blocking the critical rendering path.

Layout, paint, and the LCP element

With CSS parsed and the DOM partially constructed, Chrome can now perform style calculation and layout. The browser computes the geometry of each element—header height, text positioning, and, crucially, the dimensions and position of the hero image.

You've been diligent about performance: the `<img>` tag for the hero image includes explicit `width` and `height` attributes, and you've added `fetchpriority="high"` to tell Chrome this image is critical. Thanks to Early Hints and `fetchpriority`, the image has been downloading at high priority and arrives quickly. If the image isn't fully loaded yet when layout happens, the browser reserves the correct space for it (because you provided its dimensions), preventing layout shift when it does arrive.

The first paint occurs around 1.0 s after navigation starts. Chrome paints text content—you've also preloaded your web font, which arrives around 0.8 s, so the initial paint likely uses your custom font without a swap. Background colors and basic layout structure appear on screen. This is first contentful paint (FCP).

At 1.2 s, the hero image finishes loading and painting. Because it's the largest element in the viewport, this moment becomes your LCP. Crucially, no layout shift occurs because you reserved the image's space in advance—so your CLS remains at zero.

Post-load interactivity

With the DOM fully parsed, the `defer` script now executes at around 1.3 s. This script contains your application logic and event handlers, and it's been architected carefully to split work into chunks. Using `scheduler.postTask()`, it schedules noncritical analytics initialization as `background` priority, ensuring it won't compete with user interactions. Critical event listeners (click handlers, form submissions) are attached immediately and run as user-blocking tasks by default.

If the user clicks an interactive element quickly after LCP, the main thread is free—the heavy analytics work is queued as background and yields periodically. The click handler executes immediately (well under 50 ms), updates the UI, and performs any necessary calculations in a yielded manner, breaking work into chunks to stay responsive. This produces an excellent INP score.

Smooth scrolling and progressive loading

As the user scrolls down the page, Chrome's compositor thread handles most of the scrolling work independently of the main thread. You've applied `content-visibility: auto` to below-the-fold content sections, which means Chrome didn't need to fully render offscreen content during initial layout—this saved memory and improved rendering performance. As content comes into view, it renders just in time. The compositor leverages GPU-accelerated tile rendering, drawing pieces of the page in parallel.

You've attached scroll event listeners with the `passive: true` option (or avoided scroll listeners altogether), so the compositor thread doesn't need to wait for the main thread to check whether you'll cancel the scroll. The result is buttery-smooth 60 fps scrolling.

For images further down the page, you've implemented lazy loading using `IntersectionObserver`. As images approach the viewport, the observer triggers network requests for them. The Network Service fetches these with lower priority than initial resources, ensuring they don't compete with more critical work. This reduces initial page weight and speeds up LCP.

Handling dynamic interactions

Suppose the user triggers an action that requires fetching data from the server—perhaps opening a details panel that loads content via API. Your code responds immediately by showing a loading spinner (instant visual feedback), then calls `fetch()` to retrieve the data. The Network Service reuses the open HTTP/3 connection to the origin, avoiding connection setup overhead and getting data back quickly.

When the response arrives, you have options for handling it efficiently. For large JSON payloads, you can parse in a web worker to avoid blocking the main thread. For smaller payloads, you can process on the main thread but use the Streams API to handle it in chunks, yielding control periodically. Either way, update the UI incrementally, showing progress to the user rather than blocking. The page remains responsive throughout the interaction.

Zero layout shift

Throughout this entire journey—from initial paint through user interactions—you'll experience zero layout shift. You've been careful about every detail: image dimensions are specified, font metrics are matched between fallback and web fonts, and dynamically loaded content has reserved space or loads below the fold where it doesn't push existing content around. Your CLS score remains perfect.

The harmonious result

All components of Chrome's architecture—the network stack, the main thread, the compositor, the task scheduler—worked in perfect harmony to deliver this experience. The network stack prioritized critical resources and used protocol features like HTTP/3 and Early Hints efficiently. The main-thread balanced parsing, layout, and script execution without blocking. The compositor enabled smooth animations and scrolling without main-thread involvement. Task scheduling ensured user interactions took priority over background work.

Achieving this level of optimization requires understanding and applying all the concepts you've covered: resource hints, priority signals, task yielding, progressive rendering, and careful measurement of real user metrics. It's not about any single silver bullet—it's about making dozens of small, informed decisions that compound into a dramatically better user experience.

Conclusion

Armed with knowledge of how Chrome schedules tasks and loads resources, you can make better performance decisions:

- You know not to flood the main thread with long tasks and that *yielding*, or breaking up tasks, allows Chrome's scheduler to do its job (like handling input).
- You know to utilize background threads (workers) for heavy work.
- You understand that certain CSS properties are cheaper (compositor-only) while others are expensive (layout).
- You appreciate how hints and protocol features can speed up loading, and how crucial it is to provide the browser with the information it needs (like resource hints and dimensions) to do its job well.

For the curious, tools like Chrome's trace viewer can show how tasks and requests were prioritized and executed: record a performance trace and look at the "Blink scheduler" and "Network" tracks. You might see a script task labeled "user-blocking" or another labeled "background" if you're using the new API.

By mastering both high-level best practices and low-level mechanics, you'll become a performance engineer—capable not only of implementing optimizations but also of debugging the thorniest performance issues and understanding *why* something helps or not.

CHAPTER 6
Trade-Offs in Performance Optimizations

> *Web development is a series of trade-offs.*
> — Tim Kadlec (*https://oreil.ly/166WM*)

Every performance enhancement comes with a cost: increasing complexity, adding maintenance, even potentially hurting some other metric. This chapter takes a pragmatic look at strategies for improving JavaScript performance—and the trade-offs they entail. The goal is to help you evaluate optimizations objectively, balancing explicit recommendations with context. As Tim Kadlec wisely points out, there is rarely a one-size-fits-all solution in web development; we operate in a "grey goo" of possibilities. You have to know your priorities (speed, accessibility, developer productivity, etc.) and choose your optimization strategies accordingly.

Balancing Different Performance Metrics

As you've seen throughout this book, performance itself isn't one metric—it's many. Sometimes you need to trade one off for another. For example, to improve largest contentful paint (LCP), you might delay some script that is needed for interactivity, which could hurt interaction to next paint (INP) if the user tries to interact quickly. Or a strategy to optimize time to interactive (TTI) might increase the total load time slightly. You have to decide which metrics are more important for your scenario.

For a concrete example: if you have heavy JavaScript that doesn't affect above-the-fold content, you might postpone it until after the first paint. This improves LCP because the image or text loads faster; it might also improve INP since it leaves the main thread free at the start. However, if the user tries to interact early, some functionality might not be ready. If that happens rarely, it's fine; if it's common, you might need to ensure that critical interaction handlers aren't being delayed and perhaps load skeleton handlers that will show a spinner until the rest is ready.

It's a game of priorities. Make sure that any trade-off still leaves the user with a *consistently good experience*. No one likes a site that loads really quickly but then is unresponsive when you tap. No one enjoys an interactive site that gives them nothing to look at for seconds at a time. So aim to get something onto the screen quickly (optimize the rendering path) *and* make sure there are no long blocks where user input is ignored (optimize main-thread scheduling).

Objective Metrics Versus Subjective Perception

When making trade-offs, rely on data. Use real performance metrics: measure load times and interactivity times using Core Web Vitals like LCP and INP (see Chapter 4). If switching to a lighter framework or removing a library improves LCP by one second on 3G, that's huge and worth maybe making a dev's life slightly harder. If an optimization changes a lab test by five ms but adds three days of work each sprint to maintain, though, it's probably not worth it.

Also consider the *distribution* of your users. If 90% of your audience is on high-end corporate laptops on fast Wi-Fi and just 10% are on mobile, you might set a different budget than if 90% are on midrange phones. Alex Russell's p75 guideline suggests paying attention to devices at the 75th percentile and above, at the least. Depending on your product, you might explicitly target certain environments sometimes. Know who's using your product and on what devices.

Common Trade-Offs

In this section, I'll discuss the trade-offs in decisions like bundling versus splitting and framework abstractions versus vanilla JavaScript, as well as when to invest effort in micro-optimizations. Then we'll move on to how to set performance budgets.

Bundle Size Versus Network Overheads

In Chapter 4, I recommended code splitting as a way to reduce the initial size of the JavaScript. That's generally a good practice, but there is a trade-off: if you split your code into too *many* small chunks, that could incur additional HTTP requests or increase the total download bytes, due to bundle overhead or because you're duplicating the runtime boilerplate in each chunk. HTTP/2 reduces the per-request cost but doesn't eliminate it completely: for example, if each chunk has its own wrapper or needs its own fetch, 100 tiny chunks might incur more overhead than 10 moderately sized chunks.

So there's a balance: you want to isolate code that can be delayed or conditionally loaded, but you don't want to split so much that the initial page ends up pulling in hundreds of files, which can cause slowdowns for other reasons. It's often helpful to analyze real user data or use tools like Webpack's Bundle Analyzer to see how your code is split and if there's duplication among chunks. Let's look at some examples:

- Sometimes splitting can *cause* code duplication. For instance, if two lazy-loaded chunks share a common library, it might get included in both, increasing total bytes. The solution in that scenario might be to factor the common code into a separate, shared chunk that loads early or on demand.

- Suppose you have a large form on your page that uses a 50 KB validation library. You could either include it in the main bundle or load it *only* when the user navigates to the form and focuses on the first input. Including it up front adds 50 KB to everyone's load—even users who never open the form. Loading it on focus means a slight delay as the chunk loads (maybe 100 ms) the first time someone interacts with the form. Which is better? If most users use the form, maybe including it in the main bundle is fine, so no one experiences an extra delay on focus. If few do, lazy loading is better: that way, most users save the 50 KB download. There isn't a universal answer; it depends on your users' behavior and priorities. If that delay on focus is acceptable in your UX, or if you can perhaps mitigate it using a small spinner or by preloading when the user navigates to the form, then lazy loading is likely the better trade-off.

- Bundling all your code into one file might simplify the build and avoid any overhead from the runtime module loader, but it fails badly for caching: if *any* part of your app's code changes, the user has to redownload the *entire* bundle. With chunking, if you change one feature's code, only that chunk's hash changes. The others can be pulled from cache. So code splitting improves cache efficiency. The trade-off is making the build process a bit more complex and maybe adding some runtime complexity, but most would consider that worth it.

Consider bundle size against development speed too. Maybe you're only using two functions from a utility library like lodash. Importing the whole library would be wasteful, but you could cherry-pick just those modules. The trade-off is trivial with modern bundlers, but if you don't configure them properly, you might unintentionally include more of the library than needed.

Some teams disallow large utility libraries, preferring instead to write small helper functions by hand to save bytes. That's a trade-off too: writing that code might take more time or be more error-prone than using a battle-tested library. One approach is to use those libraries during development, then measure. If it looks like size is an issue, remove or replace the heaviest usages.

Frameworks Versus Vanilla JavaScript

A decision with one of the biggest trade-offs in web development is whether to use frameworks or heavy libraries to speed up development, or write more optimized, perhaps leaner code by hand. It's ultimately a question of prioritizing the developer experience versus the user experience. Frameworks like React, Angular, and Vue provide immense productivity and consistency benefits, but a very developer-friendly approach—like using lots of high-level abstractions or multiple analytics scripts for every need—might harm UX if it bloats the app.

However, as Tim Kadlec's analysis shows (*https://oreil.ly/dYcmq*), sites that use large frameworks often incur a significant performance penalty in terms of JavaScript bytes and CPU time. To quantify this, Kadlec pulled data from HTTP Archive. He found that median scripting time for React sites was about 9.3 s on mobile versus about 2.3 s for all sites. That's a huge difference. Angular and Vue had similarly heavy costs, while jQuery sites were closer to average (jQuery is smaller and not a full SPA framework).

This doesn't mean that "frameworks are bad" outright. It highlights a trade-off: those frameworks make it easier to build complex apps, but you're trading initial performance for that convenience (*https://oreil.ly/Hqhz2*). You can mitigate their cost through techniques like tree-shaking or server-side rendering (SSR), but there's always some overhead, since the framework's own code and abstractions must run.

If raw performance was the only goal, you might write an app with vanilla JavaScript or a minimal library, tuned to exactly what you need. But that could take much longer to develop and be harder for a team to maintain. The trick is finding balance. Some options to consider:

Use frameworks, but be disciplined
> For example, use a framework for the main UI but not for a simple landing page—maybe that page can be mostly static HTML. You could use a lighter-weight framework like Preact (*https://preactjs.com*), Solid (*https://solidjs.com*), or Svelte (*https://svelte.dev*) when possible to reduce runtime overhead. You could also trim parts of a framework you don't use or augment it with performance improvements, like using web workers for certain tasks or virtualization for long lists.

Embrace performance budgets
> If you choose to use a framework, Tim Kadlec and others strongly advocate setting a performance budget to keep yourself accountable. I'll discuss performance budgets in more detail later in the chapter.

Use progressive bootstrapping
> Consider using an app shell architecture, where the initial page is server-rendered and not all features are active until they're needed. This way, you use a framework but don't initialize the whole app on first load.

Developers have to advocate for the users. As Alex Russell writes (*https://oreil.ly/_7E31*), we need to shift from thinking in "developer experience mantras" to user-centered thinking. That doesn't mean you should never use frameworks—it means you should use them judiciously and be aware of the costs.

Micro-Optimizations Versus Maintainability

It's easy to get obsessed with micro-optimizations in JavaScript: things like "`for` loops are faster than `forEach`" or "avoid `try/catch` blocks because they can deoptimize your code" (*https://oreil.ly/-3SmC*) or "bitwise ~~ for `Math.floor`." Thanks to recent engine improvements, many of these micro-optimizations yield only tiny gains—or none at all. Worse, they can make code less readable and more bug-prone.

Donald Knuth's famous statement in *The Art of Computer Programming* (Addison-Wesley, 1968) that "premature optimization is the root of all evil" is a bit hyperbolic, but the core idea is that you shouldn't sacrifice clear design for minor performance tweaks without evidence that it will pay off. It's easier to refactor a well-structured codebase for big performance gains than a messy one littered with hacks that save a few milliseconds.

That said, in hot code paths, micro-optimizations can matter. If you've identified through profiling that a certain function is being called millions of times and is a bottleneck, then, yes, optimize it, even if you have to use a more complex but faster algorithm or cache results. Just make sure you always measure the impact. For example, you might find that eliminating a deeply nested closure or avoiding an object allocation in a tight loop gives that function a 20% performance boost, which might translate to a 5% gain in overall performance. If that 5% is meaningful (like if you're trying to get from 55 fps to 60 fps on an animation), then it's justified. If not, maybe skip it.

Frameworks often encourage certain patterns that might not be maximally efficient but are easier to reason about. For instance, in React, it's common to update state—which triggers a rerender of a component subtree. That might re-run rendering logic for many components, even if only one small part has changed. The React team provides tools like Memo and useCallback to help optimize this, but using them everywhere makes your code more complex. If your performance is fine, you could skip adding memoization to keep the code simpler. If your profiling reveals that wasted rerenders are making performance janky, *then* invest in those optimizations. In a sense, this is about applying complexity (like memoization or manual `shouldComponentUpdate`) selectively, where it pays off the most.

Long-term maintainability is also affected by how easily new team members can understand and modify code. Highly optimized code can be like assembly code—very fast, but very hard to work with. If a slightly slower, clearer approach means fewer bugs and faster iteration, that may be better. This is a trade-off where people often lean toward favoring maintainability, unless the performance impact is truly significant.

Performance Budgets and Culture

Setting a performance budget is one of the best ways to manage trade-offs. A budget might say something like this:

> Our home page should not exceed 200 KB of JavaScript and should hit a time to interactive of less than five seconds on a slow 4G network or a midtier device.

Everyone needs to agree on this and evaluate every decision (like adding a new library) against the budget. If adding something will break the budget, the team should either find a lighter alternative or agree to increase the budget (which should be rare and deliberate).

Budgets create a culture of accountability. They turn performance into a requirement, not a "nice to have." Tim Kadlec notes (*https://oreil.ly/-FmlZ*) that budgets are vital guardrails for preventing performance from degrading over time as features pile on. Of course, budgets themselves are a trade-off: you might sometimes say, "We can't meet this budget unless we drop feature X. Is that acceptable?" Maybe yes, maybe no. It's important to at least discuss it.

Building a performance-aware organizational culture (see Chapter 11) also means including performance in your definition of "done" or acceptance criteria. You don't want to ship a product and then, a month later, find your dashboards showing slower speeds. Instead, you want to catch those issues in PR reviews or testing.

There are also trade-offs around *when* to optimize. If you follow an Agile approach, you might first get something working, then iterate to optimize and improve speed. This is often practical: why spend a week micro-optimizing code that might change due to user feedback next sprint? Instead, you could measure after the initial implementation, then fix any bottlenecks. The risk here is that if you wait for too long, you accumulate more "performance debt" and it's harder to pay down. Ideally, include at least some baseline optimization from the start. Go especially for the low-hanging fruit, like not loading huge things unnecessarily. Then you can tune performance continually.

Third-party scripts like analytics, ads, tag managers, and A/B testing snippets are infamous performance killers. They often load additional resources and can even block the main thread or cause layout jank. Each one may be small, but together they add up. It's enough of a concern that I've devoted Part IV of the book to this topic, but for the moment, I want to draw your attention to the trade-off between the business value they add and their impact on performance. How can you find a balance?

Sometimes you have to educate stakeholders about why adding that fancy chat widget will slow the site for users, potentially reducing conversions more than the chat increases them. These are tricky discussions, but framing your argument in terms of user experience ("we might lose X% of users because of slower loads") can help you argue against purely feature-driven impulses. (See Chapter 11 for more about building a performance culture.)

Over the years, third-party code can accumulate, even if it isn't used anymore. If your site has been around for a while, one approach is to audit all of your third-party scripts and remove any that aren't truly providing value. For those you want to keep, you can also look for lighter alternatives or consolidate—maybe using one analytics platform instead of three.

It's also a good idea to use `async/defer` (*https://oreil.ly/LD5qK*) and other performance-focused techniques to load third-party code after the important stuff. For instance, you might put analytics loading at the end of the code body using `defer`, and perhaps wrap it in a `requestIdleCallback` to make sure it waits until the main thread is idle. If it's A/B testing that must run early to avoid flashing the original content, see if you can use server-side testing or at least a very optimized implementation.

There's also an emerging concept of performance contracts with third-party providers. Tim Kadlec mentions (*https://oreil.ly/gaoJH*) putting guardrails and monitoring around third-party performance. For example, if you find when using PerformanceObserver that a third-party script is causing a long task (tasks that take more than 50 ms to run, as defined by the long tasks API (*https://oreil.ly/xdqb3*)) or delays TTI, you might push back on the vendor to improve its performance or even dynamically unload scripts that misbehave.

Knowing When to Stop Optimizing

Another subtle trade-off to consider is your time. Could you spend infinite time squeezing out performance gains? Probably—but you have other features to build and bugs to fix. Once your site is within acceptable thresholds for most users, further improvements might yield diminishing returns. For example, if your site's already scoring a 90 in Lighthouse, chasing 100 might not noticeably help users—but it *could* consume a lot of effort that might be better spent elsewhere (and perhaps compromise your code's clarity too). Especially when optimizations require complex refactoring, they might only be worth it if there is a clear need, like user complaints or a competitive analysis showing that your site lags behind the competitors.

However, sometimes performance issues are *silent* killers—that is, users leave without complaining, so you never learn about the issue. Rely on your analytics and field data (see Chapter 2). If 20% of users have very slow times, that's a sizable chunk you could improve, even if the average looks good. Decide what level of user experience you consider acceptable (Google Chrome's guidelines (*https://web.dev/articles/vitals*), which include "p75 LCP < 2.5 s," are a good starting point). Once you hit "good" for most metrics for most users, you may declare victory and only revisit performance periodically or when adding big changes.

Conclusion

Performance optimization isn't about making everything as fast as possible at all costs. It's about making things fast *enough* that users are happy, in a way that's sustainable for development. By understanding the trade-offs and using data to inform decisions, you can find the right balance between speed and everything else you care about, like features, ease of coding, and code clarity.

To quote Tim Kadlec's advice (*https://oreil.ly/DfzNN*) one more time: "Find a solid base to build from, determine the considerations most important to the project and always keep those in mind as you make your decisions about what trade-offs to make." Keep user experience at the forefront, but also consider the viability of your team's workflow. The optimizations that stick (and don't get reverted or bypassed) are usually those that balance these factors well.

PART III
Optimizing JavaScript

CHAPTER 7
The Cost of JavaScript

> *It has never been easier to deliver pages quickly, but we are not collectively hitting the mark.*
> — Alex Russell (*https://oreil.ly/NhsKj*)

JavaScript is a double-edged sword: its performance can determine whether your users are delighted or frustrated. While it enables rich interactive experiences and is essential for creating the dynamic web experiences discussed in Part II, its costs are paid in CPU cycles, network bandwidth, and precious seconds of user time. Part III of this book explores what slows down JavaScript web applications and how to deliver great user experiences by mitigating those costs.

This chapter takes a deep, pragmatic look at JavaScript performance in the browser, focusing on real-world constraints and modern solutions. You've seen in Chapters 5 and 6 how new techniques like code splitting, hydration, and scheduling can improve perceived performance. Here, I'll examine how hardware and browser internals affect JavaScript execution and how JavaScript engines themselves have evolved to run code faster. My goal is to give you a high-level framework for thinking about JavaScript performance and a set of concrete techniques to apply.

Understanding the Constraints

To understand the cost of JavaScript, you must first understand *why* JavaScript can be so costly on some devices and networks. This chapter explores how CPUs, networks, and browser architectures shape its performance, often in surprising ways.

Device Performance: CPUs, Memory, and the Mobile Gap

As Alex Russell warns, if you build assuming ideal conditions, you risk excluding the many users on suboptimal devices or connections. Not all users have the latest iPhone or a high-end desktop. In fact, as discussed in Chapter 1, a huge portion of the world accesses the web on budget Android phones or older devices. The disparity in computing power is *stark*, and it directly impacts JavaScript execution.

JavaScript is CPU-bound during parsing and execution. A script that runs in one second on a high-end device might take three, four, or even six seconds on a low-end one. One 2019 study (*https://oreil.ly/dspHb*) found that in loading a typical site like Reddit's web app on a midrange phone, script execution took three to four times longer than on a flagship phone. It took more than *six* times longer on a low-end budget Android phone. In other words, a page that is "fine" on your MacBook Pro might be nearly unusable on an inexpensive Android handset.

Why such a big gap? Late-model high-end CPUs have multiple cores, higher clock speeds, bigger caches, and more advanced microarchitectures. Low-end and older devices often have fewer and slower cores and may throttle performance to save battery or prevent overheating (this is called *thermal throttling*). So not only do cheap devices have slower baseline speeds, but their sustained performance can degrade over time. JavaScript that "pegs the main thread," or fully occupies a CPU, on these devices can easily cause noticeable lag or jank. It's not just raw speed either; memory and garbage collection (GC) can also be constraints. Low-end devices have less RAM, which can lead browsers to collect garbage more frequently or to struggle with large script files in memory.

Russell's research into this performance inequality gap highlights that, to serve users at the 75th percentile of devices, developers and engineers need to rein in our resource usage significantly. The assumption that Moore's law (*https://oreil.ly/B9OlD*) means "devices will keep getting faster" simply hasn't panned out for the majority of users (*https://oreil.ly/IQXFi*). In Russell's blunt words, "It was all bullsh!t." The reality is, device performance improvements have slowed (*https://oreil.ly/oJXX7*), and the lower end of the market has not caught up. Today's fancy framework might run smoothly on the latest iPhone, but if your site bogs down an older Android or a Chromebook, you're *excluding* that user from your digital product.

Device constraints mean we must be conscious of how much JavaScript we send and how intensive our scripts are. In fact, one study (*https://oreil.ly/m22il*) found that mobile devices could experience long tasks (tasks that block the main thread for 50 ms or more) that take 12 times longer than on desktop hardware. Under heavy load, "older devices could be spending half of their load-time running Long Tasks" (*https://oreil.ly/1E6a_*), which implies the browser's main thread is tied up doing JavaScript when it should be responding to user input or rendering updates. This paints a clear picture: more JavaScript equals more CPU work, and not all CPUs are equal. For performance, the budget device should be your baseline—*not* the latest iPhone.

Network Constraints: Bandwidth and (Especially) Latency

Even before JavaScript reaches the CPU, it has to be delivered to the device. *Network constraints*—how fast code can download—are a major part of the cost of JavaScript. Developers in places with ubiquitous broadband may forget that many users are on slow or spotty connections. Mobile networks in particular introduce high latency and variability: despite the expansion of 4G and 5G, in practice many users still experience 3G-equivalent speeds or high latency regularly when on the go. This disparity is especially pronounced between urban and rural areas (*https://oreil.ly/j_OFx*), where rural users continue to face slower speeds and limited infrastructure. The *effective* bandwidth might be OK, but latency (the delay for each request) and network reliability often lag behind.

The browser can't execute a script until it's downloaded (unless using progressive streaming techniques, which we'll discuss later). So large script files directly translate to longer time before code can run. As Ilya Grigorik has famously noted (*https://oreil.ly/4eKWp*), "Round trips matter. They are the biggest bottleneck to mobile performance." Each HTTP request on a mobile network requires a radio handshake and multiple round trips that can easily total hundreds of milliseconds even before any data flows. If your page is making dozens of requests (for scripts, JavaScriptON, and so on), those latencies add up.

For instance, on a 4G network with good signal, the *setup latency* for a single request might be around 100 ms; on a 3G network, it could be 600 ms or more. And that's *per request*. If your site fetches many small JavaScript chunks sequentially, users could be waiting through many round-trip delays. This is why performance best practices often advise bundling resources to reduce requests—though, as you saw in Chapter 6, bundling has its own trade-offs.

Bandwidth is the other piece. After the initial latency, how fast can the bytes of the JavaScript file travel? Modern networks like 4G do provide higher bandwidth, but user conditions vary wildly. A user who has "full bars" of LTE but is in a congested network cell might find that a connection with a usual speed of tens of MB per second (Mbps) yields only 1 Mbps. Or they might get a strong connection that suddenly drops or fluctuates. Unlike wired broadband, mobile bandwidth can change second to second. Moreover, users on limited data plans or in "Save Data" mode explicitly *prefer* sites to be lightweight. If your site ships megabytes of JavaScript, it could exhaust some users' monthly data, literally costing them money. That's why developers should consider payload size as part of the cost of JavaScript.

Browser networking optimizations (like HTTP/2 multiplexing and caching) help mitigate some of these issues. HTTP/2, for example, allows multiple files to be downloaded in parallel over one connection, so splitting a bundle into pieces doesn't incur as much extra latency overhead as it would under HTTP/1.1. But there are limits to what protocol improvements can do. The bottom line is that smaller scripts and fewer of them mean faster loads, especially on slow networks.

One practical guideline from performance experts is to keep initial JavaScript payloads under certain size budgets (for example, <200 KB compressed for mobile initial load remains a reasonable guideline as discussed in 2018 (*https://oreil.ly/dR04E*)). And as a Google study of news sites (*https://oreil.ly/_nIRZ*) found, complexity kills performance: some slow pages made 500+ network requests, leading to load times of 10 to 30 s. Much of that overhead comes from third-party scripts and large JavaScript bundles.

Remember that "the best network request is one that you don't make." Every script you choose to load should be justified by its benefit to the user.

Networks—particularly mobile networks—are a fundamental limit. Even with a powerful chip, a device can't run code it hasn't downloaded. And if that download is stuck behind a slow 3G connection or 300 ms latency per request, the user will be waiting. Thus, the cost of JavaScript begins even before execution: large scripts cost time on the wire.

Browser Architecture: The Main Thread, Parsing, and Execution

Finally, we have to understand how browsers handle JavaScript under the hood. As you learned in Chapter 5, the main thread is a busy place: it's not only running JavaScript, but it's also doing layout, style calculations, painting pixels to the screen, and handling user-input events. When your JavaScript finally arrives over the network, the browser must parse it from text into bytecode or an abstract syntax tree (AST), compile or interpret it, and execute it—typically on the main thread. If JavaScript takes too long on the main thread, it blocks everything else, delaying other work.

Parsing JavaScript is surprisingly expensive. It's CPU-intensive and must happen before the code can run. According to the team that runs V8 (Chrome's engine, also used in Node.JavaScript), raw JavaScript parsing speed has improved significantly, but it still can consume a lot of time on a slow CPU. If you send huge scripts, you force the browser to do a lot of parsing work up front.

Modern JavaScript engines (as discussed later in this chapter) do many clever things to reduce parse and compile overhead on the main thread. For instance, V8 can perform streaming parsing (parsing the script incrementally as it downloads) and can offload some compilation work to a background thread. These optimizations have cut down main-thread parse/compile time dramatically. V8 has reduced main-thread parse/compile work by about 40% (*https://oreil.ly/KODuh*) on average for real websites compared to earlier versions by doing work off the main thread. Some sites saw even bigger improvements (Pinterest saw around 62% less main-thread compile work, YouTube around 81%). This means the browser tries hard to make loading

JavaScript less likely to block the main thread. But there are limits; certain phases (like initial parsing and handling syntax errors) still happen on the main thread, and of course code is always executed on the main thread.

Once parsed, the JavaScript engine either interprets the code or just-in-time (JIT) compiles it and begins running it. If your code immediately does a lot of work (like a big loop or complex calculations on load), that's going to tie up the main thread, delaying user interactivity. Chrome's parsing and compiling might be happening off-thread, but the moment your code calls `function initApp() { ...heavy work... }`, that heavy work is on the main thread, potentially causing what users perceive as slow loading or input lag.

Recent measurements show that script execution (not just download) can account for a significant portion of total load time (*https://oreil.ly/kg0ZD*)—30% or more on JavaScript-heavy single-page apps. In other words, even after the bytes are delivered and parsed, *running* the code is a major cost. A complex web app might run tens of thousands of JavaScript operations during startup, and all of that competes with rendering and input handling.

Browsers typically execute JavaScript in a single thread (the main thread, unless you explicitly use web workers), effectively making it single-threaded (in the context of the page) and cooperative. Only one JavaScript task runs at a time. If a task doesn't yield, nothing else can run. The browser can't, for example, scroll the page or process a button click while your script is crunching numbers. This is why I emphasize breaking up long tasks and yielding control (covered in Chapters 5 and 6).

Like devices, not all browsers are equal. Each major browser has its own JavaScript engine and performance characteristics. Most have similar main-thread constraints, but some lower-end browsers (or older versions) lack certain optimizations. Also, if the user has many tabs open or the device is under load, your page has to contend for CPU, so its performance could be affected. You can't control those external factors, but you *can* at least avoid being the thing that maxes out the CPU.

The JavaScript Engine

Modern JavaScript engines are marvels of optimization, squeezing every millisecond out of our code.

While we developers optimize our code loading and scheduling, the browser's JavaScript engine works tirelessly in the background to run that code faster. Over the past decade, JavaScript engines like Chrome's V8, Firefox's SpiderMonkey, WebKit's JavaScriptCore, and others have made astonishing progress. They have introduced JIT compilation, multitiered execution strategies, concurrent garbage collectors, and myriad micro-optimizations.

This chapter explores how JavaScript engines have evolved to mitigate JavaScript's performance costs. Understanding these internals will help you appreciate what the runtime does—and what it *cannot do*. Engines have reduced many bottlenecks (like parsing and function call overhead), but they can't magically speed up a bloated 5 MB bundle or eliminate the logic cost of an app. Once you understand the engine's strengths and weaknesses, you can write code that works with the engine, not against it.

From Interpretation to JIT Compilation: Engine Evolution

In the early days, JavaScript was purely an interpreted language. The engine would parse the source code and execute it directly, via a tree walker or similar mechanism. That was fine in the 1990s, when scripts were tiny. As JavaScript use grew, though, the engines became more sophisticated.

The big leap came in the mid-2000s with JIT compilation. Modern engines use a *tiered JIT* architecture. The basic idea of JIT is to compile JavaScript to native machine code *at runtime*, so it runs faster than interpretation. But doing this optimally is tricky, because JavaScript is a dynamic language.

Let's use V8 (Chrome's engine) as an example. V8 has at least three execution tiers (*https://oreil.ly/r8ipj*):

Ignition (interpreter)
  When code is first loaded, V8's Ignition interpreter turns JavaScript source into bytecode and executes it immediately. Interpretation has low startup costs: it starts running quickly, which is good for initial load. But interpreted code runs slower than compiled code.

Baseline JIT (Sparkplug)
  V8 added an internal baseline compiler called Sparkplug. This kicks in after the interpreter, taking the bytecode and compiling it to machine code without heavy optimizations. The goal is to get to faster-than-interpreter code quickly but without spending a lot of time optimizing. Sparkplug-generated code isn't as fast as fully optimized code, but it's a step up and can be produced quickly.

Optimizing JIT (TurboFan)
  As the code runs, V8 collects profiling information, like the types of variables and which branches are taken. When it identifies *hot functions* (code that runs frequently), it invokes TurboFan, the optimizing compiler. TurboFan uses the type feedback to generate highly optimized machine code for that function. This code can inline functions, unbox objects, and do all sorts of optimizations under the hood, all tailored to the types of variables it observes. The result is often an order-of-magnitude speedup for hot code.

This tiered approach means that code starts running quickly, with no big pause to compile everything fully up front, and gets faster as it runs. There is a warm-up period: a function might run a bit slower at first, while it is interpreted or baseline compiled, and then speed up after a few iterations, once it's been optimized. Surma (*https://surma.dev*), a Chrome DevRel engineer, explains that under ideal conditions, both WebAssembly and JavaScript end up as machine code and can reach similar peak performance, but JavaScript has this dynamic compilation path to get there. The engine trades initial performance for eventual performance: first make it work, then make it fast.

However, JITs also can *deoptimize*. If the assumptions used to optimize the code break—say, a variable that was always a number suddenly becomes a string—the optimized code might no longer be valid. V8 then deoptimizes and falls back to baseline or interpreter. It might attempt to reoptimize the code later, if conditions stabilize. All this happens under the hood, without developers realizing it.

Other engines, like SpiderMonkey and JavaScriptCore, have similarly tiered systems. While the specifics differ, conceptually, they all aim to balance startup and peak performance.

This optimization pipeline means that your JavaScript often runs much faster than you might expect. It also means that certain patterns can be friendly or hostile to JIT. For example, if you write functions that consistently receive the same types and shapes of objects, JITs can optimize them well. If your function sometimes gets a number, sometimes a string, sometimes an object, the JIT will have a harder time optimizing, because it has to handle all cases. Thus, it's a good idea to avoid "shape-shifting" your variables: try to use a consistent structure. That's not to say you need TypeScript (the JIT will figure types out at runtime); it's just that at runtime, you shouldn't mix and match too radically in hot code paths.

If your code runs only once (like initialization code), it might never get optimized by the JIT because it's not "hot" enough. In these cases, interpreter performance matters. In contrast, a tight loop that runs thousands of times *will* get optimized. This is why microbenchmarking a small loop might not show benefit if it doesn't run enough to trigger the optimizer. It also suggests an interesting paradox: if you break your code into too many small functions, each of which is called only a few times, they might not get optimized individually. Sometimes inlining can help (whether it's done manually or by the engine) because it makes one function hotter.

Modern JavaScript engines are also increasingly incorporating machine learning to improve their optimization decisions. For example, engines can use profiling data and ML models to predict which functions are likely to become hot and should be optimized earlier or which branches are likely to be taken. While still an emerging area, AI-assisted JIT compilation represents the next frontier in JavaScript performance optimization, potentially making engines even smarter about when and how to optimize code.

Background Compilation, Parsing, and GC

I've touched on moving work off the main thread, but let's look deeper. Parsing and compiling JavaScript on the main thread *directly* competes with the critical rendering path. To mitigate that, engines have introduced background threads to handle these tasks. V8, for example, can parse and compile scripts on a worker thread as they are being downloaded (this is called *streaming compilation*). By the time the script is fully downloaded, a good chunk of it might already be parsed or even compiled—without blocking the main thread. The V8 team has reported (*https://oreil.ly/4Cw1z*) that these efforts "reduc[ed] the amount of time spent compiling on the main thread by between 5% to 20% on typical websites."

This translates to pages loading faster because it frees the main thread to do other stuff (like process HTML/CSS or handle interactions) while the heavy JavaScript prep work is done in parallel. Why not parse on one core while executing on another? Background compilation isn't trivial—thread safety and coordination are major considerations—but the payoff is big on multicore devices (which is basically all devices today).

Another improvement has been *lazy parsing*. Engines don't always fully parse every function on initial load. Many employ a lazy strategy: parse just enough to know where functions start and end, but only fully parse the function's code when and if it's actually invoked. This way, if you have a large library but only use a portion of it, the unused parts might never be fully parsed (saving time). For example, V8 has had lazy parsing for years. Not parsing inner functions until they're called can reduce parsing overhead significantly if many functions are never used. Of course, if eventually they are all used, the cost comes anyway—it's just deferred.

Memory management has also become more efficient. JavaScript has automatic GC, and early on, this sometimes caused noticeable pauses. Modern engines have highly optimized garbage collectors that often do a lot of work incrementally or on background threads. GC matters to performance because a GC pause is a pause in JavaScript execution. Engines try to make GC pauses so short that you don't notice them: ideally, under one or two ms, in incremental slices. Efficient memory management also means the engine can allocate and free objects quickly, which is important for object-heavy code. However, if you allocate enormous numbers of objects very quickly or hold onto a lot of memory, this may cause long GC pauses occasionally. Memory leaks in your code, like forgetting to drop references, can also hurt performance, since the engine may have to scan a larger heap.

Engine improvements also target *power efficiency*. On mobile, doing the same work faster means the CPU can idle sooner, saving battery and reducing thermal strain (less chance of hitting that thermal throttle point). So optimizing JavaScript isn't just about raw speed but about using fewer CPU cycles overall, which is good for energy.

The Limits of Engine Magic

For all the engine's smarts, it still has limitations. If a site is slow because it's executing huge scripts, the engine can only optimize so much. No matter how good the JIT, on a low-end phone, executing 5 MB of minified (compressed and optimized) code that initializes a complex app will take a noticeable time. Engines also can't eliminate logic that's fundamentally unnecessary to the user; they won't, for instance, decide, "this framework is doing extra work, so I'll skip those calls." It's a developer's job to avoid sending unnecessary code. Engines just make each individual operation faster.

Another limitation is that certain JavaScript behaviors are inherently hard to optimize. For instance, with `eval` or dynamic code generation (function constructors), the engine has to treat the resulting code as new and unknown, preventing some optimizations. Similarly, if you modify the prototypes of built-in objects (known as *monkey-patching*), the engine's assumptions about, say, `Array.prototype.map` might become invalid, which will affect its ability to optimize calls to that object. Engines generally optimize for the idiomatic common cases—the well-trodden path. So if you avoid too much dynamic trickery and use normal prototypes and standard patterns for classes or closures, you'll maximize optimization. If you do weird stuff like using a single object to store lots of unrelated properties dynamically, the engine might fall back to slower, more general paths.

There are also trade-offs between engines' startup performance and their long-term performance trade-off. For faster startup on repeat visits, Chrome and other browsers use a technique called *bytecode caching*: the engine can cache the compiled bytecode of scripts in a database so that the next page load can skip parsing that script. However, this cache can be invalidated if the script changes. It's especially helpful on mobile, where parsing large scripts repeatedly is expensive. As a developer, you don't manage this, but you should know that it exists.

Finally, consider multithreading and parallel JavaScript. Apart from web workers, JavaScript in a single page remains single-threaded, and we don't yet have a way to utilize multiple cores for computation in JavaScript. If you have a compute-heavy task, using a web worker that runs on another thread is a way to leverage another core. But writing multithreaded code is complex. The typical approach is to offload distinct tasks to workers and communicate via messages, so the main thread (and thus the UI) stays responsive. Transferring data between threads does incur overhead, but there are techniques to optimize that (*https://oreil.ly/Tmnpe*).

Today's engines execute JavaScript an order of magnitude faster than they did 10 years ago. Yet many sites still feel slow—often because developers give the engines even *more* work than we did before. Our job is to not overwhelm the engine in the first place, and the engine's job is to run our code as efficiently as possible. Now let's look beyond the browser to optimizing JavaScript on the backend.

Backend JavaScript Performance

The browser is where JavaScript's cost is most visible to users, but JavaScript is also used on the backend: in Node.js, Deno, serverless functions, and more. This brief chapter touches on considerations for JavaScript performance on the server side. Although backend JavaScript performance isn't directly visible to end users in the way the frontend is, it ultimately affects them via API latency or page generation time. For example, if you're using SSR on the backend with Node, a slow server will delay the initial HTML. So achieving good backend performance is part of delivering good UX. It's all part of the critical path, until the user sees and can interact with your content.

The backend environment is different—there's no UI to render, and the hardware is typically more consistent—but a sluggish server can harm user experience indirectly by causing slow responses. Interestingly, many of the frontend techniques discussed in this book apply conceptually to the backend, too. In a backend context, splitting code might mean not requiring modules until you need them (*lazy require*) to save memory and avoid cold-start latency (discussed later on). The backend, like the browser, can cache computations or responses in memory or a caching layer to avoid redoing work. And load shedding on the backend works somewhat like a performance budget does on the frontend: you can decide not to do certain optional work under heavy loads to preserve core performance.

One difference is that, on the backend, you usually don't need to worry about bundle size in the network sense, since the code isn't delivered to a client. But you do need to worry about dependency bloat, which can affect memory usage and startup time. It's easy to pull in many NPM packages, which can slow require time or consume a lot of RAM, which indirectly affects performance—especially in memory-constrained environments, like frontend-as-a-service containers with limited memory.

Node.js and the Event Loop

Node.js runs on Chrome's V8 engine, so all the engine optimizations discussed in Chapter 6 benefit Node as well. Parsing and JIT work similarly. One key aspect is that Node is single-threaded for JavaScript execution, except when using its Worker Threads or clustering. This means that, just like in the browser, while your Node server (*https://oreil.ly/Qgm-W*) is executing a heavy JavaScript calculation, it will not be able to handle other incoming requests on that same thread. Node excels at input/output (I/O) concurrency (thanks to its event loop and asynchronous nonblocking I/O model), but CPU concurrency requires more effort.

A principle, then: don't block the Node.js event loop. If your server has to do expensive computation (like image processing or big data crunching), consider offloading it to a separate process or thread or even a different service. For web servers, typically time is spent waiting on database or network I/O. Node handles this efficiently by not blocking during awaits or callbacks, but occasionally people misuse Node by doing CPU-heavy tasks inline.

For example, parsing a large JSON file or compressing data in pure JavaScript could freeze a Node server. The trade-off is between throughput and simplicity. You might get away with it if such tasks are rare or if the server primarily does that for one request at a time. But generally, it's better to stream and chunk such work, or use native modules (like C++ add-ons or WASM) that can sometimes do it faster and release control periodically.

Node offers worker threads, which allow you to run JavaScript in parallel threads within the same process. If you have a multicore server and a CPU-bound task, moving it to a worker thread can ensure that the main thread (event loop) keeps handling other requests. This is like using web workers in the browser.

Backend-Specific Optimizations

On the backend, performance is often about throughput (requests per second) and latency (response time). If your Node server serves an API endpoint that assembles data from various sources, how can you optimize that? You might parallelize external calls, firing off multiple awaits simultaneously to reduce overall latency. The JavaScript overhead in those orchestrations is usually minor compared to network and database times.

However, if your server does a lot of JavaScript processing per request, it needs to be efficient or it will reduce throughput. For instance, an Express middleware that does complex logic for every request could become a bottleneck at scale. Profiling your Node apps (with tools like the Node profiler or clinic.js) can help you pinpoint hotspots.

One way to mitigate heavy CPU usage is to scale out. Node processes can be clustered, with one process per CPU core. For example, a Node cluster of four processes on a four-core machine can handle four JavaScript executions in parallel, since each is single-threaded. Many Node-based servers (like PM2 or the built-in cluster module) do this to utilize all CPU cores. The trade-off is higher memory usage, since each process has its own V8 instance. But it's usually worth it for a backend service to maximize its hardware use.

Memory leaks in Node, such as holding onto request data in a global, can degrade performance over time. The process might start garbage collecting more often or even run out of memory, leading to slowdowns or crashes. In a browser, a memory leak affects just one page; on a server, it affects uptime and performance for *all* users. That's why it's important to monitor memory usage. You can connect tools like Node's `--inspect` and Chrome DevTools to do heap snapshots if needed.

GC in Node is "stop-the-world" for that process: in other words, it will pause JavaScript execution to clean up. On a server, a GC pause of 50 ms might not be noticeable, but a pause of 200 ms could delay responses slightly. V8 tries to keep pauses short, but if memory usage balloons, you may hit longer GCs. Efficient memory-management practices, like reusing objects and not creating large numbers of unnecessary objects, can improve Node performance for high-throughput servers.

Some Node performance tips:

- Use asynchronous, nonblocking calls for I/O, which is the default for most Node APIs. Synchronous file system or crypto calls will block the event loop, so avoid them except in the startup phase.
- Leverage streaming for large data. For instance, stream a file to the response rather than readFileSync into memory then send.
- If you're performing JSON serialization and deserialization a lot, note that V8's JSON.parse and JSON.stringify are quite fast if written in optimized C++ code. Still, if you parse extremely large payloads, that can be CPU-heavy. Consider using streaming JSON parsers or even lighter data formats, if applicable.
- Use efficient algorithms. This is true on the frontend, too, but on the backend, the datasets are likely to be larger and more frequent because the server might process data from many users. A naive algorithm could significantly limit throughput if called on every request.
- If you're using a database, the biggest performance wins often come from optimizing queries (such as by adding indexes) rather than optimizing the JavaScript itself. On the JavaScript side, though, you can batch queries or cache results to avoid repeating heavy operations.

In serverless (like AWS Lambda), JavaScript functions' speed can suffer from *cold starts*: the time it takes to load your JavaScript code, start V8, and initialize the runtime and code when the function is first invoked. To reduce cold-start latency, minimize the size of your deployment package so it loads faster, and avoid doing expensive setup on startup (do it lazily if possible). Some Node frameworks for serverless optimize this by bundling code efficiently.

Also, using newer JavaScript syntax and features on Node can sometimes have performance benefits. For instance, async/await is pretty well optimized in newer Node, so use it instead of older callback patterns that might have more overhead.

Node can be very fast for I/O-bound tasks, often matching or exceeding other server platforms in throughput for simple API serving, thanks to its event loop and V8's speed. But for CPU-bound tasks, languages with true multithreading or better raw CPU performance might have an edge. This is why you often see architectures that use Node for the web API layer but delegate the heavy lifting to a service written in a more system-level language or to a specialized database. However, Node is continually improving, too, and with things like worker threads and even WebAssembly, you can augment Node with high-performance code when needed.

Monitoring and Observability

Application performance monitoring (APM) does for Node backends what the Core Web Vitals do for frontends. In particular, it lets you keep an eye on event-loop lag. Node provides an API to check if the loop is being delayed, similar to the long tasks API. If you see spikes in event-loop lag, that means some code is taking too long. Monitor response times and throughput metrics to see if your Node server's JavaScript is handling the load or if it needs some optimizations or scaling.

Running memory and CPU profiles in production (with minimal overhead tools or sampling profilers) can also help you catch issues. The Node flag `--prof` lets you output profiling info that you can process to see what functions are consuming time.

In summary, while this book's primary focus is on the frontend, JavaScript performance matters on the server too. Many core ideas are the same: avoid blocking operations, optimize hot code paths, leverage concurrency, and measure. Node.js has matured to a point where it powers large-scale systems, and part of that success is due to engineers applying performance best practices to Node just as they would to any other server platform. A holistic performance strategy looks at both client and server. Your frontend optimizations could be undercut by a slow backend and vice versa—so as you optimize your web app, consider profiling and improving both ends of the stack where needed.

Conclusion

The cost of JavaScript is something every user pays, in time or device resources, and it's our job as engineers and developers to spend those bytes and cycles wisely on their behalf.

To recap a few key themes from this chapter:

Know your constraints
> Not all users have high-end devices or fast networks. CPUs aren't getting dramatically faster year over year for single-thread performance, and the gap between cheap and expensive devices is huge. Network latency is a fundamental limit (*https://oreil.ly/s_3x0*) that requires us to minimize round-trips and payload sizes. Browsers execute JavaScript on a single main thread, making well-timed, modular work crucial. Keeping these constraints in mind grounds our performance work in real user context.

Load less, do less, as late as possible
This mantra underpins many techniques. Code splitting and lazy loading help you load less code up front. Scheduling, idle work, and efficient algorithms help your code do less work for the same result. Deferring noncritical tasks and resources means doing things as late as possible and no later—you still need to meet users' needs on time. By being mindful of *when* and *how much* JavaScript runs, you can create more responsive apps. The fastest JavaScript execution (*https://oreil.ly/R7g87*) is the one you avoid entirely (or at least postpone until it's needed).

Leverage the platform and engine
Modern browsers and JavaScript engines are quite advanced. Use features like `defer`/`async` scripts, `yield` from the Scheduler API, `requestIdleCallback`, and web workers. They're specifically there to help performance. Trust the JIT to do its job, but feed it good patterns: give it consistent object shapes and don't invalidate optimizations willy-nilly. Let the browser handle heavy lifting when it can, such as by using CSS instead of JavaScript for animations, or using built-in APIs like `Array.prototype.map` that are optimized in native code. And use the browser's measurement tools, like Performance Profiler and Core Web Vitals, to see where the bottlenecks are; sometimes what you guess is slowing things down isn't the real issue.

Balance trade-offs thoughtfully
Trade-offs are rarely black-and-white. Use frameworks if they help you move faster, but rein in their costs with prudent techniques, like Next.js's SSR or Preact for smaller builds. Optimize but not to the point of obscurity or diminishing returns. Performance budgets give you a clear target and a way to say "enough." Always consider the user and business impacts of decisions too: is this new library worth the added second of load time? Is this micro-optimization worth the code complexity? Will faster speeds improve conversions?

Web engineers have more power than ever: frameworks, tools, and powerful devices. But as the saying goes, with great power comes great responsibility. The ease of adding a dependency or pushing a bunch of client-side logic can lull us into shipping more than we need. Performance work is about being responsible stewards of our users' time and resources.

The cost of JavaScript ultimately should be outweighed by the *value* it delivers. If you make deliberate, informed choices, you can ensure that every byte and every millisecond of JavaScript in your apps is worth it for your users. When you achieve that balance, you've turned JavaScript from a cost into an investment—one that pays off in rich experiences and satisfied customers.

Optimizing the JavaScript *you* write is only half the battle, though. Often, the most significant performance challenges arise from the code you *didn't* write: the third-party scripts that power analytics, ads, and widgets. Part IV focuses on providing strategies for taming the impact of external scripts.

PART IV
Managing Dependencies and Maintaining Quality

CHAPTER 8
Introduction to Third-Party Scripts

Third-party scripts are any scripts that a website includes from external sources outside of its own codebase. While Chapter 7 focused on the costs associated with the JavaScript *you* write, these external scripts often introduce even greater performance challenges. This includes both code you write manually and code generated by AI tools: AI-generated code that integrates third-party services still inherits the same performance characteristics and constraints of those external dependencies.

Third-party scripts allow developers and site owners to quickly add features or services provided by others, ranging from analytics and advertising to social media feeds and interactive widgets (*https://oreil.ly/Tc-rI*). In practice, they are often embedded by referencing a script URL or an `<iframe>` pointing to a different domain. For example, a marketing site might include Google Analytics for tracking, a Facebook software development kit (SDK) for social-sharing buttons, a YouTube iframe for an embedded video, and a chat widget from a customer-support provider or an AI customer-support chatbot. These scripts power valuable functionality without the site owner having to build it from scratch—but including them comes at a cost.

As I've written before, if you've optimized your code, but your site still loads too slowly, it's probably the fault of third-party scripts. In other words, once you've done all you can to speed up your own application code, any remaining performance bottlenecks are likely to be from third-party content. Third-party scripts are outside your direct control, but they can slow down page loads, introduce security and privacy risks, and behave unpredictably. Relying on them means trusting that external providers won't degrade your own users' experience.

This chapter begins by breaking down what third-party scripts are, where they are (everywhere), and how they affect your site. I'll look at key tools and metrics you can use to measure that impact, then finish the chapter by introducing a set of principles to guide you as you decide how best to optimize their presence.

Third-Party Code Is Everywhere

Nearly every modern website uses at least one third-party script in some form—over 94%, according to the HTTP Archive Web Almanac (*https://oreil.ly/iHI9O*). In fact, the median website on desktop pulls from 23 third-party domains, and on mobile the median is 21. On highly popular sites, the count is even higher: according to the same study (*https://oreil.ly/Ydmu6*), the top 1,000 sites use 40 to 47 third-party integrations on average. And a study in the Web Almanac (*https://oreil.ly/fTVnW*) notes that about 33% of the total scripts loaded on an average site are third-party scripts. They're ubiquitous—not edge cases but a core part of the web ecosystem. Table 8-1 shows some of the most common use cases for third-party scripts.

Table 8-1. Third-party scripts fulfill many purposes across different types of sites

Type of third-party content	Example	Script function/purpose
Analytics and tracking	Google Analytics, Mixpanel, Facebook Pixel	Log user behavior and traffic sources; measure conversions and remarketing
Advertising networks	Google AdSense, programmatic ad networks	Bidding, ad rendering, tracking impressions
Media embeds	YouTube, Vimeo, Instagram, SoundCloud	Play back and display video and audio content
Social sharing widgets	Facebook "Like" button	Social media interaction
Chat and support widgets	Intercom, Zendesk	Render the chat widget; handle messaging
Tag managers	Google Tag Manager	Manage analytics, A/B testing, and advertising tags centrally
A/B testing and personalization	Optimizely or Google Optimize	Swap out or modify page elements for different test variants; personalize content
Utility libraries	date-fns, Moment.js	A date-picker library, a video player library from a CDN
Ecommerce and SaaS integrations	Shopify, Discus	Reviews, recommendation widgets, analytics, external comment systems

Across web apps, content management system (CMS) sites (like WordPress), and ecommerce platforms (like Shopify), the patterns are similar: third-party scripts offer plug-and-play capabilities for common needs. A Shopify merchant might add an app for an upsell pop-up (which injects a script), while a WordPress blogger might paste an embed code from SoundCloud to share audio. Modern single-page applications (SPAs) also use third-party SDKs. For instance, a React app might dynamically load the Google Maps API for a map component or use Stripe's JS library for payments. In short, third-party scripts are everywhere, in every category of site.

Why Third-Party Scripts Affect Performance

Unfortunately, the convenience of third-party code comes with significant performance impacts. Introducing scripts that the browser must fetch from various origins and execute extends the critical path of page loading beyond your own code. Key reasons third-party scripts tend to slow down web pages include:

Extra network requests
  Each third-party resource often requires additional HTTP requests to different servers. This means extra DNS lookups, TLS handshakes, and data transfers. Every new domain (analytics, ads, etc.) adds latency. As the web.dev team puts it (*https://oreil.ly/xVhxM*), "the more requests a site has to make, the longer it can take to load." A page might load its own code quickly from its server but then stall while waiting on multiple calls to ad networks, analytics endpoints, and content delivery networks (CDNs) for third-party content.

Large script payloads
  It's not uncommon (*https://oreil.ly/Djmp2*) for a single embed to pull in hundreds of kilobytes or even a couple of megabytes of JavaScript: a typical social-media feed embed or video player can easily include as much as 500 KB of script. This can dominate the total bytes of the page. Users on slower connections or with limited data plans could pay a high cost to download code that isn't even part of your site's core functionality.

Main-thread execution cost
  Parsing and executing JavaScript on the browser's main thread can delay interactivity. As you learned in Chapter 7, when the browser encounters a script, by default it must pause parsing the HTML to execute the script's code. Third-party scripts often run sizable code blocks on load, which can block your own page from rendering. Even if loaded asynchronously, a large script can still hog the CPU once it runs. These "boot-up" times add to the time to interactive (TTI) and can cause jank. Analysis from web.dev shows (*https://oreil.ly/3M1cM*) that third-party scripts frequently block the main thread, delaying user interactions. If the script does heavy work (like analytics processing or building a widget UI), it may introduce noticeable lag or even frame drops.

Contention for resources
Third-party content competes with first-party content for bandwidth and CPU. If an advertisement script starts making lots of network calls or doing layout, it's competing with your own images and scripts for the main thread (and other resources). Without careful sequencing, third-party resources can consume network resources that could otherwise be fetching important images or API data for your main app scripts or CSS, potentially delaying initial render or painting.

Render-blocking
Some third-party embeds, especially older ones, use outdated techniques that outright block the page from rendering. Certain ad or tracking scripts still use the notorious `document.write()`, which can halt parsing and insert content synchronously, leading to performance hazards. Even when using modern async techniques, third-party iframes can delay the `window.onload` event if their servers respond slowly. In other words, an external script might be loading "asynchronously" but still end up gating the load event or other page milestones due to how browsers treat slow iframe loads.

When you include several third-party widgets, there's also a cumulative impact. Each widget might bring along its own miniframework or library. For instance, you might include a date-picker library in your own code, and then an A/B testing script separately injects its own copy of a similar library—doubling the bytes and work. It's possible to end up loading jQuery multiple times or loading two incompatible versions of a framework because two embeds each fetch their own copy. This duplication wastes resources and exacerbates performance issues.

Third-party code can also be unpredictable. Since it's fetched from the third party's server each time, it can change without you knowing or load additional scripts of its own (so-called fourth-party scripts). Andrew Welch notes (*https://oreil.ly/BCLlq*) that often, when you include a "tag" (really a snippet of third-party JavaScript), it can essentially do whatever it wants inside the user's browser, including loading further scripts. For example, a tag manager might load five tags, each of which then calls out to other services, ballooning the number of requests. This cascade effect can degrade performance in ways that are hard to anticipate or monitor.

Relying on external servers introduces the risk that if one of them is slow or down, your page might hang or break. This is known as the *single point of failure* (SPOF) problem. If a third-party server doesn't respond or times out, it could block parts of your site from loading. In the worst case, a crucial third-party script (like a CDN-hosted library) failing to load could even halt your site's functionality.

Third-party embeds often inject content (like an iframe of unknown size) into your page asynchronously. A classic example is an ad that loads in after the article text, moving the text. Such shifts hurt the user experience. If you don't account for them by reserving space for them in advance, this can push your content around, causing layout shifts; in fact, many third-party iframes are significant contributors to poor CLS (covered in Chapter 2).

While not a performance issue per se, it's worth noting that third-party scripts can introduce security vulnerabilities by opening the site to potential cross-site scripting (XSS) attacks, as well as privacy issues by tracking users or accessing sensitive data. Third-party tags should be reviewed not just for speed but also for compliance with privacy regulations and security.

In summary, third-party scripts make the web more dynamic, interactive, and interconnected—but using them is risky. They often execute outside the site owner's control and can significantly impact page load speed and stability. With so much code coming from elsewhere, performance optimization can't ignore this portion of the stack.

I recall a WebPageTest (WPT) trace of a news site that showed that the tracking and marketing scripts took longer to load than the page's own content. The network waterfall revealed that third-party requests dominated the timeline. Figure 8-1 shows an example of a domain breakdown chart where a huge percentage of the bytes and requests were from third-party domains. This kind of data is a wake-up call: without intervention, third-party scripts can steal the spotlight from your first-party content, leaving users waiting.

Given these stakes, web performance experts treat third-party script optimization as a critical task. In the following chapters, I'll explore how to analyze the impact of third-party scripts and optimize their loading, execution, and overall footprint.

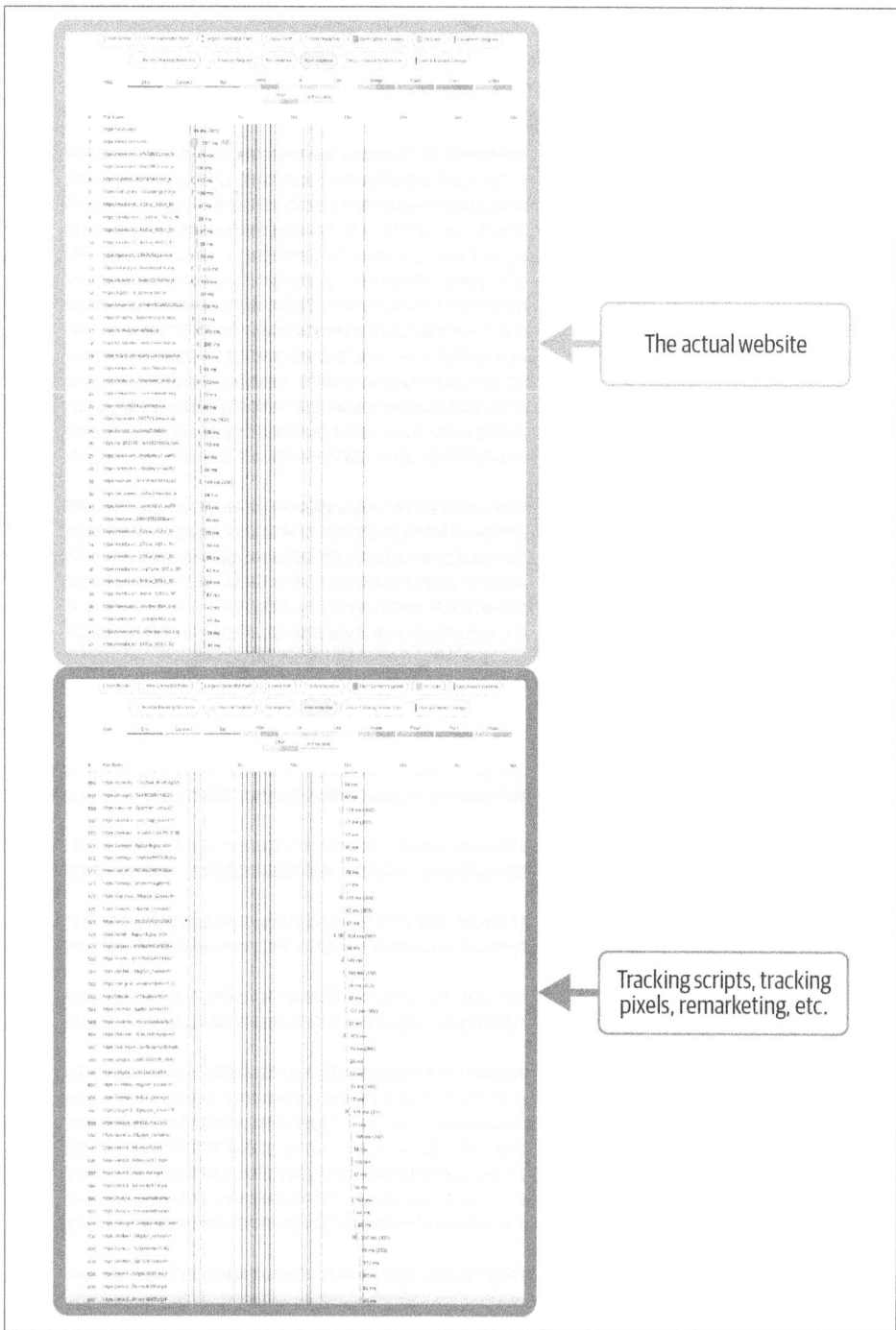

Figure 8-1. WebPageTest's waterfall view can highlight the impact of heavy third-party script use

Measuring Third-Party Scripts' Performance Impact

Before you can optimize third-party scripts, you need to identify them and quantify their impact on your site's performance. This involves using performance auditing tools and techniques to see what third-party code is present and how it affects loading metrics. You're already familiar with tools like Chrome DevTools, Lighthouse, and WPT from Chapter 2. Here, I'll focus on applying them specifically to third-party script analysis, highlighting what to look for and how to interpret the results.

Inventory and Identification: Key Metrics and Indicators

The first step is to inventory all third-party scripts on a given page. This includes both scripts added directly into your HTML (like a `<script src="https://third-party.com/script.js">` tag) and those dynamically injected by other scripts or tag managers.

The key is to establish a baseline: know what third-party scripts are on the page, where they come from, and some measure of their cost in bytes, load time, execution time, and so on. When evaluating third-party scripts, metrics to pay attention to include:

- How many HTTP requests are coming from third-party domains? (Generally, more requests mean more overhead.)
- How much data is being transferred from third parties, in total KB/MB? This affects load on slow networks. If third parties dominate the bytes, that's a red flag.
- How many milliseconds on the main thread (CPU) are spent executing third-party JavaScript? This directly affects TTI and responsiveness.
- Do third-party requests start after your main content, or are they interfering by starting too early? Ideally, critical content should load first, and third-party scripts or embeds should be loaded later or at a more appropriate time.
- Do your most third-party-heavy pages show worse Core Web Vitals? For instance, compare FCP or LCP on a page with heavy embeds versus a simpler page. If third-party scripts are blocking rendering, the LCP may be delayed. Likewise, if they delay interactivity, the INP might suffer.
- Do one or two scripts stand out as the worst offenders? Those should be your first candidates for optimization or removal. Often, a minority of third-party scripts cause the majority of impact.

It's important to interpret your audits with appropriate context. For example, an ad script might show one second of main-thread time. If ads are business critical, you probably can't cut all of that, but this quantification can help you justify your efforts to defer or optimize it. Lighthouse scores can help you track improvement as you implement optimizations too.

Special Considerations for AI-Based Third-Party Scripts

AI-based third-party scripts, such as chatbots and customer-support tools, deserve special attention in your performance audits. These scripts often bundle LLMs or make frequent API calls to external AI services, which can significantly impact performance. When evaluating AI-powered third-party integrations:

- Monitor the size of the initial JavaScript payload—many AI chatbot SDKs can exceed 500 KB or even 1 MB.
- Track the frequency and size of API calls to AI backends, especially during user interactions.
- Measure the latency impact of round trips to AI services, which can be substantial if the service is geographically distant or under heavy load.
- Be particularly cautious with AI-generated code that integrates third-party services. As noted in Chapter 4, AI tools don't inherently optimize for performance. If you're using AI to generate integration code for third-party services, you must manually review it for performance best practices: check if the code uses async loading, uses proper error handling, and doesn't block critical rendering paths.

When reviewing any third-party code (whether AI-generated or manually written), ensure it follows the optimization patterns discussed in later sections of this chapter.

Lighthouse and Chrome DevTools

In Chrome DevTools, the Network panel is a great starting point: you can load your page and filter and group requests by domain. Any requests to domains that aren't yours (or your CDN's) are third-party, so they're easy to spot.

Tools like PageSpeed Insights and Lighthouse (which is integrated into Chrome DevTools) offer automatic analyses that list third-party resources. For example, Lighthouse has an audit called "Reduce the impact of third-party code," which enumerates third-party scripts, showing their sizes and main-thread execution times. It's an easy way to get a quick list of all external script providers and how costly each one is. Other useful Lighthouse audits include:

- "Reduce JavaScript execution time" (previously "JavaScript boot-up time")
- "Avoid enormous network payloads"
- "Eliminate render-blocking resources"
- "Reduce unused JavaScript"

Another way to identify third-party script execution in Chrome DevTools' Performance panel is to record a performance trace while loading the page, then group your profiling data by script origin. To do this, go to the "Bottom-Up" or "Call Tree" view, group by "Product." Chrome will label groups like "Google Analytics" or "Facebook SDK" if it recognizes them. This tells you how much CPU time was spent executing script from each domain. Sorting by total time quickly shows which third-party scripts are consuming the most CPU during page load.

The Coverage tab in DevTools' Sources panel shows how *much* of each script was executed. This can sometimes reveal that you loaded a big third-party library but that only a small portion of it actually ran.

You can also use DevTools throttling to mimic real-world conditions by turning on network and CPU throttling when measuring third-party impact. On a fast local machine with no throttling, a third-party script might seem to load innocuously in 100 ms. But on a typical midtier smartphone on slow 4G, that could be 500 ms or more plus slower execution. By testing under "Regular 4G" and a fourfold CPU slowdown (which approximates a low-end device), you'll see what users really experience. Many third-party scripts (especially heavy analytics and visual widgets) have a disproportionate impact under constrained conditions, so it's crucial to measure with throttling for an accurate picture.

The Performance panel recording can also reveal long tasks caused by third-party script execution. DevTools even supports a long task API in pages themselves: you can use `PerformanceObserver` to log long tasks in real time, which can include identifying the culprit frame or script. Some advanced RUM setups use this to track third-party slowdowns on real user devices.

WebPageTest (WPT)

WPT is a powerful ally in understanding third-party impact. It can produce a handy waterfall chart showing the percentage of requests and bytes coming from each domain on your page. Figure 8-2 shows an example of such a chart. If you see that, say, 50% of the bytes are from `*.doubleclick.net` or `*.facebook.com`, you know that third-party ads or widgets are dominating your payload. WPT's breakdown clearly distinguishes first-party from third-party content and can be quite eye-opening.

The waterfall chart of requests also shows when each third-party resource is loaded relative to the rest of the page. Often, you'll notice clumps of requests to different domains. For instance, a waterfall might show your initial HTML and CSS loading, then a pause, then a bunch of requests to analytics and ad servers kicking in. This timing visualization can reveal if third-party requests are delaying the onload or if they're firing in parallel with other content.

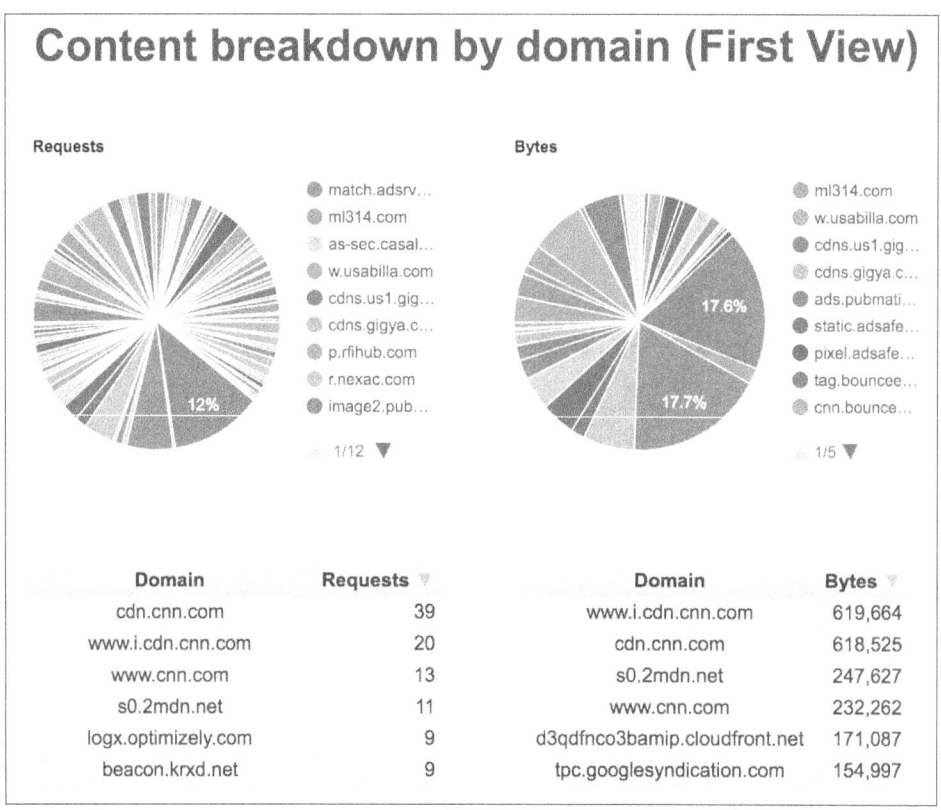

Figure 8-2. A WPT chart with domain breakdown, highlighting the proportion of third-party versus first-party requests and bytes

Another valuable WPT feature is request blocking, which allows you to simulate the page load with certain domains blocked. A recommended workflow is this:

1. Run a test normally (no blocking) to get baseline load times.
2. Go into Advanced settings. In the "Block" field, list the hostnames of known third-party domains (like ad networks) to block.
3. Run a second test blocking those domains.
4. Compare the two results using WPT's filmstrip and comparison features.

By doing this A/B test, you can quantify the impact of those third parties. For example, you might find that the page visually completes two seconds faster without the ad scripts. That delta is essentially the "performance tax" of those scripts. Andy Davies, a web performance expert, has demonstrated using WPT comparisons (*https://oreil.ly/PPpDK*) to measure third-party costs and found it very insightful for prioritizing what to optimize or remove.

Chrome DevTools lets you perform similar experiments: in the Network panel, you can right-click a request and choose "Block request domain." This will prevent any request to that domain from loading, and you can then reload the page to see the effect. While this is a manual test (and won't give you a filmstrip like WPT does), it's a quick way to check during development: "What if I remove this tag? Does my load time improve dramatically?" Remember to disable caching in DevTools when doing this to simulate first-load conditions.

WPT also has a special SPOF simulation (*https://oreil.ly/Vf7uP*). Instead of outright blocking a domain, SPOF mode simulates what happens if that domain is slow or times out. This is useful because third-party problems often manifest as slow servers rather than complete failures. Using the SPOF tool, you can see, for instance, how your page behaves if the analytics server takes five seconds to respond. Does it delay the whole page? Does the page eventually load without it? This helps you assess risk and ensure you have proper timeouts and fallbacks.

By thoroughly auditing with the tools and methods covered in this section, you will gain a deep understanding of your site's third-party landscape. Keep logs of these findings: they'll inform the strategies you choose and help you track improvements as you begin optimizing.

Principles of Third-Party Optimization

Before I dive into any specific techniques, it's useful to establish some guiding principles and a mindset for optimizing third-party scripts. Unlike your own code, you can't edit an analytics script to make it execute faster—it's someone else's code. So the kind of optimization you'll do here revolves around how and when you load those scripts and how you manage their impact on the page.

When you're dealing with a third-party script that hurts performance, you have two options, broadly speaking: you can get rid of it (by removing it or replacing it with a more efficient alternative), or you can optimize its loading and execution to minimize its interference with your page's critical path. This includes deferring it, loading it asynchronously, conditionally loading it, and otherwise managing its execution timing and environment. A holistic strategy may involve a bit of both: maybe removing a few tags that aren't needed and heavily optimizing the rest.

Remove, Reduce, Replace

Now that you have a list of third-party inclusions and their costs, start with a critical look at each one. What does it do? Is it worth it? Is it truly needed? The most effective optimization is elimination. There's no script that loads faster than the script you don't load at all. So part of measuring impact is arming yourself with data to make the case: "This chat widget adds 300 KB and 0.5 s load, but only one in a thousand users clicks it. Perhaps we should load it differently or remove it."

It's easy for sites to accumulate third-party scripts over time (from various teams and experiments) and never remove them. Periodic audits often find tags that no one in the organization owns or uses anymore. Eliminating those frees your site from unnecessary baggage. Consolidating and removing duplicates is also low-hanging fruit—you might, for example, find two analytics doing similar tracking because the marketing department added one and sales added another.

Guidance from web.dev (*https://oreil.ly/zMl2L*) suggests running A/B tests to balance each inclusion's "perceived value versus its impact on key metrics." You might experiment by removing a third-party script (or use a tool like DevTools or WPT to simulate removing it) to see if there's any effect on user engagement or revenue. If not, maybe you can drop it permanently.

For scripts that provide some value, are there lighter alternatives? Perhaps you're using a heavy third-party date-picker library for a certain form; could you use a native `<input type="date">` or a lighter-weight library instead? If an embed provides something fancy but not critical, maybe a simpler embed would do. Or maybe a one-time static integration could replace that live embed. For example, instead of loading a live Instagram feed through a script, maybe you could fetch and embed a few images at build time. (I'll discuss this concept, called *static facades*, more in the next few chapters.)

As you've seen throughout this book, optimization is often about trade-offs. Weigh the value of each third-party script against its cost. A script that is crucial to revenue might justify a 200 ms delay, whereas one that's marginal probably does not.

Think in Performance Budgets

Adopting a performance budget mindset can be helpful. Set quantitative goals for third-party impact, such as "Third-party scripts should consume no more than one second of main-thread time on mobile" or "Total third-party bytes should total less than 500 KB." Treat these as budgets. This approach turns optimization into a continuous effort: whenever a new script is proposed, you evaluate it against the budget. If adding it would exceed the budget, you must optimize elsewhere or reconsider the addition.

Many organizations include performance budgets in their CI/CD processes, for instance, by running the "Reduce third-party impact" Lighthouse audit in CI and failing builds if certain metrics regress beyond the budgeted threshold. This is effective at preventing new third-party bloat from slipping in unnoticed.

Shifting Left: Involving Everyone

It's crucial to understand that third-party optimization is as much about culture as technology. Often, the teams adding third-party tags (marketing, analytics, third-party vendors) are different from the performance engineers or core developers. So when deciding on what to remove and/or replace, involve your stakeholders. Marketing might be reluctant to remove a tracking pixel until you show that it slows the site without any demonstrable ROI. Here's where data helps: present the performance impact (as you've measured it) alongside any business metrics. It could be worth running an A/B test measuring conversion or engagement with the script and without it. If removing the script has no negative impact on business metrics, that's a win-win: you've sped up the site *and* removed complexity.

Fostering a culture where performance is a shared responsibility will ensure your optimizations persist. Chapter 11 will discuss this in detail.

The Goal: Fast and Functional

Our goal is to have our cake and eat it too: preserve the useful functionality of third-party integrations while dramatically reducing their impact on performance. This often means loading them in smarter ways so that they don't block or delay what the user cares about most: the primary content or interaction of your site.

In the next chapters, I'll explore optimization patterns and techniques for third-party scripts, including:

- Explicitly controlling the loading sequence
- Asynchronous and deferred loading
- Lazy loading
- Click-to-load (import on interaction) patterns
- Conditional loading based on device or network conditions
- Scheduling loads during idle times or after initial load
- Offloading work to web workers or the server/edge
- Utilizing framework-specific optimizations
- Tuning tag managers

From there, I'll turn to what it means to build a performance culture in your organization.

CHAPTER 9
Loading Third-Party Scripts

Third-party scripts—from analytics platforms to advertising networks, social-media widgets to customer-support chatbots—are essential to modern websites, but they come with a cost. While Chapter 8 covered what third-party scripts are and why they matter, this chapter focuses on *how* to load them efficiently. The common thread throughout is *sequencing*: prioritizing what loads first, delaying what can wait, loading conditionally based on user context, and implementing click-to-load patterns that defer heavy resources until they're actually needed.

Loading third-party scripts effectively requires balancing functionality with performance. Load them too early or carelessly, and they can block your critical content, slowing down the initial page render and frustrating users. Load them too late, and you might miss capturing important analytics data or delay features users expect. The techniques in this chapter—like using `async` and `defer` attributes and implementing lazy loading with facades—give you fine-grained control over when and how third-party content appears on your pages. By the end, you'll understand how to sequence third-party loading to minimize their performance impact while maintaining the functionality your site needs.

Sequencing and Prioritizing

One of the fundamental aspects of optimizing third-party scripts is controlling when they load and execute relative to your page's critical content. AI-generated HTML often simply includes third-party `<script>` tags without consideration for when they load, which means the browser might load and run them at inconvenient times, potentially delaying other important tasks. You need to take manual control over sequencing to ensure that third-party code doesn't interfere with the initial page render.

Identify Critical Scripts

First, categorize your third-party scripts into critical and noncritical. *Critical* third-party scripts are those absolutely required for the page to function or render properly. These should be loaded early, albeit carefully. For example, if you use a third-party library to render part of your UI (say, a map component that uses an external JavaScript API), that might be critical to showing content above the fold.

Noncritical third-party scripts provide enhancements or tracking but are not needed for the page to work initially. This includes analytics, advertising, heatmaps, social widgets, and so on. The user experience is usually fine if these load a bit later or after the main interface is up. They should almost always be deferred or delayed until after the main content loads or becomes interactive.

A well-optimized site prioritizes the main content over third-party extras. As I've written for Web.dev (*https://oreil.ly/ErmUb*), as a best practice, "the main content should load quickly and before any other supporting content." For instance, on a news article page, the article text and images are critical first-party content; the social share buttons and ad frames are noncritical content that can load afterward.

Positioning Script Tags

Where you place third-party script tags in your HTML matters a lot. By default, when the browser encounters a normal `<script>` tag without any special attributes, it will pause HTML parsing to download and execute that script. This means that if you put a third-party script in the `<head>` of your document, it can block everything that comes after from rendering until it's done.

Here's an example of what *not* to do:

```html
<head>

  ... your CSS/metadata ...

  <!-- Third-party script -->
  <script src="https://example.com/3p-library.js"></script>

</head>

<body>

  <!-- Main content -->

</body>
```

Instead, as a rule of thumb, place third-party `<script>` tags *as low in the HTML as possible*, after your important scripts/content—ideally just before the closing `</body>` tag, unless they are critical and truly needed earlier. This allows the HTML and other resources to load first. For example:

```
<head>
  ... your CSS/metadata ...
</head>
<body>
  <!-- Main content -->
  <script src="https://example.com/3p-library.js" async></script>
</body>
```

Moving the script to the bottom (and adding an `async` or `defer`, which I'll discuss next) ensures it doesn't block the initial DOM from parsing and rendering content.

Some third-party snippets (such as Google Analytics) instruct you to put them in the head. In such cases, they usually also instruct you to use `async`. If you have to include something in head, always mark it as nonblocking (`async`/`defer`).

Nonblocking Scripts: async and defer

Using the `async` or `defer` attributes on script tags are the primary ways to load JavaScript without blocking the HTML parser. Let's clarify these attributes:

defer
: With `defer`, the script is fetched in parallel while the document is parsing, but its execution is deferred until after the HTML parsing is complete. Deferred scripts also preserve execution order relative to each other: if you have two scripts with defer, they will execute in the order they appear in the document (after parsing).

async
: With `async`, the script is fetched in parallel and executed as soon as it's downloaded and available, without waiting for HTML parsing to finish. Critically, async scripts do *not* guarantee execution order: two async scripts can finish and execute out of order if one downloads faster. When an async script executes, it can still pause the parser, but at least downloading it doesn't block the parser initially. In modern browsers, async works a bit differently for module scripts, which will defer execution to maintain order among dependencies. For classic scripts, though, think of async as "download in the background, execute ASAP."

For third-party scripts, I generally recommend using `defer` by default for noncritical scripts (any script that is not needed before the DOM is ready). This ensures it won't interfere with HTML parsing and will run after the document is done, which is usually what you want for things like analytics or ads. In contrast, `async` is useful for scripts that you want to load in parallel and run as soon as possible but that aren't dependent on other scripts. For example, if you have an early analytics snippet that you want to start recording data immediately, you could use `async` so that it fires whenever it's ready, possibly even before the page is fully parsed. (It still won't block parsing while downloading.) For example:

```
<script src="https://analytics.example.com/tracker.js" async></script>

<script src="https://cdn.example.com/widget.js" defer></script>
```

In this snippet, `tracker.js` might start executing as soon as it's loaded (maybe capturing early page timing), whereas `widget.js` will definitely execute after HTML parsing. `widget.js` will also execute after `tracker.js` if parsing finishes before `tracker.js` arrives, since `tracker.js` is async and might execute earlier unpredictably. If both used `defer`, they'd execute in order after parsing.

Both `async` and `defer` will prevent the script from blocking other downloads while it's downloading. But scripts loaded with `async` or `defer` are assigned a lower download priority by the browser since they're considered nonblocking. In some cases, this means a deferred script might actually load *later* than you'd like. Trust the browser's scheduling. If a script is truly high priority, you might not want to defer it at all.

Key takeaway: always add `async` or `defer` to third-party `<script>` tags unless you have an extremely compelling reason not to. By doing so, as Jonathan Osemekhian notes (*https://oreil.ly/iFL2z*), you prevent them from blocking the parser. For multiscript scenarios, prefer `defer` to maintain their order. For standalone scripts that need to run ASAP but shouldn't block parsing, `async` is fine.

Load Critical Third-Party Scripts Early (but Not Too Early)

What about *critical* third-party scripts? Maybe you have a frontend built in React, and you rely on an external analytics tool that actually needs to run *before* your app (maybe it tracks page views even before hydration). Or maybe you have a GDPR cookie-consent-management script that should run at the very start to prevent other scripts firing before consent has been handled. (Consent managers are often optimized by their providers to be as lightweight as possible, but keep an eye on it.) These are scenarios where a third-party script might be considered critical to a page's logic or compliance.

In such cases, you might include the script in the `<head>` with `defer`, so it executes as soon as parsing is done, before other deferred scripts. You might even consider loading the script inline or by a preload. Some frameworks (*https://oreil.ly/G2Pq-*), like Next.js, allow you to mark scripts you want to run before others.

Only treat a script as critical if it's absolutely necessary. You should still use `defer` so that it doesn't block HTML parsing, and if it's very large, see if you can split or reduce it.

Preserving Script Order

If you have multiple third-party scripts that depend on each other or must run in a specific order, include them carefully. For example, maybe you include jQuery from a CDN (third-party) and then a third-party plug-in that assumes jQuery is present. In such a case, if you use `async` on both, they might execute out of order: if the plug-in loads first, it'll error, because jQuery hasn't loaded yet. If you use `defer` on both, they will execute in the order they appear in the HTML, which solves the dependency order issue. Alternatively, you might combine them or use a single script that includes both. Let's assume for this example that they're separate.

If script B depends on script A, then, you have two options. You could put script A before script B and use `defer` so they don't block but still preserve order. Or you could use `async`, but that's not recommended for dependencies. If you do so anyway, you may need to implement a callback or onload to load the next script.

In modern development, bundlers or module loaders handle dependencies, so it's rare to manage them manually, but it can certainly happen on legacy or simple sites.

Establish Early Connections with Resource Hints

Sequencing isn't just about where you put script tags; it's also about preparing the browser for third-party loads. If you know a third-party domain will be needed, you can use resource hints in your HTML, like `<link rel="dns-prefetch" href="...">` and `<link rel="preconnect" href="...">`. These hints establish early network connections to the third-party servers, so that when you later initiate the script fetch, some of the networking handshake is already done.

For example, you might add to the head:

```
<link rel="preconnect" href="https://example-third-party.com">
```

This tells the browser to start the DNS lookup, TCP connection, and TLS negotiation to *example-third-party.com* as early as possible. By the time you actually load the script from that domain, it can fetch the bytes more quickly. A weaker hint, `dns-prefetch`, does only the DNS lookup early; this can be useful for older browsers or for less crucial domains.

This technique is part of sequence optimization because it's about ordering network operations: you essentially pull some work to earlier in the timeline (during the idle time at start) so that the actual script request, when it comes, will be faster.

Andy Davies reports a real case (*https://oreil.ly/GT03B*) where using `preconnect` for an image CDN improved median load times by 400 ms and 95th percentile by over 1 s. While that example was for images, the same idea applies to third-party scripts: preconnecting to your analytics domain could shave a few hundred milliseconds off the user's network latency to that server.

As you plan sequencing, remember to add preconnects for critical third-party origins you know you will call. This way, you get the benefit of an early start even before loading the full script.

Summarizing Sequencing Best Practices

In summary, best practices for sequencing third-party scripts include:

Prioritize first-party content
: Always load your site's core content and critical resources before noncritical third-party scripts. Structure the HTML accordingly.

Place scripts late
: Put third-party script tags at the bottom of the body or load them dynamically after content, unless it's absolutely necessary to do otherwise.

Use `async` and `defer`
: Mark third-party scripts as `async` or `defer` so they don't block the parser. Use `defer` for most cases, especially if there are multiple scripts or if a script must run after the DOM is ready. If order matters, rely on `defer` (or manage load via callbacks). Avoid relying on chance with `async` ordering.

Load critical third-party scripts early
: For the rare third-party script that's critical, still load it asynchronously, but do so as early as needed (deferred in the head). Ask if it truly *must* be head-loaded.

Preconnect if possible
: Use `<link rel="preconnect">` for key third-party domains to reduce connection-setup time.

One at a time (maybe)
: Don't flood the page with a dozen third-party loads all at once, especially early on. Even async scripts can contend for bandwidth, if many start downloading simultaneously. Stagger them if possible by using priorities or initiating some later.

Next, I'll explore techniques to delay third-party loading even further when appropriate.

Lazy Loading Third-Party Content

As you learned in Chapter 4, *lazy loading* is a technique to delay loading a resource until the moment it's actually needed. It's often applied to only load images as the user scrolls down, but the same concept can be applied to third-party scripts and embeds. By lazy loading third-party content, you reduce the amount of work the browser has to do up front, which leads to faster initial load times. Users who never interact or scroll to certain features might never incur the cost of those third-party scripts at all, saving data and time.

Consider a typical scenario: you have social-media widgets or video embeds in a sidebar or further down the page, not immediately visible on initial load ("below the fold"). There is no need to fetch and render them until the user scrolls to them or interacts. Loading them immediately would slow down the page for every user, even those who might never scroll to the widget. Lazy loading such content optimizes the initial load and reduces unnecessary downloads for users who don't engage with that part of the page.

Lazy loading third-party scripts can lead to substantial performance improvements, including: reducing initial page weight by not loading heavy scripts up front; speeding the time to first render and interactive, since the browser has less to do initially; and lowering data usage for users who don't engage beyond initial content.

For example, YouTube's iframe embed is known to be heavy. Simply adding `loading="lazy"` to a below-the-fold YouTube embed can save approximately 500 KB on the initial page load. That's enormous, especially on mobile. Similarly, if you had three social embeds that total 1 MB of scripts, lazy loading them means a user who doesn't scroll will load 1 MB less data, which is important for users on limited data plans.

Browser-Native Lazy Loading for Iframes

Many third-party embeds, like YouTube videos and maps, are in iframes. The easiest way to lazy load these is to use the native `loading="lazy"` attribute on the `<iframe>` tag, much like you'd add `loading="lazy"` on an `<img>`. For example:

```
<iframe src="https://www.youtube.com/embed/VIDEO_ID"
        width="560" height="315"
        loading="lazy"
        title="YouTube video player"
        frameborder="0" allowfullscreen></iframe>
```

All modern browsers support iframe lazy loading via this attribute. The browser will hold off on loading the iframe's content until it's close to being in the viewport. The exact distance threshold varies by browser but is measured in screen heights. The nice thing is that the browser automatically handles this one line of code as a hint.

One important consideration when lazy loading iframes is to reserve space for the content. If you don't specify its `width` and `height` (or CSS dimensions), when the iframe eventually loads, it might cause a layout shift, harming CLS, because the browser didn't allocate space for it initially. Always set explicit size attributes or CSS for lazy-loaded iframes.

Browser-native lazy loading is completely passive—you don't need JavaScript to handle it. This is great for simplicity and reliability. However, there are a few caveats:

- Some browsers load conservatively to avoid popping content in late. If an iframe is just below the fold, one browser might load it eagerly, while another might wait until the user scrolls.
- Older browsers that don't support lazy loading will just ignore this code and load the iframe immediately, as usual. There's no harm; they just won't benefit from this optimization. This has become less of an issue as browser support has become far more widespread.
- If you need more precise control, perhaps to load at a specific threshold or condition, you might need a script-based lazy-load solution.

Custom Lazy Loading with IntersectionObserver

For more control, or to lazy load elements beyond images/iframes (like a script or any element), the IntersectionObserver API is the go-to solution. It can notify you when an element enters or exits the viewport (or a defined threshold of it).

This technique lets you control exactly when to load the script (in this case). Here is a typical pattern for lazy loading via IntersectionObserver:

1. Put an empty container `div` or a lightweight placeholder element in your HTML where the third-party content will go.
2. Set up IntersectionObserver (*https://oreil.ly/iWWQz*) in your script to watch that placeholder.
3. When the placeholder comes into view (that is, the observer callback fires), the browser will inject the `<script>` or `<iframe>` element for the third-party content and then stop observing the element.

Here's an example in plain JavaScript that loads the script when at least 10% of the placeholder is visible:

```javascript
const placeholder = document.getElementById('social-feed-placeholder');

if ('IntersectionObserver' in window) {

  let observer = new IntersectionObserver(entries => {

    entries.forEach(entry => {

      if (entry.isIntersecting) {

        // Placeholder is now visible or near-visible, load the actual content

        loadSocialFeed();    // e.g., replace placeholder innerHTML
                             // with embed code or append script

        observer.unobserve(entry.target);

      }

    });

  }, { root: null, threshold: 0.1 });

  observer.observe(placeholder);

} else {

  // Fallback for older browsers: just load immediately or after a timeout

  loadSocialFeed();

}
```

The `loadSocialFeed()` function would contain the logic to create an iframe or script tag for the actual third-party content. If you have multiple items, like a list of video embeds, it would observe them all and load them as each comes into view. Facebook's SDK supports a `data-lazy="true"` attribute on its embed code to enable internal lazy loading. If such an option exists, use it: it essentially tells the third-party script itself to defer work.

Since writing IntersectionObserver logic can be repetitive, the `lazysizes` library abstracts this, using IntersectionObserver under the hood for modern browsers. You can use it to automatically lazy load images and iframes with certain classes and data attributes. It provides a consistent threshold and behavior, whereas native `loading` might differ slightly by browser.

Here's the previous iframe example, this time using `lazysizes`:

```
<script src="lazysizes.min.js" async></script>

<iframe data-src="https://www.youtube.com/embed/VIDEO_ID"

        width="560" height="315"

        class="lazyload"

        frameborder="0" allowfullscreen></iframe>
```

Here, you put the real URL in `data-src` and `lazysizes` swaps it into `src` when needed. The class `lazyload` signals `lazysizes` to track it. This saves you from writing IntersectionObserver logic yourself and ensures that even very old browsers without IntersectionObserver still get some behavior (`lazysizes` falls back to a scroll event check). To tune these thresholds and conditions, use the options in Intersection Observer or data attributes in `lazysizes`.

Trade-Offs

While lazy loading is great, be mindful of its potential downsides. These include:

User experience
    If lazy loading is implemented poorly, users might notice content appearing late as they scroll. Ideally, it should load by the time they get there or slightly before. Setting a reasonable threshold in IntersectionObserver helps.

SEO
    Lazy loading content that is important for SEO (text content or certain images) can be problematic if search engines don't see it. Generally, for purely third-party content that's not your primary text, it's fine. Google Search can execute some JavaScript, but it's best not to lazy load critical textual content. Use these techniques only for nonprimary content so that critical content is still indexed.

Analytics impact
    If you use scrolling-based lazy loading, your analytics may still need to account for when a lazy-loaded component actually appears or is viewed, if that matters. Some analytics tools don't automatically know about content loaded later.

Browser differences
    As noted, different effective connection types might cause different behavior. Chrome's native lazy loading might load a bit earlier on a fast connection than it would on slow 3G. If consistency is key, use IntersectionObserver (with your own logic) or `lazysizes` to make behavior uniform across conditions.

Example: Lazy Loading an Analytics Script

Thus far, I've spoken of lazy loading visible widgets. But you can lazy load even nonvisual scripts like analytics in some cases. If your site's primary content is very performance-sensitive, you might choose to lazy load Google Analytics—meaning you don't load it until after the main content is shown or even until the user interacts (since Google Analytics can technically miss initial page view timing if loaded late, one must weigh trade-offs).

A pattern some use is to load analytics with `defer` (so it's after parse), or even wait for the `load` event (using `window.onload = function(){ loadAnalytics() }`). This is a form of lazy loading by event. It ensures that the analytics script doesn't interfere with page load, though it might miss capturing some early data, like the page's own load timing. Many modern analytics actually can be loaded deferred without issue, but it's something to consider.

Facades and Click-to-Load Patterns

Even with lazy loading, some third-party content can still be resource-intensive once it loads. Facades take lazy loading a step further by providing a lightweight stand-in for a heavy third-party embed, only loading the real thing if the user interacts. This approach is also known as "click-to-load" or "import-on-interaction." The idea is to not load the third party at all unless the user explicitly requests it (usually by clicking a placeholder).

A *facade* in this context is a static or simpler element (*https://oreil.ly/HuWJU*) that mimics the appearance of a richer, interactive embed. It gives the user a visual cue or partial functionality, but it doesn't actually include the full third-party content. Because it's static, it's much lighter and has no significant performance overhead. For example, you might show a static-image preview of a video (a play button over a thumbnail) as a placeholder. The video-player script only loads when the user clicks.

In a simple lazy load, the content is empty until it's triggered by scrolling, then it loads the actual content. Lazy loading with a facade can further improve perceived performance since the user at least sees something instead of nothing.

With the facade approach, the browser shows some lightweight placeholder content that looks like or hints at the real content but only loads the real one on interaction (click or hover). This is especially useful for heavy interactive embeds like video players, maps, and chat widgets, because users might not interact with them at all. A facade caters to those who won't interact by giving them a noninteractive preview that's faster and only engages the full feature for those who do interact.

Implementing Click-to-Load

The click-to-load pattern typically involves three phases:

Page load
   This is when the facade renders. No third-party scripts or iframes are loaded yet, just your own lightweight placeholder elements.

Preconnect on hover
   Optionally, if you want to be extra slick, when the user hovers over or touches the facade to indicate interest, you can initiate a `preconnect` to the third-party domain. This preestablishes network connections so that if they click, the actual load is faster. This improves perceived speed.

Load on-click (or interaction)
   When the user clicks the facade, dynamically load the third-party content. This might mean inserting a `<script>` tag, creating an `<iframe>` with the real `src`, or otherwise initializing the embed. The facade is then replaced by the real thing, which the user can now interact with.

For instance, for a YouTube video, in the page-load phase the page shows `<img src="thumbnail.jpg">` with a play-button overlay (CSS or a small image). On hover, it will establish a preconnect with `<link rel="preconnect" href="https://www.youtube.com">` or even begin loading the YouTube iframe in a hidden way. When the user clicks, the browser replaces the `<img>` with the actual video: `<iframe src="https://www.youtube.com/embed/VIDEOID?autoplay=1">`. The video then loads and (if autoplay is enabled) begins playing.

Generative AI-powered customer support chatbots, like those from Intercom, Zendesk, or specialized AI chat providers, deserve special attention when implementing click-to-load patterns. These tools have become increasingly popular for providing instant customer support, but they come with significant performance costs. AI chatbots typically require:

- Loading substantial JavaScript frameworks for natural language processing interfaces
- Establishing WebSocket or long-polling connections for real-time communication
- Loading additional assets like avatars, typing indicators, and suggestion interfaces
- Sometimes preloading model data or conversation context

This can easily add 500 KB, 1 MB, or more to your initial page load, plus ongoing network activity. For a customer-support chatbot, using a facade pattern is particularly effective because:

Most visitors won't need support
　Typically only 1% to 5% of visitors actually engage with support chat. Loading the full chat widget for everyone wastes resources for the 95%+ who never use it.

Support is user-initiated
　Unlike analytics, which needs to load early to capture page views, users explicitly seek out chat when they need help. A slight delay after clicking is acceptable and expected.

Alternative contact methods exist
　You can show a lightweight "Need help?" button as your facade, which opens the chat widget on-click. If the widget fails to load, you can provide a fallback email or contact form link.

Here's a typical implementation approach:

```
// Show a lightweight chat button

const chatButton = document.getElementById('chat-button');

chatButton.addEventListener('click', async () => {

  // Show loading state

  chatButton.textContent = 'Loading chat...';

  // Load the actual chat widget

  const script = document.createElement('script');

  script.src = 'https://widget.intercom.io/widget/YOUR_APP_ID';

  script.async = true;

  document.head.appendChild(script);

  // Initialize when loaded

  script.onload = () => {

    window.Intercom('boot', { app_id: 'YOUR_APP_ID' });

    chatButton.textContent = 'Chat with us';

  };

});
```

The performance benefits are substantial: instead of loading chat scripts for all users on every page, you only load them for the small percentage who click. This can improve your LCP and TTI metrics significantly, especially on mobile devices where chat widgets are particularly heavyweight.

Similarly, for a chat widget, the page would initially show a chat icon, probably at the bottom right. On hover or after some idle time, it could preconnect or preload the script. And when the user clicks the icon, the browser would insert the chat provider's `<script>` tag or call its initialization function. The chat widget would then appear. While there could be some delay while loading, this is acceptable, since it's user-initiated.

The react-live-chat-loader (*https://oreil.ly/dpjXW*) library is a React component for chat widgets that shows a fake chat button and only loads the actual chat code on interaction or idle time. Lite YouTube Embed (*https://oreil.ly/FZddF*), by Paul Irish and coworkers, is a web component that implements the YouTube facade pattern. You use a `<lite-youtube>` element with a video ID, and it takes care of showing a clickable preview and loading the real player on-click. It is "224x faster" than the standard embed (*https://oreil.ly/deKof*) (when not played)—which makes sense, since it defers loading all that YouTube JavaScript. The lite embed is basically just an image and some small code, whereas the official embed loads the whole player iframe and all the JavaScript needed to make it interactive. There are similar lite embed projects for Vimeo and other content.

The email service Postmark previously discussed how they improved user experience by implementing a click-to-load chat widget using `react-live-chat-loader`. This meant its site didn't load the chat vendor's scripts until the user clicked the "Chat" button. The result was a faster page load for everyone, and users who needed chat just experienced a short delay after clicking. Postmark found this to be an acceptable trade-off that improved page-load metrics significantly. This underlines that these patterns work in real business scenarios without harming user support or sales, as long as the functionality is still accessible.

In essence, facades often go hand-in-hand with *progressive enhancement*: they deliver a simpler, faster version of content by default, and enhance to the full version only if needed.

Facades themselves ensure you don't load the heavy stuff until interaction. You can also lazily load the facade's content on scroll if needed. For example, you might not even load the facade's image until it's in view (though a simple image is usually fine to load anytime). But if you have many video thumbnails, lazy loading those images is fine. More importantly, you might also want to lazy load the *real* embed if the user has scrolled it into view and hasn't clicked.

Trade-Offs

The advantages of using facades include:

- Massive performance savings, since if the user doesn't interact, you never load the big scripts at all. This can save seconds of load time.
- The user sees a placeholder (maybe a preview image or icon), which signals that they can load content if they wish, and is better than just an empty space.
- The user essentially opts into the heavier experience.
- Mobile users especially benefit by not downloading media-heavy content unless they want it.

The downsides include:

- The user has to perform an action (an extra click) to get the content, which might not be expected in some contexts. For video, users are used to clicking play, but if you replaced an autoloaded Instagram feed with a "Load Instagram feed" button, some might not bother or realize.
- Implementing facades is more work than simply embedding. You have to design the placeholder and write a script to handle loading on interaction, adding to complexity.
- A static image map doesn't allow zooming until you click and load the real one or go offsite. That's usually fine, but consider whether any core functionality could be lost or delayed.

If a third-party embed is core to the page (like the primary video on a video-streaming site's page), you might not want a facade: after all, the user came specifically for that content. In that case, a better strategy might be to optimize that embed as much as possible, maybe lazy loading only if what's above the fold is a thumbnail anyway. Facades shine when the third-party content is supplemental.

Next, I'll examine another axis of control: tailoring third-party loading based on the environment—specifically, device capabilities and network conditions.

Conditional Loading

As you learned in Chapter 1, not all users are equal when it comes to performance: a visitor on a high-end desktop with fiber internet can handle more scripts without noticing a slowdown, whereas someone on a low-end Android with a 3G connection will struggle with the same payload. *Conditional loading* involves adjusting which third-party scripts to load (and how to load them) based on the user's device characteristics, network speed, and other contextual signals. Some frameworks define "low-end device" by certain thresholds, like less than 1 GB RAM or older chipsets. The goal is to serve each user an optimal experience, and for users on low-end devices or slow networks, sometimes that means omitting or delaying certain third-party content.

Device Detection for Performance

Detecting a user's device capabilities can be a way to decide if a third-party script should load at all. For example, if a user is on a low-end mobile device, you might choose not to load a heavy background video or a complex interactive widget, or you might disable some noncritical third-party scripts (like some fancy analytics or nice-to-have personalization).

There are a number of ways to detect what device a user is on. Options include:

User agent strings (not recommended)
    User agent strings are an older approach that can hint at device type, but this method is unreliable and being deprecated in favor of Client Hints. Avoid using user agent parsing for new code.

Concurrency or hardware concurrency
    The `navigator.hardwareConcurrency` API returns the number of logical processors available to run threads on the user's device. You can use this to gauge device capability: a device with one or two CPU cores is likely weaker than one with eight. However, core count isn't a perfect measure of performance—CPU architecture and other factors matter too.

Client Hints
    There is a Client Hint header for "Save-Data" that users can enable in Chrome Lite mode. If that's on, it's a strong signal that the user wants to save data, so you might aggressively cut down on third-party scripts. Client Hints can give device info if you request it.

Device Memory API
    The API `navigator.deviceMemory` gives an approximation of a user's RAM. If `deviceMemory < 2` (meaning the device has less than 2 GB RAM), you know to treat it as low-end and skip some scripts. Here's an example:

    ```
    if ('deviceMemory' in navigator && navigator.deviceMemory < 2) {

        // Don't load heavy third-party

    } else {

        // Load as normal

    }
    ```

A practical use case: suppose you have an elaborate chat widget that is known to slow down low-end phones. You could conditionally not load it on phones under a certain memory threshold, possibly showing a simple "Contact us" link instead for those users (progressive enhancement approach). Yes, a few users might miss out on live chat, but they likely wouldn't have had a great experience with it anyway on their device, and providing an alternative contact method is better than giving them a slow site.

Network-Aware Loading

The browser's Network Information API (`navigator.connection`) provides info about the user's connection type and effective bandwidth. For instance, `navigator.connection.effectiveType` might return values like `'5g'`, `'4g'`, `'3g'`, `'2g'`, `'slow-2g'`, etc., based on throughput and RTT estimates. And `navigator.connection.saveData` indicates if the user has explicitly enabled a "data saver" mode in the browser. The Network Information API is not available in all browsers (Safari doesn't support it), so use it as a progressive enhancement.

You can use this information to make decisions. The following code tells the browser that if `effectiveType is '2g'` or `'slow-2g'` (a very slow connection), maybe do not load heavy third-party scripts at all, or at least defer them until absolutely needed. If `saveData is true`, be very conservative and disable all noncritical third-party scripts, loading only the absolutely essential ones):

```
if ('connection' in navigator) {
  const conn = navigator.connection;
  if (conn.saveData || (conn.effectiveType || '').includes('2g')) {
    // Save-Data is on or it's a 2G connection, avoid large third-party scripts
    window.__enableMinimalMode = true;
  }
}

if (!window.__enableMinimalMode) {
  loadThirdPartyScripts();
}
```

In this snippet, the `loadThirdPartyScripts()` function might dynamically load ads or large analytics, but could be skipped for very slow connections or data-saver users.

Even without the Network Information API, you can approximate some information, though this indirect method isn't ideal. If the initial page load takes a very long time (you might measure this by TTFB), that might hint at a slow network. Alternatively, you could provide users a manual toggle like "Basic mode," but that's more UI complexity.

Trade-Offs

Like all of the techniques discussed here, conditional loading has its trade-offs. Here are its advantages:

- The experience is better for users on slower networks or less powerful devices, as they get a lighter, faster page.
- Data savings are available for users with limited bandwidth or pay-per-use plans.
- Core Web Vitals metrics are improved across diverse user segments.
- You can still provide alternative contact methods or simpler versions of features, ensuring no user is completely left out.

Downsides include:

- It's hard to perfectly detect capability. Some midrange phones might still struggle; some fast connections have high latency; but the network might be congested even though the `effectiveType` says `'4g'`. So your rules won't be perfect. Aim to cover the clear extremes (very slow, very low-end) and be moderate with others.
- Testing can be complex, since you essentially create multiple possible code paths for different users. It's important to test thoroughly that the site still works when those third-party scripts are absent. For instance, if you skip a tag manager on slow connections, ensure no essential tag only works through that.
- Deciding not to load ads to protect certain users' experience might reduce ad impressions (and thus revenue). You'd need to justify that: maybe those users wouldn't contribute much anyway if they're leaving due to slow performance? Often there's a threshold where user experience outweighs revenue; you might skip ads only if the site would truly be unusable otherwise.
- Some privacy-focused browser modes and tools might block trackers automatically, which means your conditional loading logic might not have a chance to run. However, this usually isn't a downside—if a privacy tool is blocking trackers, that aligns with your goal of reducing third-party script overhead for users who want a lighter experience.

Conclusion

In sum, conditional loading is about being smart and empathetic: give every user as much as they can comfortably get, and no more. It's a nuanced optimization: less straightforward than lazy loading or defer, but powerful, especially for global sites with users on widely varying devices.

Chapter 10 looks at how to use scheduling techniques to ensure that third-party tasks don't compete with critical tasks.

CHAPTER 10
Scheduling and Optimizing Third-Party Scripts (and AI's Role)

Even after deciding which third-party scripts to load and when, there's an additional layer of optimization in terms of when to execute certain work. Browsers have the capability to schedule tasks during idle periods or after the main load is done, which can help in handling third-party tasks that are not urgent. This approach ensures that noncritical third-party code runs when it won't interfere with responsiveness or rendering.

Scheduling Third-Party Scripts

The primary tool for scheduling nonurgent work in the browser is `window.requestIdleCallback`.

The requestIdleCallback API

This API allows you to register a function that should run when the browser's event loop is idle (when it has no more urgent work like layout, painting, or user input handling to do). The browser will try to execute your callback in idle gaps. You can also provide a timeout to ensure it runs eventually, even if idle time is scarce.

Here's how to use `window.requestIdleCallback`:

```
if ('requestIdleCallback' in window) {

  requestIdleCallback(() => {

    // Execute non-critical third-party init here

    loadThirdPartyAnalytics();
```

```
    }, { timeout: 3000 });
  } else {
    // Fallback: if no support, run after a delay
    setTimeout(() => loadThirdPartyAnalytics(), 2000);
  }
```

This snippet schedules `loadThirdPartyAnalytics()` to run when the browser is idle or after a maximum of three seconds. On a fast device, it might run fairly soon (once the page is done processing); on a busy device, it might wait a bit, but will definitely run by the three-second mark. This is great for things like initializing analytics or widgets that truly don't need to execute immediately. For example, maybe you've deferred loading an analytics script file, but even then, it executes and starts doing work (like sending page data). You could wrap that initialization in a `requestIdleCallback` to ensure it starts sending data only when the main thread is free.

Caveat: `requestIdleCallback` is not available in all browsers (Safari added support in version 18.2, released in December 2024, but older versions still lack it). That's why a fallback to `setTimeout` is often used. The fallback ensures the code does run eventually but with a slight delay to avoid blocking critical tasks.

After Onload or First Interaction

A simpler approach is to wait for the page's "load" event. The `window.onload` event fires when all resources (like images and scripts) have finished loading. By deferring third-party initialization until this event, you guarantee it doesn't compete with loading critical resources. For example:

```
window.addEventListener('load', () => {
  // Now load non-critical third-parties
  injectThirdPartyScriptTag();
});
```

This is less fine-grained than idle callback since it waits until the whole page has fully loaded, but it's widely supported and easy. The downside is that if a page has lots of resources, it might delay longer than necessary.

Similarly, you could trigger loading on first user interaction. Suppose the user hasn't interacted at all (they might just be reading). You might decide to hold off certain scripts until the user scrolls or clicks something (which presumably means they're engaged and the initial quiet period is over). For instance:

```
function onFirstInteraction() {

  document.removeEventListener('keydown', onFirstInteraction);

  document.removeEventListener('mousedown', onFirstInteraction);

  // now load some third-party

  loadExpensiveThirdParty();

}

// Listen for first user input

document.addEventListener('keydown', onFirstInteraction, { once: true });

document.addEventListener('mousedown', onFirstInteraction, { once: true });
```

This way, if the user immediately interacts (meaning the page has likely finished loading and they want to do stuff), your page loads the third-party scripts after that. If the user never interacts further with the page—for example, perhaps they just read what's in the viewport—the loading process for your third-party scripts might hold off or eventually load using a timeout.

Idle Until Urgent (IUU) Pattern

Google's Aurora team often talks about "idle until urgent" as a pattern. This essentially means doing nothing (especially nothing heavy) until either it's idle time or something becomes urgent. Many third-party tasks are never truly urgent from the page's perspective: sending analytics can happen a bit later without harm; loading a recommendation widget can wait a moment. So design your third-party loading such that it's delayed until an idle period, or it's chunked into smaller pieces that can run during multiple idle slots if needed.

For example, if a third-party library does heavy computation on load, you might not have control to split it, but you can at least schedule its loading for idle time.

Breaking Up Long Tasks

While this section focuses on advanced techniques typically more relevant for first-party scripts, these principles can also apply when you have control over third-party integrations or wrapper code.

If you have control over a third-party integration (like a custom script or your wrapper around it) and it needs to do something heavy, consider breaking it into smaller tasks, spaced out by `requestIdleCallback` or `setTimeout(, 0)` (to yield to the event loop). This prevents it blocking the main thread for too long in one go, improving interactivity.

This is advanced and typically more relevant for first-party scripts, but if, say, a tag manager triggers a bunch of custom JavaScript that you wrote, ensure those tasks yield periodically. For example, Google Tag Manager (GTM), by default, injects its content as fast as possible. However, you might configure some tags within GTM to trigger on the `window.load` event rather than earlier. Some developers choose to load the GTM snippet itself after a delay (though Google's official snippet doesn't do that). There's a balance, since delaying GTM might delay important tags (like analytics or ads firing). But if certain tags aren't urgent, you could incorporate an idle strategy.

One idea is to put critical tags in one container that loads normally and heavy noncritical tags in another container loaded via a delayed mechanism. But GTM doesn't directly support `requestIdleCallback` in its interface; this would be a custom integration.

Using setTimeout as a Fallback or Simpler Option

If `requestIdleCallback` feels too fancy or isn't supported widely, a crude but sometimes effective method is to use `setTimeout` with a few seconds' delay:

```
setTimeout(() => {

  loadExtraThirdParties();

}, 5000);
```

This just waits five seconds after the page starts to load something. The assumption is that, by five seconds, the page is likely settled. (On fast connections, it may be done at two seconds; on slower ones, it may still be in progress, but hopefully at least the critical content has loaded.) It's not perfect, but ensures the initial experience isn't marred by those extras.

When scheduling for idle or after load, monitor to see whether those tasks ever interfere. If a user is on a slow device, the CPU is churning, maybe even after page load. Using `requestIdleCallback` provides a deadline to your callback about how much idle time the system has, which you can use for chunked processing. If idle time never happens (some pages are continuously busy, such as with an animation), consider a fallback strategy where these tasks run after a maximum time, to avoid starvation—meaning that some tasks never run because the browser never becomes idle (as shown with the timeout option).

The *Telegraph* case study (*https://oreil.ly/XgyNe*) did something conceptually similar. Those developers deferred all third-party scripts and found that not only did it not harm metrics, but it improved the time the first ad appeared by four seconds on average. That's an example where deferring helped both performance and business metrics: the ads still got loaded, but just faster, since the page overall loaded faster.

By scheduling noncritical third-party work for idle periods, you ensure that critical interactions, like the user trying to scroll or click during initial load, aren't forced to compete with those scripts. The user perceives the page as more responsive, and the third-party scripts still eventually run.

Now that I've covered strategies for when and whether to load third-party scripts, the next question is where they execute. Can you offload their work away from the main thread or even to other environments like web workers or servers?

Offloading and Sandboxing Third-Party Scripts

One of the more advanced approaches to mitigating third-party scripts' impact is to run them in a different context where they won't interfere with your page's main thread as much. *Sandboxing* refers to isolating third-party code in a restricted environment (like an iframe or web worker) to limit its access to your main application and prevent it from negatively affecting page performance or security. This can involve using web workers to execute scripts off the main thread, or even server-side or edge processing to handle work that otherwise would happen in the browser. Additionally, sandboxing third-party scripts in iframes can contain their effects.

Web Workers and Partytown

Web workers allow JavaScript to run in a background thread separate from the main UI thread. Normally, third-party scripts interact with the DOM. That isn't directly possible from a plain web worker, since workers don't have access to the DOM API. However, an innovative library called Partytown (*https://partytown.builder.io*) (by Builder.io) addresses this by running third-party scripts in a worker and proxying any needed interactions back to the main thread when necessary.

Partytown's philosophy is that the main thread should be reserved for your first-party code, and that all those heavy third-party scripts like analytics and trackers can be moved to a worker so they don't block the main thread. It intercepts access to globals like `window` and delegates them.

To use Partytown, you self-host the Partytown library and then mark your third-party script includes with `type="text/partytown"` instead of `"text/javascript"`. Partytown will load those in the worker environment. For example:

```
<!-- Partytown initialization in head -->

<script src="/~partytown/partytown.js" defer></script>

<!-- Third-party script configured for Partytown -->

<script type="text/partytown"
    src="https://third-party.com/analytics.js"
    data-partytown-config></script>
```

Under the hood, Partytown sets up proxies so that if the third-party script tries to do `document.cookie` or other main-thread actions, it will forward those calls in a controlled manner to the main thread. The heavy lifting, like crunching data and preparing requests, stays in the worker thread.

It's a clever concept: third-party code often doesn't need to alter your page synchronously; it mostly logs data or inserts some element eventually. (Ads might be an exception, where they add iframes, but even that can be coordinated.) If successful, this means that third-party scripts no longer jank the main thread. Your page stays responsive because the busy work is in a worker. It's a sandbox, too, so any crashes or slowdowns are isolated.

Of course, there are trade-offs: Partytown is actively maintained and has matured since its initial release. Not all scripts will work perfectly with it, especially if they require immediate DOM access or assume certain synchronous behaviors. It also requires you to host the Partytown scripts and set up that integration, which isn't trivial. There's also a slight overhead in proxying calls between the worker and main thread. The library provides React components to integrate with frameworks, like a `<Partytown/>` component to include in Next.js heads, and specific components for GTM. Because it's new, use it experimentally: test thoroughly and be prepared for occasional issues. It might not support every API a third-party script uses, though it covers cookies, `localStorage`, and so on via proxies.

Partytown is most appealing if you have a lot of third-party scripts that heavily tax the main thread, like multiple analytics or A/B testing libraries. If those can run in a worker, it frees up the main thread significantly. It's one of those "next-gen" approaches that, if it becomes robust, could change how we include third-party code.

Sandboxing in Iframes

A simpler, older method is to sandbox third-party scripts in an `<iframe>` so they don't directly affect your page. For example, some sites put large third-party bundles in an invisible iframe (like an ad iframe). The advantage is that whatever happens in that iframe, such as long tasks or reflows, might not directly interfere with your main page's scripting. If it hogs CPU, however, it still affects overall device performance.

Accelerated Mobile Pages (AMP), a framework by Google designed to create fast-loading mobile web pages, used this idea by loading all third-party JavaScript inside sandboxed iframes, freeing the main page from their direct influence. However, managing communication between the iframe and main page, if needed, can be complex. Also, an iframe still runs on the main thread—just with an isolated scope—so CPU usage isn't offloaded; it's just that blocking operations might not block the parent document's parsing.

GTM also has a setting to sandbox scripts that use `document.write()` so they don't block the main document (found in GTM under Variables > Configure > Enable Document Write Support with Sandboxing). It basically intercepts them and writes to its own context.

Handling Third-Party Logic on the Server Side

Moving beyond the browser, consider if some work could be done on the server or via edge workers. As Patterns.dev mentions (*https://oreil.ly/LtQNI*), the ideal for A/B testing is to do it server side. Instead of running a heavy Optimizely (*https://optimizely.com*) script on the client to swap content, you determine the variant on the server (based on cookies or user ID) and render the appropriate variant directly in HTML. That eliminates the need for experimental client-side scripts and avoids making the original content flicker. Similarly, if you have dynamic content for user segments, doing that classification and rendering on the server avoids the need to run large personalization scripts in the browser.

Some performance engineers route certain third-party calls through an edge worker or content delivery network (CDN). For example, instead of loading a third-party resource on the client, they have an edge worker fetch data from that third party and embed it in the page. This can reduce the payload or at least avoid blocking the client.

Here's a concrete example. There was a concept of server-side GTM (server-side tagging) (*https://oreil.ly/C2fZI*), which routes tag data through your own server infrastructure instead of loading multiple third-party scripts directly in the browser, where the idea is the client includes only a small script that sends data to your server (or cloud function), and that server then fans out to all the marketing endpoints. The user's browser isn't running all those scripts; it just does one network call. This shifts load to your server (and the network, of course) but can significantly lighten the browser load. It also has privacy benefits, since third-party domains aren't directly loaded in the browser.

Here's another example. To show social media content (like latest X posts) on your page, instead of using the embed script, you could call X's API on your server periodically, cache it, and output the content in HTML. That offloads the work to the server side and avoids the user's browser pulling in X's widgets script). Real-time interactivity, like buttons to repost, might not work in a static render, but often that's acceptable.

> **Service Workers for Caching**
>
> Using a service worker doesn't offload execution, but it can offload repeated network costs. Patterns.dev suggests using service workers to intercept and cache frequently changing third-party scripts. For instance, if a third-party script isn't well cached by the provider, you could cache it in the service worker so that subsequent page loads get it from cache instantly and can maybe even inject it early. This doesn't reduce the first load cost but helps on repeat visits. You could also use service workers to delay or schedule third-party loads after certain events by intercepting requests and responding when convenient (though that can get complicated; it is easier to control via normal code, as we have discussed).

Server-side solutions often require more engineering effort and coordination with backend systems. Not every third-party can be moved server side either: for example, Google Analytics relies on the client side to measure things like page timings and user interactions. However, the cultural shift is interesting: for a long time, developers accepted that "third party" meant "runs in client." Now tools like Partytown challenge that, showing we can reimpose control and decide where code runs.

Adopting these strategies might also require convincing stakeholders. For instance, to perform server-side experiments, product teams need to move logic out of marketing tools and into engineering's domain—it's often a collaboration between frontend and backend teams.

Next, I'll discuss how modern frameworks and tools support some of these patterns out of the box, making it easier to implement best practices without reinventing the wheel each time.

Framework-Specific Optimizations: Next.js and Beyond

Modern web-development frameworks have begun to incorporate performance best practices for loading third-party scripts, so developers don't have to implement everything from scratch. This section looks at how frameworks like Next.js provide built-in solutions like the `<Script>` component to manage third-party scripts. I'll mostly focus on Next.js (*https://nextjs.org*) here but will touch on other frameworks and tools where relevant.

The Script Component in Next.js

Managing third-party scripts is crucial for Next.js applications because improper loading can block hydration, delay interactivity, and hurt Core Web Vitals. The `<Script>` component provides a declarative way to control when and how third-party scripts load, ensuring they don't negatively impact the user experience.

Next.js introduced a `<Script>` component in version 11 specifically to make third-party script management easier and more efficient (*https://oreil.ly/JkK0t*). This component wraps an external script and allows you to set a `strategy` prop to control when and how it loads.

The `strategy` prop can be loaded in any of three ways, as Table 10-1 summarizes.

Table 10-1. Loading the strategy prop

Strategy	When it loads	Use cases
`beforeInteractive`	Before page becomes interactive (during SSR/in head, before hydration)	Critical scripts needed early: polyfills, consent banners, critical A/B testing. Caution: overusing this defeats optimization purposes by blocking interactivity. Use sparingly.
`afterInteractive`	After page becomes interactive (like `defer`)	Default choice for most scripts: analytics, monitoring, noncritical functionality.
`lazyOnload`	During idle time (after `onload` event)	Lowest-priority scripts: chat widgets, social embeds, optional features.

The `strategy` prop accepts three possible values:

Before the page becomes interactive
Use `beforeInteractive` to load a script before the page becomes interactive, such as during server-side rendering (SSR) or in the head, before hydration. Use this for critical scripts that are needed early, such as a necessary polyfill or must-run early code like a consent banner that blocks other things. A note of caution, though: overusing `beforeInteractive` defeats the purpose of optimizing third-party loading, as it forces scripts to load before your page becomes interactive, potentially blocking critical rendering and hydration. Reserve it only for truly essential scripts.

After the page becomes interactive
The default setting, `afterInteractive`, works like `defer`. This essentially means the script is injected on the client side and runs after hydration is complete. Use this for typical analytics or any script that can wait until the initial render is done.

Lazy loading
If you use `lazyOnload`, the script will load during idle time, essentially waiting until the browser is free (after an `onload` event). This is for the lowest-priority scripts, like chat widgets and social embeds that you truly don't need until later.

Here's what this looks like in a Next.js page:

```
import Script from 'next/script';

function MyPage() {
  return (
    <>
      <h1>My Page Content</h1>
      {/* Google Analytics script, after interactive */}
      <Script
        src="https://www.googletagmanager.com/gtag/js?id=GA_ID"
        strategy="afterInteractive"
      />
      <Script id="ga-init" strategy="afterInteractive">
        {`window.dataLayer = window.dataLayer || [];
          function gtag(){dataLayer.push(arguments);}
          gtag('js', new Date());
          gtag('config', 'GA_ID');`}
      </Script>
      {/* Chat widget script, lazy load */}
      <Script
        src="https://example.com/chat.js"
        strategy="lazyOnload"
      />
    </>
  );
}
```

In this snippet, Google Analytics is set to `afterInteractive` so it loads as soon as possible after Next.js hydration. A hypothetical chat script is set to `lazyOnload`, so it won't even start loading until everything else is done—similar to `window.onload` time.

Under the hood, Next.js ensures that these scripts are injected in the appropriate way and order (see Next.js Script documentation (*https://oreil.ly/F03nI*)). For instance, all `afterInteractive` scripts behave like deferred scripts (they won't block content), and any script added via this component is deferred unless Next.js is told otherwise (which is a safe default). By using this component, you avoid doing manual DOM manipulation or writing effect hooks to inject scripts. It also can prevent common mistakes like forgetting `async/defer` or accidentally blocking the main thread.

Additionally, `<Script>` helps coordinate ordering. If you mark one script `beforeInteractive` and another `afterInteractive`, Next.js knows which to do first. It also does some things automatically. For instance, if multiple scripts are set to `afterInteractive`, they all effectively load with defer to keep their order intact. And if you accidentally forget to mark a needed script as `beforeInteractive`, Next.js will warn you if it's used in a way that suggests it should load earlier.

Next.js's `<Script>` is built on the concept of *conformance patterns*: essentially, codifying best practices into the framework so that developers get it right by default. It's like having performance guardrails built in.

Optimizing in Other Frameworks

While Next.js is a leader here, other frameworks have also been optimizing their script loading story:

React
React (create-react-app) itself doesn't have a special script loader, since it's more of a library, but you can manually manage scripts with `useEffect` or include script tags in your HTML template.

Angular
Angular historically had a concept of `APP_INITIALIZER` for things that must run before bootstrapping, which could possibly be used to insert scripts. Angular also encourages using its built-in tools (like Angular Google Analytics libraries) instead of raw script tags.

Vue
In Vue, you might include third-party scripts in *index.html* with `defer`/`async`, or use `mounted()` to append script tags. Vue doesn't have a built-in component like Next.js's.

Gatsby
> Gatsby, React's static site generator, provided an API (in older versions) in `gatsby-ssr.js` or `gatsby-browser.js` to include scripts at certain points (like onInitialClientRender). For example, one could include an analytics script after the page hydrates using Gatsby's APIs.

Optimizing by Site Type

The strategies for managing third-party scripts often need to be tailored based on the specific characteristics and constraints of your website's architecture and platform. Different types of websites face distinct challenges with third-party scripts. This section discusses tailored strategies for a few common scenarios: single-page applications (SPAs) and modern JavaScript apps, WordPress and other content sites driven by content management systems (CMSs), and ecommerce platforms (like Shopify). Each has unique constraints and opportunities for optimization.

Handling Third-Party Scripts in SPAs Versus Multipage Applications (MPAs)

SPAs built with frameworks like React, Angular, and Vue often deliver a rich client-side experience. They may rely on third-party SDKs for services like authentication (Auth0), analytics (Segment, Google Analytics), and media (video players).

There are some challenges with SPAs. For instance, since the initial load already includes your framework bundle, adding third-party scripts on top might worsen the initial load if not handled carefully. Because the navigation is client-side, third-party scripts that normally fire on each page load might need manual handling on route changes. This could mean manually triggering pageview in analytics on a route change, since no full page reload occurs. Memory can also be an issue: an SPA that accumulates many scripts for different sections and features might hold them in memory once loaded, even if they're not used frequently after that.

Another pitfall with SPAs is that if a third-party script runs too early, it could, say, manipulate the DOM before your framework has attached event listeners, causing those changes to be lost or overwritten. That's why Next.js's `beforeInteractive` is carefully designed to integrate with SSR (*https://oreil.ly/DT-C0*) (it actually injects the script in the HTML output on server). When rolling your own, be mindful: if you inject scripts before your framework hydrates, make sure they don't conflict. Loading analytics is usually fine, though: they don't mess with the DOM much beyond adding their own elements, which frameworks will ignore if outside their root element (the DOM element where the framework is mounted, like a `<div id="root">`) or if using nonclashing IDs.

SPAs—which load once and update content dynamically via JavaScript—and MPAs—which load new pages from the server on each navigation—have slightly different challenges. In an SPA, when navigating between "pages" (views) without a full page reload, you might need to manage adding and removing third-party scripts for certain views. For instance, a marketing embed might only be needed on the home page. In an MPA, you'd include the embed's script tag only on the home page. In an SPA, if the user goes to the home page, you might need to load that script dynamically and perhaps unload it when leaving. Unloading JavaScript is tricky, but you'd basically remove event listeners or elements, if possible.

Fortunately, there are some framework-based solutions. In an SPA, Next.js still loads each page's scripts according to the strategy, even on client transitions. But after a client-side transition, the new page's `beforeInteractive` scripts can't run retroactively before hydration, which happened when the app launched. Next.js solves that by loading critical things up front or limiting such usage to the initial load by design.

If you're using React Router or similar, you might use an effect in page components. For example:

```
useEffect(() => {
  if (!window.thirdPartyLoaded) { /* load it */ }
  return () => { maybe cleanup }
}, [])
```

Some frameworks, like Qwik, aim to pause and resume logic and handle third-party differently. Qwik actually integrates Partytown for third-party scripts by default. In a vanilla SPA, however, you have to be careful not to double-load scripts. If a script is needed globally, consider loading it once at app start (with async) so it's available.

One good practice for SPAs is to encapsulate third-party integration in a service or a custom hook like `useChatWidget()` to ensure that it loads and that any necessary initialization happens once. For example, your components can call `useChatWidget()` when needed, and will insert the script, if it's not already present, and handle showing and hiding the widget.

Code splitting by route is also helpful. Use dynamic imports to only load code (including third-party libraries packaged in your app) for routes where needed. For example, if the admin dashboard uses a heavy charts library, don't include it in the main bundle: split it and load it when the user navigates to the dashboard. Similarly, for external scripts: if you need a third-party widget only on a certain route, load it on entering that route. In React, you might put a `<Script>` (if using Next.js) or `useEffect` in that page component to inject the script. Be sure not to double-load it if the user leaves and comes back; you might check a global flag or simply keep it loaded.

Decide which third-party scripts should be loaded globally (on app startup) and which lazily. For example, analytics might load at startup (with `defer`) to capture all pages. But a feedback widget can wait until the user triggers it or reaches a certain page. For example, say a React app uses Stripe.js for payments on the checkout page only. Instead of putting Stripe's script in *index.html*, which would load it for every user, even if they never buy anything, the app can load it dynamically when the user proceeds to checkout, using the `loadStripe()` function from `@stripe/stripe-js` (which internally handles injecting the script). This approach also works well for embedded maps.

You can also leverage service workers for caching. In an SPA, subsequent navigations are within the same app instance, but a service worker can help cache static third-party requests, such as caching data you fetch from a third-party API.

Tag Manager Performance Tuning

If you're using something like GTM, here are a few tips:

- GTM itself loads asynchronously by default (the snippet uses an async script tag). But once loaded, it immediately executes any tags—some of which might be third-party scripts inside.

- You can configure triggers for tags. For performance, you might set some tags to fire on "Window Loaded" rather than immediately. For example, an analytics tag could be on "Page View (Window Loaded)" instead of "Page View (DOM Ready)" if you want to delay it a bit. You could also only fire certain heavy tags on specific pages rather than doing it sitewide.

- If you have many tags in GTM (say, more than 20 tags with heavy scripts), consider splitting them into multiple containers based on page type or priority. However, be aware that this adds the overhead of loading multiple container snippets. Alternatively, you can audit and remove tags that aren't truly used.

- GTM now offers a server-side container option (*https://oreil.ly/i6qRY*). That way, the client gets a small script that sends data to your server container, which then distributes to endpoints. This requires infrastructure (a Google Cloud setup) but can vastly reduce client load. The trade-offs are cost and complexity on the server side.

Frameworks like Next.js can integrate with GTM easily by loading the snippet in *_app.js* using `<Script strategy="afterInteractive">`, which is an example of combining framework with tag manager knowledge.

WordPress and Content Management System (CMS) Platforms

WordPress sites (and similarly Joomla, Drupal, and the like) often owe a significant portion of their third-party scripts to plug-ins and embedded content. CMSs, while not frameworks in the JavaScript sense, have their own approaches to third-party scripts, and this comes with challenges. Plug-ins (such as a contact-form plug-in) may add scripts everywhere, even if they're only used on one page. Site owners often include many marketing scripts via theme settings or tag managers, and might not have the development expertise to fine-tune how they load. Updates can also be challenging: WordPress might update a plug-in and re-add some code you removed. Let's look at some strategies for dealing with these issues:

Use WordPress's scripting system
    WordPress has a scripting system (`wp_enqueue_script`) that lets you specify if a script is in the header or footer, and whether to load `async/defer` (see the WordPress Developer Resources for adding script attributes (*htttps://oreil.ly/jaQe5*)). In recent WordPress versions, you can add the `async` or `defer` attribute via certain filters or using the `wp_enqueue_script` parameters. Many performance-minded WordPress themes put third-party includes in the footer and defer them. WordPress asset management plug-ins like Flying Scripts, Asset CleanUp, and Perfmatters allow you to disable specific scripts (CSS or JS) on pages where they are not needed, like disabling a slider plug-in's JavaScript on pages that don't have a slider. They also specifically let you delay JavaScript until user interaction or a timeout, essentially implementing idle loading for any script by wrapping it.

Manual conditional load in theme
    If you code your theme, use WordPress's `wp_enqueue_script` with conditions such as `is_page('contact')` to load scripts only on relevant pages. Also mark them as `defer` if appropriate by adding the attribute (there are small snippet techniques to add `defer` to enqueued scripts).

Lazy load embeds
    WordPress 5.7+ (released March 2021) enabled lazy loading for iframes by default by adding `loading="lazy"` to iframe embeds, which remains the default behavior in current versions. Make sure this hasn't been disabled by your theme or plug-ins.

Use updated official widgets
    Some third-party features can be achieved via server-side solutions. For instance, instead of a JavaScript-powered "related posts" widget that fetches after page load, use a plug-in that computes related posts server side and outputs them directly, eliminating the need for an extra script call on client.

Limit plug-ins
    The simplest advice: fewer plug-ins generally means fewer third-party scripts. Audit your plug-ins and remove any that aren't providing significant value. Sometimes multiple plug-ins add overlapping third-party tags; consolidate those if possible.

Leverage caching/CDN
    Many third-party scripts might be cached by the user's browser if they visit multiple pages. Encourage caching by using a CDN or service worker for your static assets, and set the third-party scripts to expire in the far future (most do already, via their CDN).

Use GTM carefully
> If you're using GTM on WordPress, remove any tags not in use, and configure triggers not to fire on pages where they're not needed.

Convert third-party content to first-party
> Instead of embedding a YouTube video player, consider using a preview image that links to YouTube or a lightbox that loads the video on click. Or use plug-ins like Embed Privacy that implement facades for you, like a placeholder for YouTube, until the user gives consent or clicks.

Smaller Dependency Options

Some smaller tools and polyfills to consider include:

Head manager libraries
> Tools that manage `<head>` injection in single-page contexts, like React's Helmet and Next.js's Head, allow you to update `<head>` on navigation, including adding and removing script tags.

Dynamic import for components
> For third-party libraries that are not just scripts but packages, using dynamic `import()` in frameworks like React can split the code, so you only load those packages when needed. For example, if a page uses a third-party chart library, doing `import('charting-library')` on demand will ensure it's not in the initial bundle.

CDNs versus self-hosting
> If you're using a framework with bundling (such as Webpack), sometimes you need to decide whether to bundle a third-party library or include it through a CDN. Bundling means one less HTTP request and keeps it under your control (and maybe tree-shakable if it's modular). Using a CDN, however, might allow for parallel loading and separate caching. Measure what's better for your case.

Ecommerce Sites

Shopify doesn't give merchants fine-grained control over load timing; if a third-party app adds a script, it typically loads as it wants (often in the head). Shopify injects scripts via "apps" that merchants install with one click, often without understanding their potential impact on the site's performance. However, a developer creating a Shopify theme can choose to add scripts at the bottom with attributes or use Shopify's script tag API to insert scripts with `async`. Some Shopify merchants resort to custom code to move scripts around after load, which is not ideal. Magento and Drupal work similarly: they allow you to add scripts in a page template, so a savvy developer can position them after the main content and add `async/defer`.

Ecommerce sites also tend to suffer from a plethora of marketing tags: analytics, tracking pixels, A/B testing, review widgets, recommendation engines, chat, and so on. Business teams frequently add these to track campaigns, affiliate links, and the like. Each might be a third-party script added via the platform's integration or by adding a snippet in the theme. Removing scripts can conflict with your organization's revenue goals, so be careful. For instance, an A/B testing tool might be slow but drive improvements in conversion rates.

Here are some optimization strategies for ecommerce sites:

Monitor performance against a budget
    Constantly measure the impact of third-party scripts using synthetic and RUM, and set a performance budget to help developers make decisions (see Chapter 2).

Audit ROI
    Periodically review all third-party integrations to determine if they are delivering enough value to justify their performance cost. For instance, if you have two analytics tools, consider dropping one. If a fancy personalization script isn't proving beneficial, remove it.

Use a tag manager
    Wrangle as many scripts as possible under one control. If marketing insists on many tags, putting them through GTM or a tag manager at least centralizes where to optimize them, uses one network request instead of many, and makes it easier to remove them. However, tag managers can amplify the issue if misused—for example, by loading dozens of tags on every page regardless of necessity, creating a "fire everything" approach that hurts performance more than having a few well-placed scripts. Regularly audit your tags, remove unused ones, and configure appropriate triggers. Consider using server-side GTM for ecommerce where possible.

Load conditionally by page type
    On the checkout pages or critical conversion flows, load minimal third-party content to avoid any disruption. Many ecommerce platforms allow separate control for checkout pages and storefronts: for example, in Shopify, you can use the theme's conditional logic (like `{% if template == 'product' %}`) to load product review widgets only on product pages, or disable chat widgets on the checkout page using app settings or custom code in your theme's *checkout.liquid* file.

Defer ads and marketing until after user action
    Something like an exit-intent pop-up script to capture emails might be heavy; you could load it only after the user has spent X seconds or viewed Y pages rather than on first page load.

Optimize core third-party scripts
> For example, product recommendation carousels sometimes offer the option to prerender some content, so the script doesn't have to do as much.

Use Shopify's native features
> Avoid installing too many apps that add their own JavaScript. For instance, using Shopify's native customer-reviews system might be leaner than a third-party reviews widget. If an app is simple, like adding a tracking pixel, sometimes you can add its code manually in the theme and remove the heavy app integration.

Shopify's case study (*https://oreil.ly/H7cVQ*) touches on these ideas: when the company removed or deferred noncritical scripts, it saw conversions improve. Speed can directly correlate to conversion in ecommerce. Use that data to argue for performance: "Yes, that chat widget might capture some leads, but if it's slowing every page, maybe our overall sales will drop. Let's implement it in a smarter way."

AI's Role in Third-Party Script Optimization

As the title of this chapter suggests, artificial intelligence is beginning to play a meaningful role in helping developers manage and optimize third-party scripts. Let's explore how AI tools can assist in this challenging area of web performance.

Modern AI tools, including LLMs and specialized performance-analysis tools, can help identify problematic third-party scripts and suggest optimizations.

Automated script auditing is a big innovation: AI tools can analyze your website's loading behavior and identify which third-party scripts are causing the most performance impact. Tools like Chrome DevTools and Lighthouse already provide some of this analysis, and AI-enhanced versions can provide more contextual recommendations. For example, an AI assistant could analyze your Lighthouse report and suggest specific loading strategies for each third-party script based on its purpose and impact.

When implementing third-party integrations, AI coding assistants (like GitHub Copilot, ChatGPT, or Claude) can help you by:

- Suggesting appropriate loading strategies (`async`, `defer`, `lazyOnload`)
- Generating wrapper code that implements idle callbacks or conditional loading
- Identifying when you're accidentally loading the same library multiple times
- Recommending framework-specific solutions, like Next.js's `<Script>` component

For example, if you paste a vendor-provided script snippet into an AI assistant, you could ask: "How should I optimize this for performance in a React application?" The AI can suggest wrapping it in a `useEffect` with proper cleanup, using dynamic imports, or implementing lazy loading.

AI tools can also help you quickly create facade implementations for common third-party embeds. For instance, you could ask an AI assistant to "create a YouTube embed facade that shows a thumbnail and only loads the iframe when clicked," and it will generate the HTML, CSS, and JavaScript needed, saving you implementation time.

Machine-learning models can be trained to detect anomalies in third-party script behavior. For instance, AI systems can monitor your RUM data and alert you when a third-party script suddenly starts causing performance issues. For example, if your analytics script typically takes 50 ms to execute but suddenly jumps to 500 ms, an AI system could flag this anomaly automatically.

AI tools are also helpful for predictive analysis. By analyzing patterns in how third-party scripts affect UX metrics such as bounce rate and conversion, AI models can help predict the ROI impact of adding or removing specific scripts, making it easier to have data-driven conversations with stakeholders.

When third-party scripts are too heavy or problematic, AI can help generate alternatives, such as converting client-side third-party functionality to server-side implementations. For example, you could ask an AI to "convert this client-side A/B testing script to run on an edge function instead," and it can generate the appropriate server-side code.

Additionally, for some third-party functionality, AI can help you build lighter first-party alternatives. For instance, instead of loading a heavy feedback widget, you could use AI to generate a simple, performant custom solution that meets your specific needs.

While AI is a powerful tool for optimization, keep these cautions in mind:

Verification is required
　Always test AI-generated code thoroughly. AI suggestions may not account for your specific edge cases or security requirements.

Know third parties' policies
　Some third-party services have specific requirements about how their scripts must be loaded. AI might suggest optimizations that violate terms of service.

Context matters
　AI tools don't have full context about your business requirements. A script that seems slow might be essential for revenue, so human judgment is still necessary.

Keep learning
　Use AI as a learning tool. Don't just copy-paste solutions—understand why the AI recommends a particular approach so you can make informed decisions.

The role of AI in web performance optimization is evolving rapidly. As these tools improve, they'll become increasingly helpful for the complex task of managing third-party scripts, but they work best as assistants to knowledgeable developers rather than as replacements for human expertise.

In all cases, it's important to foster a performance culture within the organization, so that developers, marketers, and content creators understand the cost of adding that "one more script." I'll dive into that topic in Chapter 11.

PART V
The Future of Web Performance

CHAPTER 11
Building a Performance Culture

Technology and metrics aside, lasting performance gains come from having the right team culture and processes. In this chapter, I discuss how organizations and teams can ensure that performance remains a priority throughout the product lifecycle—and thus UX does too. As someone who has advocated for performance within large teams at Google, I'll share my insights into making speed part of the conversation at all levels.

A culture that values performance will naturally produce better UX. It's an attitude of caring about the user's time and experience at every step. When everyone from engineering to design to management is on the same page that "fast is part of your product's identity," the results will show in the final UX. Sustaining the benefits of optimization requires a performance-aware culture and processes that govern third-party usage over time. In this brief chapter, I discuss how teams can institutionalize good practices, monitor performance, avoid regressions, and ensure that they prioritize performance and UX throughout the product lifecycle.

Performance as a Feature

Adopting a user-first mindset to performance can drive positive change in your projects. It's not always easy—sometimes it requires convincing colleagues or rethinking existing practices—but the rewards in user satisfaction and business outcomes are worth it.

One mindset shift is to treat performance as a *feature with user value*, not just a technical detail. Ask yourself: is this optimization truly user-focused? Does it serve the needs and constraints of real users, or is it just technical perfectionism? Keeping the user at the center of performance decisions ensures that your efforts translate into meaningful improvements in their experience. That means, when planning projects or new pages, explicitly including performance goals as part of the acceptance criteria. For example, if you're building a new checkout flow, define your performance goals: "the checkout page should have LCP under two seconds on a midtier mobile device," or "we will aim for a Lighthouse performance score of at least X." Making these goals explicit brings them to the attention of the design and development teams, just like accessibility, security, or any other feature requirement. At Google, some teams set quarterly Objectives and Key Results (OKRs) for improving Core Web Vitals (CWVs) for key pages. This helps them dedicate resources to it and signals that leadership cares about UX quality metrics.

If a design comes that would be beautiful but extremely heavy, engineers should feel empowered to push back and find alternatives that are more balanced. Likewise, product managers should understand that a faster site can directly improve key performance indicators, as you've seen throughout this book. When making the case to prioritize performance work—whether to leadership, product managers, or other stakeholders—frame it as a growth or quality investment that directly impacts user satisfaction and business metrics, not just technical cleanup.

Educating and Equipping the Team

Working on Chrome and CWV taught me that the tiniest details in performance can have huge ripple effects on users. It's rewarding to see how a technical improvement translates to people having a better day (even if in a small way, like saving them time or preventing frustration). This is what makes performance work meaningful. I encourage you to take pride in making your users' lives a bit easier through faster experiences. Sharing success stories reinforces the value of the work and keeps everyone motivated to maintain discipline.

Beyond education, it's crucial to equip your team with the right tools and resources to build performant experiences. This includes providing access to performance monitoring tools, creating reusable component libraries optimized for speed, and establishing clear documentation on performance best practices. Modern AI-powered tools can significantly accelerate this process. For example, AI coding assistants like GitHub Copilot can help developers write more efficient code by suggesting optimized patterns, identifying performance antipatterns in real-time, and even generating performance-focused tests. AI-based code review tools can automatically flag potential performance issues before code is merged, such as unnecessarily large bundle sizes, inefficient rendering patterns, or blocking scripts. Similarly, AI-powered performance analysis tools can help identify optimization opportunities by analyzing user behavior patterns and suggesting targeted improvements based on real-world data. By equipping your team with these modern tools—both traditional performance monitoring solutions and AI-enhanced development aids—you enable them to build faster experiences more efficiently.

To get the whole team on board, share real user feedback or session recordings that highlight the impact of slow performance. For example, if a user-testing session shows people getting frustrated at a slow prototype, show that to stakeholders—empathy can drive change. Sometimes sharing a performance budget document can go a long way. Consider holding a simple training session on web performance for the designers and content writers too: if you teach them that uploading super high-resolution images will hurt mobile users, they'll know to consider optimizing such assets from the start.

Marketers, in particular, have incentives to add new third-party code but often simply don't know the technical options or the issues involved, so bridge that gap and help them understand. Culturally, it may be necessary to accept that some third-party features might need to be removed for the greater good. This requires backing from leadership, who must be shown the data that the performance improvement (leading to more user engagement or conversions) outweighs the feature's benefit. The *Telegraph*—a UK newspaper—found it crucial to educate nontech stakeholders about why every tag slowed their site and get them to *collaborate* on deciding what was truly necessary. Over time, this changed people's attitudes from "add all the tags" to "add carefully and measure the impact."

Ensure that everyone involved understands the impact of third-party scripts. Show them the data you've gleaned from the techniques in this book: if your site's load time is 2.5 s, and you've now learned that third-party scripts account for 1 s of that, tell the team. Share wins too: "When we deferred script X, bounce rate improved by Y%." These concrete stats help justify the work.

Explain the *risks* of third-party scripts as well: they affect not just speed but also reliability, they bring up privacy issues, and they introduce a single point of failure. (When Google and Google Tag Manager experienced an outage in 2020 (*https://oreil.ly/lANuA*), sites around the world struggled.) Scary demos can motivate teams to avoid single points of failure by, say, using async and monitoring. WebPageTest's creator, Patrick Meenan, once famously demonstrated the dangers of having a single point of failure by simulating popular third-party domains going down, showing blank pages where trackers blocked the site.

Have a Champion Keep Performance Front of Mind

I also advocate for having a performance champion or performance budget owner on your team: someone who keeps an eye on metrics and regularly reports on them. This could be a formal, appointed role or an informal role for a performance-minded engineer. The performance champion could provide a weekly report on CWV or include a performance summary in each sprint review. Making performance budgets visible (perhaps on dashboards or in the CI/CD pipeline) helps team members stay aware of performance as a tracked metric, just like uptime or errors.

It's important to keep tracking metrics even when they're good, to catch slippage whenever it appears. Performance is an ongoing effort, not a one-time project. Websites evolve, incorporating new features, new content, redesigns. Without vigilance, it's easy for performance to regress over time. One unoptimized image here, a new script there, and suddenly things are slower.

I also recommend scheduling performance audits periodically—maybe every few months. Think of this like a "tune-up sprint." Run a deep analysis using WebPageTest, Lighthouse, or any other tools you're using, and circulate a report to the team highlighting any changes in third-party script behavior. If you notice that the marketing tag from Vendor X is now taking 100 ms more than last month, someone on the team might realize that a certain update made it slower, and you might contact the vendor or consider alternatives.

To quantify the performance costs of your third-party scripts, use WebPageTest's filmstrips feature to compare your site's performance with and without them. Presenting this visual evidence in meetings with stakeholders can be powerful.

Integrating Performance into Your CI/CD Pipeline and Workflow

It's much easier to maintain good performance than to regain it after losing it. There's a truism in the industry you might hear people quoting: "It's cheaper to fix performance in the design phase than after product launch." By catching issues in code review or automated tests, you avoid expensive refactoring later. Modern AI tools are making this even more effective: AI-powered code analysis can predict performance impacts before code is deployed, suggest optimizations automatically, and even generate performance test cases based on user behavior patterns. Some teams are experimenting with AI agents that continuously monitor code repositories and proactively suggest performance improvements based on emerging patterns across the codebase. Integrate performance tests into your CI/CD pipeline, so no one can accidentally merge something that slows things drastically without the team noticing. This could include:

- If using Lighthouse CI, include the "Reduce third-party impact" audit and set it to fail if the score drops or specific heavy third-party usage is detected.
- Create automated tests to block common mistakes: for instance, a test that scans the HTML for any `<script>` without `async/defer` and fails the build to ensure no one accidentally introduces a blocking script.
- Maintain a list of allowed third-party domains. If someone adds a script from a new vendor or domain, trigger a review. Tools like SpeedCurve and Calibre can parse a test run's network requests and compare them to a whitelist, automatically flagging unauthorized third-party domains.

Another effective cultural practice is establishing a governance policy for third-party scripts to support your performance budget. This means creating guidelines for what kinds of third-party scripts are allowed and under what conditions: maybe scripts must support async loading or must not exceed X number of KBs. With such guidelines in place, team members learn to evaluate the cost of adding any significant third-party script or library.

It's also worth considering requiring developers to obtain review and approval before adding a new third-party script. Some companies have a "tag review board" or require developers to file a request to add a new script, explaining why it's needed and measuring its potential impact on performance. This encourages the team to default to due diligence rather than ad hoc inclusion.

Get the team into the habit of asking third-party providers if they can give you performance-optimized options. For example, some analytics solutions allow sampling, reducing how much script runs on every user. Ad networks might offer a lighter tag for certain placements or a new async version. If a script is particularly problematic, reach out to the vendor's support team. The team might have best practices or alternative integration modes, like a webhook or server-side API. You won't find out if you don't ask.

Leveraging AI for Performance Culture

As AI continues to transform how we build and optimize web applications, it's also changing how teams approach performance culture. Modern AI-powered tools can help democratize performance expertise across your team, making it easier for developers of all skill levels to build fast experiences.

AI coding assistants can serve as "performance mentors" during development, offering real-time suggestions for optimization opportunities. For instance, when a developer writes code that could impact performance—such as inefficient loops, unnecessary rerenders in React, or blocking operations—AI tools can flag these issues immediately and suggest better alternatives. This continuous feedback loop helps developers learn performance best practices organically rather than only discovering issues during code review or after deployment.

AI can also help with performance monitoring and alerting. Machine learning models can establish baselines for normal performance patterns and automatically detect anomalies that might indicate regressions. Rather than setting static thresholds (which can be brittle), AI-powered monitoring can adapt to your site's natural patterns and alert you only when something truly unusual occurs. This reduces alert fatigue and helps teams focus on genuine issues.

Furthermore, AI tools can help prioritize performance work by analyzing user behavior data to identify which optimizations would have the biggest impact. By understanding which pages users visit most, where they experience friction, and which device types are most common among your user base, AI can help you allocate resources more effectively. This data-driven approach makes it easier to justify performance investments to stakeholders.

However, it's important to remember that AI is a tool to augment human judgment, not replace it. Performance culture still requires human leadership, clear communication, and organizational commitment. AI can provide insights and automation, but building a culture that truly values performance requires people who care about the user experience and are willing to make tough trade-offs when necessary.

Conclusion

Web technology is always evolving. We'll keep getting new modalities, devices, network infrastructures, and metrics, but users will always prefer faster, more responsive experiences. The goal is the same: minimize waiting. Regardless of the tools, your mindset should be to start with what's best for the user.

Performance is a journey, not a destination. Just like UX work in general, you continuously gather feedback and improve. We recommend staying user-centric by, for instance, periodically experiencing your site the way a user with a slow phone would (something as simple as throttling your network in DevTools or using your site on a $100 Android device can be eye-opening).

The best technologies succeed because they serve people, not the other way around. By starting with a focus on UX—where speed, responsiveness, and stability are top of mind—and then implementing the technology to achieve it, you'll build better products.

The web can be a fantastic platform that reaches everyone, but only if we care about how it *feels* to use. So let's build a web that is fast, responsive, and delightful for users on every device and connection. When you prioritize performance as part of UX, you're respecting your users' time and enabling them to do more, which is ultimately the goal of any product.

CHAPTER 12
Web Performance Case Studies and Success Stories

Theory and techniques are essential, but seeing principles applied in practice provides invaluable context and motivation. This final part of the book shifts from *how* to optimize to *what happens when you do*. I will explore a collection of real-world case studies from the first half of the 2020s, drawn from diverse industries like ecommerce, media, travel, and finance.

Each case study examines how companies identified performance bottlenecks (often related to Core Web Vitals), implemented specific optimization strategies discussed in earlier parts of this book, and measured the resulting impact—not just on technical metrics but on crucial business outcomes like conversion rates, user engagement, and revenue. These stories highlight the tangible benefits of investing in web performance and offer practical inspiration for your own optimization efforts. Table 12-1 provides a high-level summary.

Each case study includes an overview of the site, the Core Web Vitals (CWV) and other metrics targeted (especially LCP, CLS, and INP), the technical strategies the organization implemented, and the business outcomes achieved. The focus is on how in-depth, production-level optimizations yielded tangible user experience and business improvements.

Table 12-1. Summary of case studies by vertical

Vertical	Company/site	Metrics improved	Key optimizations	Business outcomes
Ecommerce/ Retail	Rakuten 24 (online marketplace)	LCP (faster by ~0.4 s); CLS (−93%); FID (−8%)	A/B tested a version of the site with a focus on CWV. Optimizations included eliminating render-blocking resources, code splitting, lazy loading, and image optimization.	53.37% increase in revenue per visitor and a 33.13% increase in conversion rate.
	Vodafone (Telco ecommerce)	LCP (5.7 s → 3.9 s, 31% faster); DCL (+15%)[a]	Focused on improving LCP on a key landing page through an A/B test. Key changes involved moving a client-side rendered widget to SSR and optimizing images.	An 8% increase in sales, a 15% improvement in the lead-to-visit rate, and an 11% improvement in the cart-to-visit rate.
	Carpe (D2C skincare)	LCP (−52%); CLS (−41%); TTFB (−1.5 s)	Addressed issues with lazy loading, converted background images to `<img>` tags for preloading, and added `fetchpriority="high"`. Carpe also optimized server-side liquid template logic.	+5% conversion, +10% traffic, and +15% revenue.
	Sunday Citizen (Shopify D2C)	LCP (−25%); CLS (−61%); FCP (−0.3 s)	Preloaded hero images, removed lazy loading on above-fold images, and ensured responsive image formats. The company also reserved space for navigation and carousel elements to fix CLS.	+6% conversion rate and a 4% decrease in bounce rate.
	Swappie (refurbished phones)	LCP (−55%); CLS (−91%); FID (−90%)	A comprehensive overhaul of CWV with a focus on mobile performance.	42% increase in mobile revenue and a 10% higher mobile conversion rate.
	Ray-Ban (luxury retail)	(Page prerendering)	Utilized the Speculation Rules API for prerendering key pages to anticipate user navigation.	Doubled conversion rate and a 13% decrease in exit rate.
Media/ Publishing	*Economic Times* (news)	LCP (4.5 s → 2.5 s)[b]; CLS (0.25 → 0.09)	Prioritized critical resources by deferring nonessential scripts and loading the hero image and article content first. The *Economic Times* also optimized fonts, used Brotli compression, and implemented CDN caching.	Passed all CWV and achieved a 43% decrease in bounce rate.
	Yahoo! JAPAN News	CLS (improved by 0.2)	Identified and fixed layout instability on article pages by adding placeholders and explicit dimensions for images and ads.	15% increase in page views per session, 13% longer session duration, and a 1.7 percentage point decrease in bounce rate.
	iCook (content/ recipes)	CLS (−15%)	Reserved image slots and optimized the timing of ad embeds to avoid shifts.	10% increase in ad revenue.

Vertical	Company/site	Metrics improved	Key optimizations	Business outcomes
Travel/ Hospitality	redBus (online ticketing)	INP (−72% on critical page); TTI (faster)	Reduced expensive JavaScript work on the search input by managing form state locally. redBus also optimized infinite scroll by triggering next batch loads earlier and fetching smaller chunks.	7% increase in overall sales.
	Bookaway (travel booking)	LCP (−15% p75); TTFB (2.0 s → 1.24 s)	Migrated to static prerendered pages with Stale-While-Revalidate caching on a CDN.	Improved SEO "Page Experience" scores with 79% of URLs rated as "Good" in Search Console.
	TUI (Tourism)	Load time (−78%)	Fostered a company-wide focus on performance and cross-team collaboration to streamline pages.	Faster page loads made visitors 34% more likely to convert.
Finance/ Fintech	Financer.com (fintech aggregator)	LCP, FID (improved via WP Rocket)	Implemented a full caching and optimization plug-in (WP Rocket) for WordPress.	45% increase in conversion rate and a 110% year-on-year increase in revenue.
Education/ EdTech	Private University (USA)	(General site speed and UX)	A comprehensive web overhaul focused on intuitive navigation and faster content loading, likely including home page simplification, caching, and media optimization.	35% higher website conversion in the first year and a 64% increase in users proceeding from the home page to key pages.
Social/ Community	Yelp (local reviews platform)	FCP (3 s → ~1.5 s); TTI (substantial reduction)	Introduced performance budgets after new ad features doubled load time. Yelp optimized the critical rendering path by improving server response and eliminating render-blocking resources.	15% boost in conversion rate.
	Trendyol (ecommerce marketplace)	INP (−50% on product listings)	Focused on runtime interaction performance in a large React application by optimizing component performance and leveraging modern browser features.	1% increase in internal click-through rate on search results.
AI/ML	Vercel (platform)	LCP (−20% to −35%)	AI-powered image optimization that automatically selects formats, compression levels, and responsive breakpoints based on ML models.	Up to 40% bandwidth savings with no quality degradation.
	Cloudflare (CDN)	TTFB (−15% to −25%)	ML-powered predictive caching and intelligent traffic management to prewarm edge caches.	Three to five times more traffic handled without infrastructure upgrades.
	Shopify AI (platform)	LCP (−18%)	AI-powered performance analysis, prioritized recommendations, and one-click automated fixes for merchant stores.	12% higher conversion rates for stores implementing recommendations.

[a] DCL = DOM content loaded. In Vodafone's case, DCL increased slightly due to moving work to the server, but LCP improved significantly.

[b] *Economic Times* LCP improvement of "80%" is as reported, roughly from ~4.5 s to ~2.5 s at p75.

Ecommerce and Retail Performance Wins

Ecommerce websites often have rich content and third-party scripts that can slow down load times. The following case studies illustrate how focusing on CWV and other performance metrics led to better user engagement and higher sales.

Rakuten 24: A/B Testing for CWV ROI

Rakuten 24, a Japanese online marketplace, undertook a major performance optimization project to improve CWV scores on its mobile site. By running an A/B test, it quantified the business impact of its optimizations.

Problem

Initially, over 75% of Rakuten 24's users had "good" LCP, FID, and FCP, but CLS was problematic. Real-user data showed a strong correlation between LCP and conversion rates, which convinced the team to invest in improvements.

Optimizations

To optimize the site, the Rakuten 24 team did the following:

Eliminated render-blocking resources
: The team audited and deferred or inlined critical CSS/JS and used resource hints for important assets.

Implemented code splitting and lazy loading
: The JavaScript bundle was split, and less critical UI pieces were dynamically imported. The team also lazy loaded below-the-fold HTML content.

Optimized images
: The team removed above-the-fold images from lazy loading and served them through a CDN, with proper compression and sizing.

Improved CLS
: The team reserved space for images and other content using the CSS `aspect-ratio` property and set minimum heights on certain containers.

Improved caching and infrastructure
: The team used a service worker to cache assets and pages for offline and returning visits, and employed a CDN to serve content faster.

Implemented RUM
: The team integrated the web-vitals JavaScript library to collect field data on CWV and feed it into an in-house analytics dashboard.

Results

After the A/B test ran for a month, the optimized version showed a ~0.4 s faster LCP and 92% better CLS. This led to the following:

- There was a gain of 53.4% revenue per visitor on the optimized version.
- Conversion rate increased by 33.1%.
- Average order value increased by 15.2%.
- Visitors spent 10% longer on the site.
- Exit rates dropped by about 35%.

Vodafone: Faster Landing Page, Higher Sales

Telecom company Vodafone's ecommerce team partnered with Google to improve the LCP on a critical landing page, using A/B testing to measure the business impact of the change.

Problem

The target page's LCP was about 8.3 s, well above the 2.5 s "good" threshold.

Optimizations

The Vodafone team moved a heavy client-side rendered widget to server-side rendering. Server side rendered the critical HTML for a faster initial paint. The team also optimized images by resizing and compressing files, and used CSS media queries to avoid loading offscreen images.

Results

After these optimizations, LCP on the Vodafone improved by roughly 31%, going from 8.3 s to 5.7 s. Vodafone also saw:

- An 8% increase in sales
- A 15% jump in the "lead to visit" rate, which measures how many site visitors take an initial action like submitting a form or starting a quote request
- An 11% jump in the "cart to visit" rate, which measures how many visitors add a product to their shopping cart during the session

Shopify's Merchant Stores: Sunday Citizen

Shopify's web performance team has published several case studies of improving independent merchants' stores. I'll look at two such stores here: Sunday Citizen and Carpe.

Sunday Citizen is a business that makes and sells luxury bedding and loungewear.

Problem

The Shopify team identified that Sunday Citizen's main banner image was being lazily loaded via the CSS background, harming LCP and CLS.

Optimizations

To improve these, Shopify implemented several fixes, including:

- Loading images earlier, refactoring to remove them from the CSS backgrounds and instead use standard HTML `<img>` tags
- Using modern image enhancements, such as applying `srcset/sizes` for responsive loading and `fetchpriority="high"` to important images
- Stabilizing the layout, adding explicit image heights and widths or CSS minimum heights for the navigation bar and product image galleries

Results

After these changes, Sunday Citizen saw improvements:

- Its LCP dropped by 1.1 s.
- Its CLS improved significantly due to the layout stabilization changes, particularly from adding explicit dimensions to navigation bars and product galleries.
- Its conversion rate rose by more than 6%.
- The bounce rate dropped by 4%.

Shopify's Merchant Stores: Carpe

Another Shopify merchant, Carpe, sells customized deodorant and antiperspirant products.

Problem

Carpe's site had a high LCP and a TTFB exceeding one second, indicating server-side slowness.

Optimizations

Key optimizations for Carpe included tweaks to the frontend and backend. On the frontend, to address LCP and CLS, the Shopify team:

- Removed improper lazy loading
- Converted CSS background images to proper `<img>` tags

On the backend, to address TTFB, the Shopify team:

- Reduced the data serialized in Carpe's theme's code
- Added a caching layer

Results

As a result, Carpe's TTFB dropped by about 1.5 s and its LCP dropped by about 2.5 s. Business-wise, it saw:

- A 5% increase in conversion rates
- 10% more organic traffic
- A total revenue increase of 15%

Ray-Ban: Prerendering

In 2025, the engineering team at sunglasses brand Ray-Ban implemented the new Speculation Rules API in browsers to prerender pages the team predicted the user might click next.

Problem

Ray-Ban's ecommerce site had a classic navigation performance challenge: users browsing product listings would experience a noticeable delay when clicking through to product detail pages. Each page transition required a full page load, including fetching HTML, CSS, JavaScript, and high-resolution product images. This friction during the shopping journey meant potential customers would sometimes abandon their browsing session before finding the product they wanted, directly impacting conversion rates and revenue.

Optimizations

By prerendering the next page in the background, such as a product detail page when the user is on a category listing, the Ray-Ban team ensured that if the user clicked, the page would load nearly instantly.

Results

This technique is advanced and needs careful logic to avoid wrong guesses, but it paid off: Ray-Ban reported doubling its conversion rates (*https://oreil.ly/vKgUP*) on pages where it enabled prerendering, and exit rates dropped 13%.

Essentially, users who experienced near-instant transitions were far more likely to complete a purchase than those who had to wait for a page load. This case is a cutting-edge example of how even the last few hundred milliseconds can drastically improve user behavior in ecommerce, especially when using modern platform capabilities.

News and Media: Boosting Engagement with Speed

Online news and media sites face the challenge of balancing rich content (images, videos, ads) with performance. They often serve millions of users, so small improvements in speed can have large aggregate effects. The following studies show how several media companies improved their sites' CWV at scale, leading to longer reader sessions and lower bounce rates.

The Telegraph Media Group

I've referenced the *Telegraph*'s journey throughout this book. To summarize, the *Telegraph* (*https://oreil.ly/UsbtZ*), a major British news publisher, undertook a project to improve its web performance, focusing heavily on third-party scripts used for advertising and analytics.

Problem

The *Telegraph* discovered that its own first-party code accounted for only about 5% of the requests made during page load. The overwhelming majority came from third-party scripts used for advertising, analytics, social media integrations, and other services. These third parties were outside the team's direct control but were having a significant negative impact on the site's loading performance. The challenge was compounded by the fact that different teams across the organization owned relationships with different third-party vendors, making coordination difficult.

Optimizations

Telegraph engineer Gareth Clubb emphasized (*https://oreil.ly/UsbtZ*) that initially, the team's own code optimizations only affected about "5% of the requests." The rest were third parties outside their direct control. This realization shifted the *Telegraph* engineering team's focus to broader organizational involvement. The team created a performance task force and managed to defer almost all third-party scripts.

Results

Not only did site speed improve, but the *Telegraph*'s business metrics did not suffer. In fact, its case study observed (*https://oreil.ly/UsbtZ*) that "We can say with confidence though that deferring our JavaScript hasn't skewed any existing analytics and it certainly hasn't delayed any advertising. By using custom performance marks in the advertising code, deferring JavaScript and reducing bundle sizes, the First Ad Loaded metric improved by an average of four seconds." This is a powerful validation that speeding up the site did not harm ad revenue; it likely improved user engagement so much that everything still tracked fine.

The *Telegraph*'s approach combined technical deferral with cross-team collaboration to review tags regularly. It's a prime example of culture and technique working hand in hand to achieve success.

The Economic Times: Passing CWV at Scale

The *Economic Times* (ET) is one of India's largest news websites.

Problem

In 2021, many of the ET's pages failed Google's CWV criteria, which could potentially hurt its search rankings. ET's pages are content-heavy and include third-party elements like ads and social embeds. Initially, only around 62% of page views were in the "Good" CLS range; about 26% were "Poor" (CLS over 0.25). LCP was around 4.5 s at the 75th percentile, also poor. The team identified slow server response, unoptimized fonts, and late-loading ads as key issues.

Optimizations

Over nine months, ET's development team overhauled the site's performance (*https://oreil.ly/fbfz1*), including:

Optimizing server response (TTFB)
    ET switched to a faster DNS provider and added a caching layer (using Redis) for frontend templates, so repeat visits or heavy traffic surges could be served from cache instead of hitting the origin server each time.

Putting "critical requests first"
    ET prioritized critical above-the-fold content in the loading sequence. This involved deferring scripts that weren't needed for initial render, like analytics and below-the-fold widgets, as well as using `<link rel="preload">` for key resources like large images and critical CSS. ET also reduced the number of concurrent requests by bundling where possible, since the browser can only handle so many at once.

Switching the font-loading strategy
   Text rendering was being delayed by custom web fonts. By changing from default `font-display:auto` to `font-display:swap`, the team allowed the text to show in a system font immediately then swap to the custom font when ready. This eliminated blank text flashes and made content readable faster, improving both LCP and CLS (since late font swaps can shift layout).

Using Brotli compression
   On the server, the ET team switched from GZip to Brotli compression for text assets. Brotli made JavaScript, HTML, CSS, and font files 15% to 18% smaller, reducing download times.

Preconnecting strategically
   The team audited third-party domains and added `<link rel="dns-prefetch">` or `preconnect` for those that are always needed. This saved precious time in establishing network connections. However, the team was cautious to use preconnect only for domains that would certainly be used to avoid wasting resources.

Code splitting and deferring scripts
   The ET team broke its JavaScript bundles into smaller chunks, loading only what was needed for initial content and deferring the rest to later. ET also deferred any unused scripts; for example, heavy analytics or slideshow scripts were loaded after the main content.

Reserving space for ads and embeds
   A major source of ET's CLS problem was advertisements loading in and pushing content, so the team created styled placeholders with dimensions for ad slots and other embed containers to prevent layout jump.

Adding explicit image dimensions
   Similar to ads, ET added explicit width and height attributes or CSS for all images and video containers. This was crucial to eliminate cumulative shifts on article pages with many inline images that loaded progressively.

Optimizing long tasks (FID/INP)
   While the primary focus was on LCP and CLS, the team also broke up long JavaScript tasks to improve interactivity (FID). The team used techniques like `requestIdleCallback` and splitting heavy loops into smaller chunks. The team deferred loading third-party scripts until after user interaction if possible, such as lazy loading social share buttons. The team also lazy loaded below-the-fold ads so that the main thread wasn't tied up loading ads while the user was trying to interact. Finally, the team trimmed polyfills for old browsers to reduce JavaScript payloads.

Results

By July 2021, ET had achieved substantial performance improvements:

- User engagement metrics improved dramatically: ET reported an overall 43% reduction in bounce rate after the changes. In other words, far fewer users landed on a page and left immediately—likely because the pages now loaded quickly and without jarring shifts, encouraging users to stay and read.
- LCP "Poor" occurrences fell by 33%, and average LCP improved about 80%, from 4.5 s to 2.5 s at p75.
- CLS "Poor" occurrences dropped by 65% (from 25.9% of sessions to just 9%), and average CLS went from 0.25 to 0.09, a 90% improvement that places this metric well within the "good" zone.
- Internally, the team also noted better pages per session and time on site. The smoother experience, especially on mobile (where networks are slower), kept readers on the site longer.
- Consequently, the site as a whole passed all CWV thresholds, which was a big deal for ET's SEO and for Google's page experience update.

The *Economic Times* case shows that by attacking performance holistically (network, server, and frontend), even a large news site can achieve fast, app-like performance and reap the benefits in user retention.

Yahoo! Japan News: Correlating CLS Fixes to Engagement

Yahoo! Japan News (*https://oreil.ly/XILlC*) is one of Japan's largest news platforms, with around 22 billion page views a month. By fixing a CLS issue on article pages, the company saw a clear improvement: page views per session went up ~15%, session duration went up 13%, and bounce rate decreased.

Problem

Through continuous monitoring, the team noticed that pages with poor CLS were hurting user engagement. Using Google Search Console's CWV report, Yahoo's engineers pinpointed that the article detail page template was frequently in the "poor" bucket for CLS (Figure 12-1). Yahoo then used Lighthouse's CLS audit ("Avoid large layout shifts") to find which DOM elements were moving around. This revealed that certain components—specifically the article header area and ad slots within articles—were causing significant shifts.

Yahoo also instrumented the site with the web-vitals JS library to measure CLS in the field and see exactly when in the page lifecycle shifts occurred (including user scroll-triggered shifts). This combination of tools gave a full picture: the primary offenders were likely images or ads loading without reserved space.

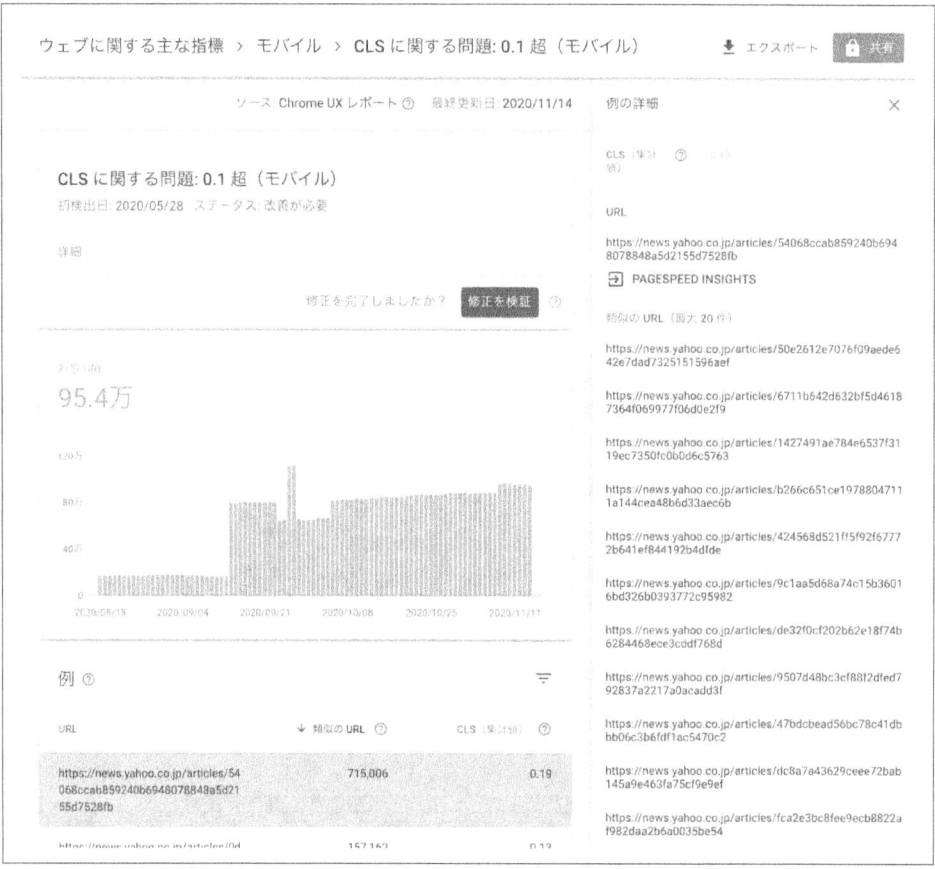

Figure 12-1. Google Search Console CWV report showing CLS status breakdown, with URLs categorized as Good, Needs Improvement, or Poor, demonstrating how Yahoo's team identified problematic page templates

Optimizations

According to Yahoo's engineering blog (*https://oreil.ly/XILlC*), the team implemented several targeted fixes:

- The team added width and height attributes or CSS aspect ratios for all images in articles. For article header images and inline content images, the team ensured the layout allocated space before the images loaded, eliminating shifts when images appeared.

- For ad iframes embedded within article content, the team inserted placeholder containers with predefined dimensions matching the expected ad sizes. This prevented the common issue of text being pushed down when ads loaded.

- The team refactored the top area of article pages—which included the headline, publication date, and share buttons—to have fixed dimensions. This prevented shifts caused by web fonts loading or dynamic content appearing.
- The team integrated automated performance testing into the Yahoo engineering team's development workflow to catch CLS regressions before they reached production. This allowed the team to continuously monitor performance across different parts of Yahoo's sites and prevent future degradation.

Results

The team achieved an improvement of about 0.2 in its average CLS score, and the impact on user behavior was immediate:

- Page views per session increased 15.1%.
- Session durations were 13.3% longer.
- Bounce rate dropped by about 1.7 percentage points from an already low base, since Yahoo News is a portal—this is significant.
- Pages flagged as poor dropped by 98%.

Virtually eliminating pages with "poor" UX likely helped ensure that Yahoo! Japan News suffered no SEO hits from its CWV rollout. The team demonstrated a tight correlation between better CLS and better engagement, which helped build a case internally that performance improvements translate to tangible audience retention.

This case is a great example of focusing on visual stability, which is often overlooked in favor of loading speed. It shows that readers are meaningfully affected by page jank: a page that jumps around will turn some users away. By smoothing out the reading experience, Yahoo! Japan News kept more eyeballs on its content—which, in turn, likely improved ad impressions and revenue.

In summary, for publishing sites, faster is stickier. Users read more and leave less when pages behave nicely. Ads, which are the revenue engine, also perform better when they load fast and without surprise shifts. These case studies reinforce that even content sites should treat performance as a core feature to keep their audience loyal.

Travel and Hospitality: Speeding Up Booking Experiences

Travel websites, like ticketing platforms and travel agencies, often have complex search and filter functionality and lots of images. They tend to be very transaction-focused. Performance improvements in this vertical can directly increase bookings, as shown by the following cases.

redBus: Improving INP for Better Sales

redBus (*https://oreil.ly/RsQWg*) is a popular bus-ticketing platform in India.

Problem

In 2023, the redBus team turned its attention to INP because certain interactive pages, like search results, were sluggish. The search result page was doing a lot of work on every user keystroke: each character typed into the search filter triggered a heavy Redux reducer and UI update, causing jank. This led to high INP: the interface would feel unresponsive as users typed or scrolled, especially on slower devices. Also, loading results as an infinite scroll was causing spikes in latency: if 30 new results loaded at once right as a user scrolled, it blocked the main thread.

Optimizations

The redBus team undertook several optimizations, including:

Debouncing state updates
: The team changed the input field logic so that it no longer updated global state on every character. Instead, the team kept the input text locally and only pushed it to the Redux store on "blur" (when the user finished typing or left the field). This eliminated a ton of intermediate renders. By "calling the reducer less frequently," the team cut out unnecessary rerenders of the large result list while the user was still typing. Essentially, typing became smooth.

Optimizing infinite scroll
: Instead of waiting until the user scrolled to the very bottom, redBus now prefetched the next batch of results earlier, when the user was on the second-to-last card. This way, the new results were ready by the time the user got there, avoiding a long wait. redBus also reduced the batch size from 30 results to 10 results per fetch. Smaller chunks meant adding content incrementally, with less lag and less JavaScript work each time.

Reducing layout thrash during load
: Though redBus don't explicitly say so, the company likely also ensured that adding new results didn't shift the page content oddly, by maintaining a consistent container height while loading spinners and the like.

Results

After these changes, redBus reported major improvements:

- The search page's INP improved by 72%. For instance, a lab test INP that was about 344 ms (needs improvement) fell to around 96 ms (excellent) after the optimizations—a huge gain in responsiveness.

- Overall sales increased by ~7% following the improvements: a faster, smoother search meant more users found and booked tickets without frustration.

This case underscores the importance of interactivity, not just loading. While earlier cases focused on loading and layout, redBus showed that if your site is interactive (lots of user input, infinite scroll, etc.), optimizing JavaScript and input handling for responsiveness can yield significant rewards.

Bookaway: Serving a Global Audience with Static Content

Bookaway is an international travel-booking service with a global user base.

Problem

Originally, Bookaway's site content (with lots of listings and search results) was dynamically generated for each request. But users around the world, many of them far from the origin server, saw high TTFB due to network latency and backend processing. A single user's experience might be fine after the first page, but cold starts were slow. The Bookaway team audited (*https://oreil.ly/_PYVi*) its CWV in 2023 and decided to focus primarily on LCP and TTFB by leveraging caching and CDNs.

Optimizations

The Bookaway team implemented a strategy of using stale-while-revalidate to serve pregenerated pages and adopted a static content-delivery approach:

- The team used AWS CloudFront (a global CDN) to serve pages from edge locations. Instead of hitting Bookaway's server for each page, most users would get a cached HTML page from a nearby edge.
- The team generated pages ahead of time or on first request, using stale-while-revalidate caching. If a page wasn't updated yet, the CDN served a potentially stale cached version immediately (so the user wouldn't have to wait) and simultaneously triggered a background update fetch to refresh the cache. The next user would get the updated content. This is great for pages that don't need to be absolutely in real time.
- By doing this, the team cut out a lot of server processing on repeat views and leveraged geographic distribution.
- Bookaway also set up rigorous monitoring with Next.js instrumentation. Bookaway piped the data into BigQuery and visualized it in Looker to track performance continuously. This helped Bookaway spot issues like a "long tail" of pages (Bookaway had ~700 K pages in seven languages, some rarely visited), indicating that Bookaway's caching strategy shouldn't attempt to prerender everything but would do better to use on-demand caching to handle that scale.

Results

These optimizations had a dramatic effect:

- TTFB dropped nearly 38%: from 2 s down to 1.24 s on average.
- LCP improved by around 15%. In essence, the first byte and first paint of pages were much faster, especially for far-flung users. Readers in Asia were now getting content from a Singapore cache, not from the US server.
- 79% of Bookaway's pages now delivered a Good page experience (up from likely much less before).
- Although he didn't cite exact conversion numbers, Liran Cohen (Bookaway's Head of Web, who wrote the case study) reported improved SEO rankings and was confident that better LCP had contributed to increased organic traffic.

This case demonstrates the power of CDN edge caching and static rendering for a dynamic site. By embracing a slightly more static architecture (even just caching HTML for a short time), you can vastly improve load times for everyone without significantly sacrificing content freshness. It also shows a forward-thinking adoption of stale-while-revalidate, a cache pattern that is becoming more popular for achieving both performance and up-to-date content. The smoother experience across regions means Bookaway can serve, say, a user in Latin America booking an Asian trip, with far less friction. That's essential for a global service.

In travel, every extra second can mean that a user leaves to a competitor or an online travel agency (OTA). Therefore, many travel sites are now setting up performance budgets and monitoring to ensure that new features don't regress their CWV. As Deloitte's "Milliseconds Make Millions" study noted (*https://oreil.ly/2V4BC*), cutting even 100 ms of load time can improve conversion by 0.5% to 1% for travel sites in competitive markets. At scale, that is huge—imagine an airline increasing bookings by 1% globally just by optimizing images and code! Thus, travel companies increasingly treat performance as a first-class feature of their booking platforms.

Finance and Fintech: Building Trust with Speed

Financial technology (fintech) platforms, such as personal finance tools or banking apps, often handle complex data and must ensure high security. Sometimes those needs can be at odds with performance, since sites often use lots of scripts for encryption or heavy analytics for compliance. But fintech users, like all users, respond well to fast, responsive interfaces. Speed can also build a perception of reliability, which is crucial in finance.

Financer.com: Speeding Up WordPress for Conversions and SEO

Financer.com (*http://financer.com*) is a global personal-finance site that allows consumers to compare loans and credit cards across 26 countries.

Problem

Financer's team ran into performance issues (*https://oreil.ly/qXJKC*) with its WordPress setup. The team had tried custom-coding its optimizations, but the optimizations had become hard to maintain as these became outdated and caused conflicts.

Optimizations

In 2021, Financer switched to using a performance plug-in, WP Rocket, and essentially applied a suite of best practices quickly. These included:

- Serving cached HTML pages to returning visitors
- Compressing, combining, and deferring CSS and JavaScript files as needed, via WP Rocket
- Lazy loading images and iframes to defer below-the-fold content
- Optimizing Financer's database for WordPress by cleaning up transients and the like

Results

Implementing these standard optimizations quickly with a tool freed Financer's developers to focus on the site's custom needs. The team achieved a remarkable turnaround:

- Financer's mobile PageSpeed Insight score jumped from around 40 to over 90, a near-perfect PSI score that indicates very low LCP/FID/CLS on key pages.
- Conversion rates increased 45%.
- Year-over-year revenue increased 110%.

With much faster page loads, Financer saw significant business growth. A 45% jump in conversion rate means many more visitors ended up completing the desired action, maybe clicking through to partners or signing up. Revenue growth of 110% year-over-year is huge. While not all of that can be credited to performance (since market factors, marketing, and other aspects play a role), Financer explicitly ties these performance improvements to better SEO (more organic traffic) and better CRO (conversion optimization).

Notably, faster site speed likely improved Financer's SEO rankings, since Google's page experience update and overall site quality signals would favor a 90+ PSI score site over a 40 score site in a competitive niche. This would bring in more organic visitors, which directly impacts revenue in affiliate-driven fintech.

Financer's case is one where using the available optimization tech instead of reinventing the wheel paid off. You don't always need a large engineering effort: often, leveraging proven solutions like a caching plug-in or CDN can get you 80% of the way to a fast site and yield major gains. This case also underscores that performance is a growth lever: improving CWV can boost both SEO and conversion metrics, which in a competitive market like finance can translate to millions in revenue.

AI and Performance: Emerging Success Stories

As artificial intelligence becomes increasingly integrated into web development and optimization workflows, a new category of case studies is emerging. These stories highlight both the challenges of AI-generated code and the opportunities that AI-powered tools present for improving web performance.

Vercel: AI-Powered Image Optimization at Scale

Vercel, the company behind Next.js, has pioneered the use of AI for automatic image optimization across millions of websites hosted on its platform.

Problem

Modern websites are image-heavy, with product photos, hero banners, and user-generated content accounting for a significant portion of page weight. Developers often struggle to choose optimal image formats, compression levels, and responsive breakpoints. Manual optimization is time-consuming, and suboptimal choices directly impact LCP and overall page load times.

Optimizations

Vercel developed an AI-powered image optimization pipeline that automatically:

- Analyzes image content to determine the optimal compression level without visible quality loss, using machine learning models trained on millions of images
- Selects the best format (WebP, AVIF, or JPEG) based on browser support and image characteristics
- Generates optimal responsive image srcsets based on actual usage patterns from analytics data
- Predicts which images are likely to be above the fold and prioritizes their delivery

The system learns continuously from real-world performance data, adjusting its optimization strategies based on measured LCP improvements across different device types and network conditions.

Results

Websites using Vercel's AI-powered image optimization saw:

- Average LCP improvements of 20%–35% compared to manually optimized images
- Bandwidth savings of up to 40% without perceptible quality degradation
- Automatic adaptation to new image formats as browser support expanded, with no developer intervention required

This case demonstrates how AI can handle repetitive optimization tasks more consistently than manual processes, while continuously improving based on real-world feedback.

Cloudflare: Machine Learning for Performance Prediction

Cloudflare has integrated machine learning into its CDN and edge computing platform to predict and preemptively optimize content delivery.

Problem

Traditional CDN caching relies on static rules and time-based expiration. This approach often results in cache misses for content that could have been precached, leading to slower TTFB for the first visitors to a page. Additionally, origin servers can become overwhelmed during traffic spikes if the CDN doesn't anticipate demand.

Optimizations

Cloudflare implemented ML-powered predictive caching and traffic management:

Predictive precaching
    Machine learning models analyze historical traffic patterns to predict which pages will be requested and prewarm edge caches before traffic arrives. This is particularly effective for news sites where breaking stories drive sudden traffic.

Intelligent bot detection
    AI distinguishes between legitimate users and bots, ensuring that performance optimizations prioritize real users while preventing bot traffic from degrading cache efficiency.

Automatic performance tuning
　The system learns optimal settings for each website, automatically adjusting compression levels, HTTP/2 priorities, and early hints based on measured performance improvements.

Results

Websites leveraging Cloudflare's AI-powered features reported:

- TTFB reductions of 15% to 25% due to improved cache hit rates
- More consistent performance during traffic spikes, with 99th percentile load times improving by up to 40%
- Reduced origin server load, enabling sites to handle three to five times more traffic without infrastructure upgrades

Google Chrome: AI-Assisted Speculation Rules

Building on the Speculation Rules API showcased in the Ray-Ban case study, Google has been developing AI-powered prediction systems to automatically determine which pages to prerender.

Problem

While the Speculation Rules API enables powerful prerendering capabilities, implementing effective speculation logic requires analyzing user behavior patterns, managing memory constraints on devices, and balancing the cost of wrong guesses against the benefit of correct ones. Most development teams lack the analytics infrastructure and expertise to implement optimal speculation strategies.

Optimizations

Google's approach uses machine learning to:

- Analyze click patterns across millions of websites to identify common navigation behaviors, such as when search result pages almost always lead to clicking a result.
- Build predictive models that estimate the probability of each possible next navigation based on current page context.
- Automatically manage resource usage by limiting speculation on memory-constrained devices.
- Learn from aggregated, anonymized user interaction data to improve predictions over time.

This AI-powered speculation is being integrated into Chrome and can work alongside custom site-specific rules defined by developers.

Results

Early implementations have shown:

- That as many as 30% to 50% of navigations are successfully prerendered when AI-powered speculation is enabled
- Near-instant page transitions for predicted navigations, with LCP effectively reduced to zero for those page loads
- Minimal wasted resources, as the ML models achieve over 80% accuracy in predicting the next navigation

AI Coding Assistants: A Performance Cautionary Tale

While AI presents opportunities for performance optimization, the rapid adoption of AI coding assistants has also created new performance challenges. Several organizations have shared their experiences optimizing AI-generated code.

Problem

A major ecommerce platform found that after widespread adoption of AI coding assistants by its development team, its CWV scores began to regress. Investigation revealed that AI-generated code, while functionally correct, often included:

- Unnecessary npm dependencies that bloated bundle sizes
- Unoptimized DOM manipulation patterns that increased INP
- Missing image optimization attributes (width, height, loading hints)
- Inefficient React component structures that caused excessive rerenders

The AI assistants were trained primarily on correctness and functionality, not performance best practices, leading to code that worked but wasn't optimized for production use.

Optimizations

The team implemented several strategies to address AI-generated code performance:

- Created custom prompts and context for AI assistants that emphasized performance requirements and included the team's coding standards
- Integrated automated performance testing into the team's CI/CD pipeline to catch regressions before deployment

- Developed AI-powered code review tools that specifically flagged common performance antipatterns in generated code
- Established a performance review checklist for AI-assisted code, including bundle size analysis and CWV impact assessment

Results

After implementing these guardrails:

- Bundle size increased from AI-generated code dropped by 60%.
- INP regressions were caught predeployment in 95% of cases.
- Developer productivity remained high while performance quality improved.
- The team created a feedback loop to improve its AI assistant prompts based on common issues found in reviews.

This case highlights that while AI can accelerate development, organizations need performance-aware processes to ensure AI-generated code meets production quality standards.

Shopify: AI for Merchant Store Optimization

Shopify has begun using AI to automatically identify and fix performance issues across its hosted merchant stores.

Problem

Shopify hosts millions of online stores, each with unique themes, apps, and content. Many merchants lack the technical expertise to optimize their stores, and Shopify's manual optimization services can only reach a fraction of stores. Poor-performing stores have lower conversion rates, which affect both merchants and Shopify's platform economics.

Optimizations

Shopify developed an AI-powered performance analysis and recommendation system with the following optimizations:

- ML models analyze store configurations, theme code, and installed apps to identify performance bottlenecks.
- AI ranks optimization opportunities by their predicted impact, helping merchants focus on the changes that will matter most.

- For common issues like missing image dimensions or unoptimized above-the-fold content, the system offers automated fixes that merchants can apply without coding.
- AI analyzes the performance impact of Shopify apps, helping merchants make informed decisions about which apps to install.

Results

Merchants who engaged with AI-powered recommendations saw:

- Average LCP improvements of 18% within the first month
- 12% higher conversion rates for stores that implemented recommended fixes
- 40% reduction in time spent diagnosing performance issues, compared to manual audits
- Improved app-ecosystem quality as developers responded to performance scores

These AI-focused case studies represent an emerging frontier in web performance optimization. As AI tools become more sophisticated, we can expect to see more organizations leveraging machine learning for everything from automated code optimization to predictive content delivery. The key insight from these early adopters is that AI works best when combined with clear performance goals, robust measurement, and human oversight to ensure that automation serves user experience rather than undermining it.

Key Takeaways

Across all these verticals and many more, real-world performance improvements lead to better user experience, which in turn drives business success. Crucially, these case studies were not about simple tweaks but about systematic, production-level changes: architectural shifts like SSR and static caching, combined with granular frontend tuning like optimizing images, managing script loading, and streamlining interactions.

A few common themes and lessons emerge from these case studies:

Measure and correlate
　For many teams, RUM data was key to finding correlations between performance metrics and business metrics. This was vital to justify working on performance and to prioritize what to fix first, depending on impact.

Optimize holistically
　Improvements often span multiple layers: server, network, and client. For instance, the *Economic Times* (ET) combined server caching, network hints, and client-side lazy loading for maximum effect. The best results came when sites attacked all major bottlenecks in the user journey.

Focus on the CWV
  LCP, CLS, and INP (or FID) were explicit targets in almost every case. This focus is well founded: as Google's research on user experience metrics (*https://oreil.ly/ 8BBxN*) shows, users are 24% less likely to abandon loads when a site meets the CWV thresholds. These case studies put that into practice, and many exceeded those threshold goals, achieving LCP below 2.0 s or even close to 0 CLS.

Expect a significant business impact
  The numbers speak loudly. Whether it's +53% revenue (Rakuten), +8% sales (Vodafone), −43% bounce (ET), or +110% revenue (Financer), there is a tangible return on performance investment. Even single-digit improvements (like +5% conversions at Carpe and +7% sales at redBus) are significant, since these optimizations are typically much cheaper than improving other features.

Focus on user experience
  Beyond raw conversions, metrics like longer session duration, more page views, and higher engagement were common. This often indicates improved customer satisfaction, which has long-term benefits in loyalty, word-of-mouth, and so on. For example, Yahoo! Japan News found that making pages stable led to users reading more, which likely reinforces the company's habit of using that site for news.

Leverage tools and processes
  Shopify's team used WebPageTest, while Yahoo! Japan News used Search Console and Lighthouse CI. Automated performance testing with Lighthouse CI and setting performance budgets are becoming standard in these organizations to prevent regressions. Pfizer's marketing team set a strict performance budget for new pages and saw a 20% drop in bounce rate when the budget was adhered to (as documented in Conductor's case study on enterprise performance optimization (*https://oreil.ly/VUcNn*)), highlighting the importance of process.

Conclusion

The case studies in this chapter demonstrate that web performance optimization delivers measurable, significant business impact across every industry. From ecommerce sites doubling conversion rates through prerendering to news publishers reducing bounce rates by over 40% through CWV improvements, the evidence is clear: faster, more stable websites directly translate to better user engagement and revenue.

These success stories also reveal common patterns: the importance of measuring real user metrics, the need for cross-functional collaboration, and the value of treating performance as an ongoing practice rather than a one-time fix. Organizations that embed performance into their culture and tooling see sustained improvements over time.

In Chapter 13, we'll look ahead to how artificial intelligence is transforming web performance—from AI-powered development tools that can inadvertently introduce performance problems to emerging AI-driven optimization techniques that promise to automate much of what these case study teams accomplished manually. The lessons from these real-world successes provide the foundation for understanding both the opportunities and challenges that AI brings to web performance.

CHAPTER 13
The Future of Web Performance with AI

The evidence is clear: performance is not merely a technical detail, it's a critical component of successful web products. Faster, smoother, and more stable experiences lead directly to happier users, increased engagement, and better business outcomes. While the web platform and optimization techniques continue to evolve, the core principle remains constant: start with the user experience and work backward to the technology.

Building high-performance websites requires a holistic approach: understanding user perception, mastering technical optimizations, managing dependencies responsibly, and fostering a culture of continuous measurement and improvement. It demands empathy for users facing diverse device and network constraints, and a commitment to delivering value efficiently.

The AI Revolution in Web Development

We stand at an inflection point in web development. AI-assisted coding tools have moved from novelty to necessity, fundamentally changing how we write code. Large language models can generate entire applications in minutes, offering unprecedented productivity gains. Yet as we've explored throughout this book, this revolution comes with a critical caveat: AI optimizes for correctness, not performance.

The paradox is stark. AI can generate code faster than ever before, but that code often embodies the "average" practices found in its training data—which includes countless examples of suboptimal performance patterns. An AI will happily produce a React component that works but will include unnecessary rerenders, heavy computations on the main thread, or layout instabilities that harm Core Web Vitals (CWV). The code passes basic tests but fails real users on real devices.

This reality demands a fundamental shift in how we think about our roles as developers. We're no longer just writing code—we're curating, verifying, and optimizing it. When you use AI assistance, you must become a performance advocate who explicitly guides the tool toward efficient solutions. The question isn't whether to use AI (that ship has sailed) but how to use it responsibly while maintaining the performance standards users deserve.

The good news is that the tooling ecosystem is evolving rapidly. AI assistants are beginning to understand performance context. DevTools integrations like the Chrome MCP server now allow AI agents to record traces, identify long tasks affecting interaction to next paint (INP), and propose targeted refactors. When you ask an AI to "improve performance," it can increasingly back that up with actual profiling data rather than generic suggestions.

However, as of today, these capabilities still require human oversight. An AI might correctly identify a performance bottleneck but propose a fix that works in isolation yet breaks existing functionality or creates new problems. The verification loop—profiling with Lighthouse, testing on real devices, measuring with RUM—remains firmly in human hands. Treat AI-generated optimizations like you would code from a junior teammate: valuable input that needs thorough validation.

We're also seeing AI become part of the performance problem itself. The ease of generating code means more code being produced overall, potentially making applications heavier if left unchecked. Industry surveys confirm that over half of development teams report increased performance problems after adopting AI-assisted development. The velocity is real but so are the risks.

Practical Strategies for the AI Era

To navigate this landscape successfully, integrate performance thinking into your AI workflows from day one:

Prompt with performance in mind
> Don't just ask for working code—ask for efficient code. Include phrases like "optimize for Core Web Vitals," "minimize JavaScript bundle size," or "ensure this doesn't block the main thread." Be specific about constraints: device types, network conditions, accessibility requirements. AI responds to explicit guidance.

Treat AI output as a starting point
> Run Lighthouse audits immediately. Profile with DevTools. Check bundle sizes. The faster you catch issues, the easier they are to fix. Build performance verification into your development workflow as a nonnegotiable step.

Leverage AI iteratively
> When the initial code has performance issues, engage in a dialogue: "This causes layout shift—how can we reserve space?" or "This computation blocks the main thread—can we use `requestIdleCallback`?" AI tools excel at iterative refinement when given clear feedback.

Maintain human judgment
> AI doesn't understand your users' context, your application's constraints, or your organization's performance budgets. It can't weigh trade-offs between feature completeness and load time. These decisions require human insight, empathy, and experience.

Share knowledge within your team
> As AI democratizes coding, performance expertise becomes even more valuable. Build a culture where performance reviews are standard, where CWV are discussed in sprint planning, and where everyone understands why performance matters. The teams that thrive will be those that combine AI's productivity with human performance discipline.

Streaming-First AI Interfaces and User Experience: A New Performance Paradigm

Beyond the challenges of AI-generated code quality, we're witnessing a more fundamental shift in how users interact with AI-powered applications. Traditional web performance optimization has long focused on the page load as the critical path: get users to interactive content as quickly as possible, then step back. But AI-driven interfaces are fundamentally different. They're long-lived sessions with multiple overlapping streams of data, where the experience extends far beyond the initial page load.

This shift demands a completely new approach to web performance. Instead of optimizing a single linear path from request to interactive, you're now juggling three concurrent loops:

The generation loop
> The AI model produces tokens, diffs, or chunks of content as it processes the user's request. This happens server side and can be unpredictable: sometimes fast, sometimes slow, depending on model complexity and prompt difficulty.

The transport loop
> Network streams carry data from server to client. Unlike traditional request-response patterns, these streams can continue for many seconds or even minutes, with data arriving in irregular bursts.

The render loop
> The UI must continuously commit updates as new data arrives, all while keeping the interface responsive to user input. A user might want to stop the generation, edit their prompt, or interact with partial results—all while tokens are still streaming in.

Success in this environment is less about "how fast can we finish loading?" and more about "how can we stay responsive while delivering useful partial results early and often?" The user's perception of speed shifts from time-to-completion to perceived responsiveness and incremental value.

Traditional performance treats the page-load lifecycle as having a clear beginning and end. You optimize for metrics like largest contentful paint (LCP) and time to interactive (TTI) because once the page is loaded and interactive, your job is largely done—at least from a performance perspective.

AI experiences are fundamentally different. They're ongoing conversations rather than discrete page loads. A user might spend several minutes in a single session, asking multiple questions, refining prompts, and working with the results. During this time, the interface needs to remain consistently responsive, even as it's actively receiving and rendering streaming data.

This changes what users care about:

- Time to first response becomes critical. Users need to know the system is working, ideally within 500 ms of submitting a prompt.
- Continuous responsiveness matters more than initial load time. The interface must remain snappy even when actively streaming.
- Progressive utility is key. Users should get value from partial results, not wait for complete answers before they can do anything.
- Graceful degradation is essential. When something is slow (model inference, network hiccup), the UI needs to communicate what's happening without freezing.

The core insight is this: in streaming AI interfaces, you're not optimizing for a moment in time—you're optimizing for a sustained experience that must feel fluid and responsive throughout its entire duration.

Streaming Text

When AI generates text responses by streaming tokens to the client, traditional performance metrics fall short.

Metrics

Time to first byte (TTFB) tells you when the stream starts but says nothing about the quality of the streaming experience itself. You need new metrics that capture the user's perception of an ongoing stream:

Time to first token
> This measures when the first nonwhitespace token arrives at the client after the user submits a prompt. It's analogous to first contentful paint for page loads: the moment when users see the system is actively responding. A fast time to first token (TTFT) is crucial for perceived responsiveness.

Time to useful token
> Not all first tokens are equally valuable. If the AI responds with "Let me think about that…" or starts with a preamble, users aren't really getting utility yet. This metric captures when the first semantically meaningful token appears: the first bullet point, the first code line, or the first sentence that addresses their query. This requires some judgment to define, but it's a better proxy for when users perceive value.

Tokens per second
> Tokens per second (TPS) is the average rate at which tokens arrive, and crucially, the 95th percentile. Users notice when token flow is consistently slow, and outliers (very slow bursts) can make the experience feel janky even if the average is good.

Stall rate
> This is the fraction of time during a stream when no tokens arrive for more than a threshold duration (typically 200 ms or more). Frequent stalls make an AI feel unreliable or struggling, even if total completion time is reasonable. A smooth, consistent flow feels more intelligent and confident.

Time to last token
> Time to last token (TTLT) is the total time from prompt submission to receiving the final token. While less critical than in traditional page loads (since users get progressive value), it still matters for completion and for planning follow-up interactions.

UI commit latency
> This is the time from when a token arrives from the network to when it appears rendered on screen. High UI commit latency means users see stuttering text or delays in updates, degrading the feel of real-time streaming.

Performance Budgets

Based on research into user perception and real-world deployments, here are starting budgets you can tune for your application:

First token under 500 ms (warm path)
On subsequent interactions in a session, when connections are already established and the model might have cached context, aim for the first token in under half a second. This maintains the conversational feel.

First token under 1 second (cold path)
On initial requests when everything is cold—no connection reuse, no cached context—one second is a reasonable target. Users are typically more forgiving on the first interaction.

Useful token under 1 second for simple prompts
If a user asks a straightforward question ("What's the capital of France?"), they should see a useful answer start to appear within a second.

UI commit latency under 50 ms (p95)
The gap between token arrival and screen update should be nearly imperceptible. Higher latencies create visible stuttering and feel laggy.

Stall gaps under 200 ms (p95)
Gaps in token flow should be rare and brief. Frequent or long stalls make the AI feel slow or stuck, even if the average TPS is acceptable.

These budgets will vary based on your model's complexity, your users' expectations, and your use case. A creative-writing assistant might tolerate slower generation if the quality is higher, while a code-completion tool needs to be snappy to maintain developer flow.

Rendering Tactics

The naive approach to rendering streaming text—that is, appending each token to the DOM as it arrives—creates serious performance problems. On fast models and good networks, tokens can arrive at 20 to 100 or more per second. Touching the DOM 100 times per second triggers layout and paint that many times, which can peg the main thread and make the entire interface sluggish:

Coalesce tokens into microbatches
Instead of rendering every single token, buffer them and commit in batches. A good rule of thumb is to update the display every 50 to 100 ms or after accumulating 5 to 10 tokens, whichever comes first. This dramatically reduces DOM thrash while maintaining the perception of smooth streaming. The difference between 50 individual DOM mutations per second and one mutation every 100 ms is the difference between a stuttering mess and silky-smooth text flow.

Keep the main thread free
> Text streaming often involves parsing markdown, applying syntax highlighting (for code responses), or formatting (for structured outputs). These operations are CPU-intensive and should never block the main thread. Move this work into a web worker. Use `postMessage` with transferable streams to send raw tokens to the worker, let it do the heavy processing, and send back ready-to-render HTML or virtual DOM diffs. The main thread can then apply these with minimal work, keeping the UI responsive.

Use fixed layouts to prevent shifts
> As text streams in and wraps to new lines, the content height changes, potentially causing a layout shift that harms cumulative layout shift (CLS) scores and is visually jarring. Reserve space for the streaming response using a fixed line-height and a reasonable estimate of maximum width. Consider using a container with `min-height` that accommodates typical responses. For really long responses, consider virtualization, as we will cover next.

Virtualize long transcripts
> In conversational interfaces where users might have dozens of exchanges, rendering every single message can bog down the page. Implement virtualization: only render messages currently visible in the viewport (plus a small buffer above and below). Collapse or completely remove offscreen content from the DOM. Libraries like `react-window` or `virtual-scroll` can help, but the principle is simple: if users can't see it, don't pay the rendering cost.

Support AbortController
> Users change their minds. They might realize halfway through a streaming response that they asked the wrong question or they want to refine their prompt. Implement cancellation via `AbortController` so streams can be terminated immediately and cleanly. This prevents wasted work and lets users quickly iterate. When they cancel, clean up state, stop rendering, and be ready for the next prompt with minimal delay.

Transport Layer Choices

How you stream data over the network matters for both performance and compatibility:

Server-sent events or fetch streaming
> These are typically the best choices for text streaming. They're simple to implement, they work over standard HTTP, they're cache-friendly, and they have broad browser support. Server-sent events (SSE) are particularly clean for server-to-client data flows. Fetch with `ReadableStream` gives you more control and works in more contexts (service workers, for example).

WebSockets
   WebSockets are overkill for simple text streaming, but they make sense if you need bidirectional communication (users can send input while the server is streaming or the server needs to push events independently) or multiplexing (multiple concurrent streams over one connection). WebSockets add complexity but can reduce latency when you need real-time back-and-forth.

Compress at the message layer
   HTTP compression (GZip or Brotli) typically works at the full response level, which isn't helpful for streaming. Instead, consider compressing chunks before sending them. Avoid tiny frames—they have overhead. Prefer line-delimited JSON (NDJSON) or a compact format like MessagePack for streaming structured data. Each chunk should be meaningfully sized (a sentence, a paragraph, a logical unit) rather than individual words or characters. This balances latency with efficiency.

Perceived Speed Patterns

Even with good technical performance, you can make streaming *feel* faster through smart UX patterns:

Emit a fast outline, then stream details
   If the AI can quickly determine the structure of its response (such as "I'll cover three main points"), send that outline immediately, then fill in each section progressively. Users see progress and structure right away, even if detailed content takes longer.

Stream metadata first
   In retrieval-augmented generation (RAG) systems, show the sources or citations as they're retrieved, before the prose starts streaming. Users see that relevant information was found and the system is working, even if synthesis takes a moment.

Optimistic UI for tool calls
   When the AI decides to call a tool or function (search a database, fetch data), immediately show a placeholder ("Searching documents…" or a skeleton UI). Replace it with actual results when they arrive. This prevents blank periods and maintains perceived momentum.

Streaming UI Components

Text streaming is just one pattern. Modern AI applications increasingly generate rich, interactive UI components on the fly: think charts, interactive tables, forms, and embedded widgets. These aren't just text; they're partial component trees and data islands that need to be progressively rendered and made interactive.

With streaming UI, you're not just appending strings to the DOM. You're receiving fragments of a component tree: "Here's a search results component with the first three items, here's a chart component with initial data, and here's a form component for the next step." Some frameworks (like React Server Components) and libraries are emerging to support this pattern natively, but the core challenge remains the same: you need to render partially, evolving UI while keeping interactivity stable.

Users expect parts of the interface that look ready to actually be ready. If a button appears on screen, they'll click it. If it's not yet interactive because you're still hydrating or waiting for more data, frustration ensues. The key is progressive enhancement: make sure each island of interactivity becomes functional as soon as possible, even if other parts of the UI are still loading.

Streaming UI Metrics

Key metrics for streaming UI include:

Time to first interactive island
When does the first component that can accept user input become actually interactive? This is analogous to TTI for pages but is scoped to streaming components. If you're streaming a search results page, when can the user click the first result link or type in a filter box?

Time to first meaningful component
This is the first component that meaningfully helps the user take action. Not just a loading skeleton or status message, but an actual useful element—the first search result, the first chart with data, the first step of a wizard interface. This is your streaming equivalent of LCP: the moment users perceive value.

Island hydration time (p95 and p99 by component class)
In a streaming component world, different types of components might arrive at different times and have different hydration costs. Track how long it takes each class of component (DataTable, Chart, FormInput) to become interactive after it arrives. High percentiles tell you about worst-case user experiences.

Suspense reveal latency
    In frameworks that use suspense boundaries, this measures the time from when data for a component arrives to when the component becomes visible (replacing its fallback). Long latencies here mean users stare at loading spinners even though the data is already on the client, which feels wasteful.

Rendering Tactics for Streaming Components

Some rendering strategies you can use include:

Stream shells first, then fill in islands
    Send a minimal HTML shell that includes layout, navigation, and placeholders for the main content areas. This gets something on screen quickly (improving perceived performance) and allows the user to start interacting with static elements (scroll, read headings, etc.). Then stream in the data-heavy or interactive islands as they become ready. Critically, ensure that users can interact with the shell (like clicking a "Cancel" button or adjusting filters) even while other components are still loading.

Hydrate in priority order
    Not all components are equally important. Input fields, primary action buttons, and navigation should hydrate first. Rich visualizations, analytics widgets, or decorative elements can wait. Tag your components with priority levels and hydrate them in that order. The user should be able to start interacting with the most critical parts of your interface immediately, even if ancillary parts take longer to become fully interactive.

Use CSS containment and content visibility properties
    Modern CSS properties like `content-visibility: auto` and `contain: layout size` can drastically reduce the rendering cost of off-screen or below-the-fold components. They tell the browser it can skip rendering work for elements that aren't currently visible. This is particularly valuable in streaming scenarios where lots of content might be arriving and being inserted into the DOM, but the user is only viewing a small portion of it.

Reserve space with intrinsic sizing
    As components stream in, you don't want layout shifts (which harm CLS). Use CSS properties like `aspect-ratio` or `min-height` to reserve space for components before they fully render. For images or charts, if you know the approximate size, set it up front. This keeps the layout stable even as content loads progressively.

Keep interactive handlers tiny
> When a component first becomes interactive, its event handlers should execute almost instantly. Offload any heavy work (data processing, API calls, complex calculations) to web workers or defer it using `requestIdleCallback`. The user's click should trigger an immediate response (visual feedback, state update), not a multi-hundred-millisecond computation that freezes the UI.

Failure Modes to Watch

Keep an eye out for:

Rapid rereconciliation causing INP spikes
> If your framework rerenders frequently as streaming data arrives—especially if you're updating multiple components simultaneously—you can trigger main-thread congestion and high INP. Batch state transitions where possible. Debounce or throttle updates if they're coming very rapidly. Measure INP during active streaming sessions, not just on initial page load.

Hidden streams still doing work
> If you're streaming components that are off-screen or in a collapsed section, but your rendering logic is still parsing and processing them, you're wasting CPU cycles and risking jank. Pause or throttle streams that aren't currently visible. When the user scrolls to that section or expands it, you can resume full-speed rendering.

Flicker from reparented nodes
> If your reconciliation logic moves DOM nodes around (changing their parent or sibling order), it can cause visible flicker, especially if those nodes contain images or iframes. Minimize DOM restructuring during streaming. Keep stable keys on list items, and avoid unnecessary reordering. If you must move nodes, do it in a batched, synchronous commit to reduce perceptible flashing.

Streaming Content and Media

Text and UI components aren't the only things that stream. AI applications might generate or fetch images, audio, video, or large data feeds on the fly. Each media type has its own performance considerations.

Lists and Feeds That Grow in Place

Think infinite scrolls or feeds where more content loads as the user reaches the bottom. In AI contexts, this might be search results that progressively improve, or a feed of generated items. Important metrics here include time to first visible item (the user shouldn't stare at a blank page), time between batches (consistent pacing feels better than sporadic bursts), and scroll hitch rate (does scrolling feel smooth even as new content is being inserted?).

To address these issues, you can server-paginate and prefetch the next batch before the user reaches the current end. Recycle DOM nodes for list items rather than continuously appending new ones (virtualization again). Crucially, avoid measuring layout during scroll events: use `IntersectionObserver` for infinite scroll triggers instead of scroll event handlers, which can block the main thread and cause jank.

Audio and Video Generation or Text to Speech (TTS)

AI-generated media like TTS audio or video synthesis can stream progressively, much like adaptive streaming for traditional video content. Key metrics are time to first playable frame or audio chunk (how quickly does playback start), stall frequency (does playback pause while waiting for more data), and buffer underrun count (how often does the client run out of data).

Techniques to try include choosing a segment size that matches the network's variability. Too large, and the user waits a long time before anything plays; too small, and you waste overhead on frequent network round trips. Keep a small client-side buffer (a second or two of media) to smooth over network hiccups, but prefer low-latency codecs to minimize the time between generation and playback. For truly real-time applications (like voice assistants), prioritize low latency over high quality. Users prefer an immediate, slightly lower-quality response over a high-quality one that takes noticeably longer.

Images That Arrive Progressively

AI image generation services often produce images over several seconds. You can stream these progressively (like progressive JPEGs) or in tiles. Reserve space for these up front. Use `width` and `height` attributes or CSS to reserve the image's space before it arrives, preventing layout shift. Use `loading="lazy"` and `fetchpriority="high"` on hero images to prioritize what matters.

Progressive or tiled delivery is also an option. If your image generator supports it, stream a low-resolution preview first, then progressively refine it. Or deliver the image in tiles (like map tiles) if it's very large. This gives users something to look at immediately, even if the final high-res version takes time. Use `opacity` or `filter` transitions to fade in refined images smoothly, avoiding jarring snaps from blurry to sharp.

Scheduling and Responsiveness Under Load

The biggest challenge in streaming AI interfaces is maintaining responsiveness while continuously processing and rendering incoming data. The main thread is your most constrained resource. It's responsible for handling user input, running JavaScript, computing layout, and painting. If you tie it up with streaming work, the entire interface becomes sluggish. Recommended strategies include:

Treat user input as the highest priority
    User input such as clicks, taps, keyboard input, and scrolling must be handled with minimal latency. In a streaming scenario, where you're constantly updating the UI, it's easy to let rendering work dominate the main thread, causing input delays.

    Always check for pending input between microbatches. Before you commit another batch of tokens or components to the DOM, yield and check if there's an input event waiting. If there is, process it first. This ensures that users' interactions are never blocked by rendering work.

Yield frequently
    If any rendering or processing task takes longer than 16 ms (one frame at 60 fps), split it up. Use `requestAnimationFrame` or `scheduler.postTask` (where available) to break work into smaller chunks and yield between them. This gives the browser a chance to process input, run animations, and keep things smooth.

    A simple pattern: if you're processing a large batch of tokens or components, split them into groups of, say, 50 items. Process one group, yield, process the next group, yield, and so on. This keeps the main thread responsive even when there's a lot of work to do.

Use a cooperative scheduler
    Implement a priority queue for work. High-priority tasks should include handling user input and rendering visible streams. Medium-priority tasks might be rendering background or less critical streams. Low-priority tasks are things like background analytics, logging, and cleanup tasks. You don't need a complex scheduler—even a simple task queue with three priority levels can make a huge difference. Run high-priority tasks first, and only proceed to medium or low-priority tasks if there's spare time and no input events pending.

Keep the main-thread budget small
    Aim for individual tasks on the main thread to take no more than 50 ms, and ideally much less. Animations, typing, and pointer interactions should all remain buttery smooth (under 16 ms frame times) even while streams are flowing. If profiling shows long tasks during streaming, that's your signal to break up work, move processing off-thread, or batch less aggressively.

Network and Server Pipeline Considerations

Performance isn't just about the client. Server-side architecture and network configuration play huge roles in streaming performance.

Remove Cold-Start Penalties

In serverless or edge compute environments, cold starts can add hundreds of milliseconds (or more) to your first token time. Users feel this as lag. To address this, keep the connections warm. Use HTTP/2 or HTTP/3 to enable connection reuse. Implement `<link rel="preconnect">` or early hints to establish connections before the user even submits a prompt.

Additionally, reuse model sessions when it's safe to do so. If your architecture loads models on demand, keep frequently used models warm in memory. For repeat users or active sessions, maintain cached model state (like context and embeddings) so subsequent requests can skip expensive initialization steps.

Implement Backpressure

If the server generates tokens faster than the client can render them, you can overwhelm the client's rendering pipeline. Monitor the size of the client's rendering queue (how many tokens or components are waiting to be processed). If it grows beyond a threshold (say, 100 pending items), signal the server to slow down generation. This is called *backpressure*. The server can pause generation, introduce small delays between chunks, or batch more tokens into fewer messages. This prevents the client from drowning in data it can't keep up with, which would lead to UI stuttering or hangs.

Cache Smartly

AI responses are often unique, but there are caching opportunities:

Semantic cache
 If two users ask essentially the same question (even if it's phrased differently), return the cached response. This is tricky, because it requires understanding semantic similarity but can massively speed up common queries.

Retrieval cache
 In RAG systems, cache the retrieved documents or embeddings for common topics. When a user asks about a popular topic, the retrieval step can be instant instead of searching a large corpus.

Response cache for nonpersonalized components
> If you're streaming UI components that are generic (like a standard chart or table format), cache the component template. Only the data needs to be streamed; the structure can be reused.

Chunk Thoughtfully

Prefer semantic boundaries. Instead of sending a fixed number of tokens or bytes, chunk by logical units—sentences for text, rows for data, paragraphs for prose. This reduces the work the client has to do to parse and display coherent content. If tokens arrive midsentence, the client might need to buffer and wait for the end of the sentence to render sensibly. Sending complete sentences or code lines simplifies client logic and improves the user experience.

Set a hard ceiling on the chunk rate too. On very fast networks with powerful servers, you might generate and send tokens so fast that the client can't keep up. Cap the rate at which you send chunks (for example, no more than one chunk every 10 ms) to ensure the client has time to process each batch without getting overwhelmed.

CWV in a Streaming World

The CWV (LCP, INP, and CLS) were designed for traditional page loads. They still matter in streaming AI interfaces, but they're interpreted somewhat differently:

LCP
> This measures when the largest piece of initial content appears, which still matters in a streaming interface. This might be the chat input area, the first message in the conversation, or a skeleton UI for the streaming response area.
>
> Optimize your shell: the initial page load (before any streaming starts) should be fast. Get the chat interface, input box, and any static UI on screen quickly. This establishes trust and readiness. Once the user submits a prompt, streaming performance takes over, but that first paint of the shell sets the tone.

INP
> INP becomes the primary guardrail. It measures the latency of user interactions throughout the page's lifetime. This is critical in streaming interfaces where users interact continuously: typing follow-up prompts, clicking buttons, scrolling, highlighting text.
>
> Measure INP during active streaming, not just at page start. Your goal is to ensure that INP remains low even when the interface is actively receiving and rendering streaming data. If INP spikes during streaming sessions, that's a sign you're blocking the main thread with rendering work. Profile these scenarios specifically and optimize the rendering pipeline (batching, web workers, yielding) to keep INP down.

CLS

CLS is easy to regress. This Core Web Vital measures unexpected layout movements. In streaming interfaces, content is constantly being added, which can easily cause shifts if not handled carefully.

To avoid this, reserve space for streaming content. If you know a response is coming, allocate space for it before it arrives. Use `min-height` or fixed-height containers. Avoid appending content above the user's current scroll position without careful handling, or it will shift everything down, hurting CLS.

Also, avoid appending above the fold without accounting for height. If you're inserting content above the viewport or above where the user is looking, you risk shifting their view. Use scroll anchoring (which is supported in modern browsers) or manually adjust the scroll position to keep the user's view stable.

In addition to the CWV, define SLOs for your streaming metrics, especially first token time, tokens per second, stall rate, and UI commit latency. Track these in production and set thresholds. Gate releases on both CWV and your streaming SLOs too. A change that improves initial load speed but degrades streaming performance is not a net win.

Observability and Debugging Streaming Systems

Streaming AI interfaces are complex and dynamic, making observability critical. You need to see what's happening across the generation, transport, and render loops in order to diagnose problems.

Instrument the Streaming Path with Performance Marks

Use the performance API to add marks at key points in the streaming lifecycle:

- `mark("prompt-sent")` when the user submits a request
- `mark("first-token")` when the first token arrives
- `mark("useful-token")` when the first meaningful token appears
- `mark("batch-commit")` each time you commit a batch of updates to the DOM
- `mark("last-token")` when the stream completes

Measure the intervals between these marks to calculate your streaming metrics. Log them to your analytics or RUM system. Aggregate across users to understand p50, p95, and p99 performance.

Track queue depth: monitor how many items are pending in your rendering pipeline at any given moment. If the queue grows large, it indicates the client is falling behind. Alert on this condition and investigate whether you need to throttle generation, optimize rendering, or both.

Be sure to capture input latency during streams as well. Instrument any user interactions (such as clicks and key presses) that occur while a stream is active. Measure the time from event to visual feedback. High latencies here indicate main-thread contention and warrant optimization.

Build a Stream Trace View

In your development and staging environments, build a tool that visualizes the streaming process end to end. Link network chunks to UI commits to long tasks on the main thread. This trace should show:

- When each chunk was sent from the server
- When it arrived at the client
- How long it sat in the rendering queue
- When it was committed to the DOM
- Any long tasks that occurred around that time

This visualization helps you identify bottlenecks: Is the server slow to generate? Is the network adding latency? Is the client's rendering pipeline backed up?

Alert on Stall Patterns

Set up monitoring for stall rates (fraction of streams with gaps longer than your threshold—say 200 ms). Rising stall rates indicate deteriorating model performance, network issues, or server overload. Repeated long gaps frustrate users and should trigger alerts so you can investigate and remediate. Similarly, alert if UI commit latency rises above your budget. This suggests client-side rendering problems.

Accessibility

Streaming interfaces present unique challenges beyond raw performance, including around accessibility. Some useful tips here are:

Use ARIA live regions for streamed text
    Use `aria-live="polite"` for long-form AI responses. This allows screen readers to announce updates as they arrive, without interrupting the user constantly. Reserve `aria-live="assertive"` for short, critical updates (like error messages or very brief confirmations). Test with actual screen readers to ensure the experience is coherent and not overwhelming.

Provide stop and pause controls
    Users—especially those using assistive technology—need the ability to halt a stream if it's moving too fast or they need a moment to process. Offer a clear, keyboard-accessible "Stop" button. Once the response stabilizes, provide a "Copy as rendered" option so users can extract the text without fighting with live-updating content.

Internationalization

For languages that read right to left (Arabic, Hebrew), ensure your streaming logic respects text direction. Use bidirectional text and line wrapping, and test with actual right-to-left content. Combine this with the proper `unicode-bidi` CSS properties and `dir` attributes. Chinese, Japanese, and Korean text, as well as some other languages with complex scripts, will require proper line breaking and font rendering. Make sure your tokenization and batching logic doesn't split words or phrases awkwardly. This might mean adjusting your microbatch sizes based on detected language.

Handle complex scripts early. Tokens might split grapheme clusters in languages like Arabic and Hindi, or even emoji. Don't render partial characters. Buffer incoming tokens until you have complete grapheme clusters, then render them. This prevents visual glitches and ensures text is readable in all writing systems.

Privacy

Avoid streaming sensitive input character by character. Some applications send user input to the server as they type (for autocomplete or real-time suggestions). Be mindful of privacy: don't stream sensitive information (passwords, credit-card numbers, personal identifiers) until the user explicitly submits it. Batch such information locally and only send it on intentional submit actions. If you use client-side preprocessing, such as using a local model to prerank, classify, or filter information before sending it to a server, it's important to disclose that. Be transparent and provide users the ability to opt out if they're uncomfortable with local processing.

Safety

Redact or drop tokens midstream. If your system has guardrails that detect unsafe content (hate speech, violence, etc.), you might detect a policy violation midstream. In such cases, gracefully end the stream, redact the problematic tokens, and show the user a message explaining that the response was filtered. Don't leave partial harmful content on screen.

End streams gracefully on errors when network failures, server errors, and timeouts happen. Handle them gracefully: show a clear error message, preserve what was streamed so far (if appropriate), and offer a retry or refinement option. Don't leave the interface in a broken or frozen state.

Energy and Cost Awareness

Streaming AI interfaces can be resource-intensive, both on the server (model inference) and the client (continuous rendering). This has real costs, both financial and environmental. While you can't directly measure device battery drain from JavaScript, you can track proxies that correlate with energy usage, such as:

Bytes sent
    More data transferred means more radio activity, which drains battery on mobile devices.

CPU time on the main thread
    More computation means more power draw. Long tasks and heavy rendering hurt battery life.

GPU time (if doing on-device inference)
    Some applications use WebGPU or WebAssembly to run models locally. This can be very power-intensive.

Instrument these and log them. Correlate them with user feedback or battery-usage reports, if it's available from your app analytics.

Cost is a factor as well. Model inference isn't free. Each token generated costs money for compute and API fees. In high-volume applications, costs can spiral quickly, so budget those per-token costs. Making the model's rate and precision configurable can help. Offer users a "fast" mode with a smaller, cheaper model for quick queries, and a "high-quality" mode with a larger model for complex tasks. Let them choose based on their needs and your cost constraints.

For users on mobile or using low-power modes, consider reducing streaming rates, using lower-quality models, or providing summaries instead of full verbose responses. This respects the user's device constraints and your infrastructure budget.

Design Patterns to Prefer

Certain UX and architectural patterns work particularly well for streaming AI interfaces:

Outline, then enrich
    Generate a fast, high-level outline or summary of the response first (within the first 500 ms to 1 s), then stream in the detailed content beneath each section. Users see structure immediately, understand what's coming, and can navigate to the parts they care about while details are still filling in. For example, for a multi-part answer, first stream "I'll cover: 1) X, 2) Y, 3) Z," and then fill in each section progressively. This provides orientation and context.

Guarded tool use
    When the AI needs to call a tool or query a database (which are common in agentic workflows), run the tool call asynchronously but reveal its status quickly. Show a placeholder: "Fetching data from database…" or "Running calculation…" If the tool is slow, give the user a retry or cancel option. When the results arrive, replace the placeholder smoothly. This keeps the user informed and in control, even when backend operations take time.

Pipelined RAG
    In RAG systems, you first retrieve relevant documents or data then generate a response based on them. Instead of waiting for retrieval to complete before showing anything, stream the retrieved sources first as they arrive ("Found 3 relevant documents: A, B, C…"), then stream the synthesized answer below. Finally, highlight or link to specific parts of the sources as the answer references them. This gives users confidence in the data and lets them explore sources while the answer is still being generated.

Streaming diffs for code or docs
    When the AI is generating or modifying code or documents, render a stable base version, then apply diffs in place. For example, show the original code with a subtle highlight around the area being changed, then animate the change smoothly. This avoids the entire code block rerendering and jumping around, which would cause scroll jumps and CLS. Users can follow along with the changes without losing their place.

Antipatterns to Avoid

Just as there are good patterns, there are common pitfalls that degrade performance and UX:

Rendering every token individually to the DOM
> This is the most common mistake. It causes excessive DOM mutations, layout thrashing, and main-thread congestion. Always batch tokens into microbatches (at 50 to 100 ms intervals) before committing to the DOM.

Blocking the main thread with parsing or highlighting
> Markdown parsing, syntax highlighting for code, and other text transformations are CPU-heavy. Doing them synchronously on the main thread as tokens arrive will freeze the UI. Move this work into a web worker. Send raw tokens to the worker, process them there, and send back formatted output.

Recomputing layout for every chunk
> If your rendering logic triggers layout recalculations on every token batch (for example, by reading `offsetHeight` or `scrollTop` frequently), it'll cause layout thrashing. Batch layout reads and writes. Use techniques like `requestAnimationFrame` to schedule layout reads once per frame, not per chunk.

Hiding slow streams behind spinners
> If something is taking a while, don't just show a spinner and wait. Show partial results. Users prefer to see incremental progress over a blank screen or indeterminate spinner. Even incomplete information is better than nothing, as long as it's clearly marked as in progress.

Ignoring network variability
> Assuming tokens will arrive at a consistent rate is naive. Network conditions fluctuate. Build your client to handle bursty, irregular data arrival gracefully. Use buffering, adaptive batching, and backpressure signals to smooth out the variability.

A Practical Checklist for Production

Before launching a streaming AI interface, ensure you've addressed these key areas.

Before launch:

- ☐ Preconnect to model and data endpoints. Use `<link rel="preconnect">` or early hints to establish connections before the user submits their first prompt.
- ☐ Ship a minimal, stable shell. The initial page load should be fast (good LCP) and provide a clear, interactive input area. Reserve space for where streaming responses will appear.
- ☐ Add streaming performance marks. Instrument your code with marks for prompt-sent, first-token, useful-token, batch-commits, and last-token.
- ☐ Set up dashboards for token timing and UI commit latency. Have visibility into p50, p95, and p99 for your streaming metrics before you launch.
- ☐ Test on low-end devices and slow networks. Don't just test on your dev machine. Throttle your network, use an old phone, and ensure the experience is acceptable.

During implementation:

- ☐ Use web workers for parsing and formatting. Keep markdown parsing, syntax highlighting, and other heavy text processing off the main thread.
- ☐ Microbatch token updates. Commit to the DOM every 50 to 100 ms, not on every single token.
- ☐ Throttle the repaint frequency. Use `requestAnimationFrame` to limit how often you trigger layout and paint.
- ☐ Prioritize input handling. Check for pending input events between rendering batches. Always let user interactions jump the queue.
- ☐ Hydrate interactive islands first. Make buttons, inputs, and navigation interactive before less critical components.
- ☐ Reserve space for streaming content. Use `min-height`, `aspect-ratio`, or fixed dimensions to prevent layout shifts.

In production:

- ☐ Monitor INP during active streams. Ensure interactivity remains low even when the interface is busiest.
- ☐ Set up stall-rate alerts. If the fraction of streams with long gaps exceeds your threshold, investigate server or network issues.

- ☐ Record stream traces for slow sessions. Sample a percentage of sessions and capture detailed timing data for analysis. Use this to identify bottlenecks.
- ☐ Tune chunk sizes and backpressure thresholds. As traffic patterns evolve, adjust how you batch tokens and when you signal the server to slow down.
- ☐ Track your streaming metrics alongside the CWV. Make sure both sets of metrics are meeting their targets. Regressions in either should block releases.

Conclusion

The future of web performance in an AI-driven world is not predetermined. We're writing that future now, with every architectural decision, every prompt to an AI assistant, every performance budget we enforce. The technology will continue to improve: AI models will get better at understanding performance implications, tools will become more sophisticated at catching issues automatically, and best practices will evolve.

But the fundamental responsibility remains unchanged: to advocate for users. Every millisecond matters to someone on a slow device or constrained network. Every layout shift frustrates a user trying to click a button. Every long task creates the perception that the web is broken.

AI is a powerful amplifier. It amplifies productivity, yes, but it also amplifies our decisions, both good and bad. Use it to amplify your commitment to performance. Make it part of your toolkit for delivering faster, more efficient experiences. But never let it replace your judgment, your empathy for users, or your standards for quality.

As you apply the knowledge gained from this book, remember that performance is an ongoing journey, now intertwined with AI assistance. Use the tools at your disposal (both traditional and AI-powered), implement the strategies, measure the impact relentlessly, and never stop advocating for the users' time and attention.

The web's future will be shaped by how we handle this transition. Will AI lead to bloated, slow applications because we prioritized velocity over quality? Or will it enable us to build faster, more accessible experiences because we learned to guide it effectively? The choice is ours.

By combining AI's capabilities with rigorous performance engineering, by treating the CWV as nonnegotiable requirements rather than nice-to-haves, and by building cultures that value speed and efficiency alongside features, we can deliver on the promises of both AI-assisted development and user-centered design.

The stakes are high, but so is the opportunity. Build fast. Test thoroughly. Optimize relentlessly. And remember: in the end, performance is still about people. By prioritizing performance in this AI-driven era, you contribute not only to the success of your own projects but also to a faster, more accessible, and more delightful web for everyone.

Index

A

accessibility
    AI limitations, 39
    AI-generated React components and, 55
    streaming AI interfaces, 222
adaptive loading, 86
AI (artificial intelligence)
    in DevTools Performance panel, 21-22, 61-64
    performance culture and, 177-178
    streaming AI interfaces (see streaming AI interfaces)
    third-party script optimization, 168-170
AI-aided optimization, 43, 61-64
AI-generated code
    case studies, 196-201
    correctness versus performance, 37-38
    CWVs (Core Web Vitals) and, 49-50
    developer responsibility for, 41-43, 44, 205-207
    hidden costs, 39-41
    optimizing, 42
        challenges in, 199-200
        React components, 56-61
    performance impact, 44
    for React components, 50-55
AI-powered chatbots, 142-144
alerts
    setup, 33
    on stall rates, 221
Angular, 161
animation (in RAIL model), 10
antipatterns and streaming AI interfaces, 225
APM (Application Performance Monitoring), 113
async keyword, 133-134
audio generation, 216
auditing AI-generated code, 42

B

backend JavaScript performance, 110-113
    monitoring, 113
    Node.js event loop, 110
    optimizing, 111-113
background compilation, 108
backpressure, 218
bandwidth, 103-104
blocking page loading, 71
Bookaway case study, 193-194
breaking up tasks, 153-154
browser-native lazy loading, 137-138
browsers
    event loop, 75
    hydration, 80-83
    JavaScript constraints, 104-105
    JavaScript engine
        JIT (just in time) compilation, 106-107
        limitations of, 109
        moving off main thread, 108
    main-thread task scheduler, 78-80
    microtasks versus macrotasks, 75-76
    multiprocess architecture, 68
    network stack and resource loading, 83-86
    page load optimization timeline, 86-90
    preload scanner, 74
    prioritizing resources, 74
    RAIL model, 76-77

rendering
  incremental, 68
  performance issues, 77-78
  pipeline for, 69-74
server-side rendering, 80-83
threads, types of, 68
bytecode caching, 109

C

caching
  resources, 85
  service workers for, 158
  in streaming AI interfaces, 218
Calibre, 26
Carpe case study, 184-185
case studies
  AI coding assistants, 199-200
  Bookaway, 193-194
  Cloudflare, 197-198
  Economic Times, 187-189
  Financer.com, 195-196
  Google Chrome, 198-199
  lessons from, 201-202
  list of, 179-181
  Rakuten 24, 182-183
  Ray-Ban, 185-186
  redBus, 192-193
  Shopify, 200-201
  Shopify Carpe, 184-185
  Shopify Sunday Citizen, 184
  Telegraph Media Group, 186-187
  Vercel, 196-197
  Vodafone, 183
  Yahoo! Japan News, 189-191
CDP (Chrome DevTools Protocol), 27
champions of performance culture, 175-176
chatbots, 142-144
Chrome (see browsers)
Chrome DevTools Protocol (CDP), 27
Chrome User Experience Report (CrUX), 14, 31
CI/CD pipeline integration, performance in, 176-177
click-to-load patterns, 141-145
client hints, 86
Cloudflare case study, 197-198
CLS (cumulative layout shift)
  AI-generated code and, 49-50
  AI-generated React components, 50-52

defined, 17
React component optimization, 61
streaming AI interfaces, 220
CMS (content management system) platforms, 164-166
code bloat, 40
code reviews for AI-generated code, 42
code splitting, 53, 92-93
cold starts, 112, 218
compositing, 70
compositor thread, 68, 74
compression, 212
conditional loading, 145-148
conformance patterns, 161
connection setup, 84
constraints in JavaScript
  browser architecture, 104-105
  devices, 101-102
  network, 103-104
content management system (CMS) platforms, 164-166
continuous monitoring (see field monitoring)
Core Web Vitals (see CWVs)
CPU constraints, 101-102
critical third-party scripts, 132, 134
CrUX (Chrome User Experience Report), 14, 31
culture (of organization)
  AI and performance, 177-178
  performance as feature, 173-174
  performance budget in, 96
  performance champions, 175-176
  performance workflow integration, 176-177
  team education, 174-175
  third-party script optimization, 129
cumulative layout shift (see CLS)
CWVs (Core Web Vitals), 13
  (see also metrics)
  AI-generated code and, 49-50
  AI-generated React components and, 50-55
  capturing with web-vitals.js, 28-31
  React component optimization, 61
  streaming AI interfaces, 219-220
  types of, 14-17

D

DebugBear, 26
debugging streaming AI interfaces, 220-221
defer keyword, 133-134

deoptimization, 107
dependencies, 135
design patterns for streaming AI interfaces, 224
device constraints in JavaScript, 101-102
device detection, 146-147
DevTools
  AI-assisted performance profiling, 21-24, 61-64
  runtime profiling with, 14
  third-party script metrics, 124-125

E

ecommerce platforms
  case studies, 182-186
  third-party script optimization, 166-168
Economic Times case study, 187-189
education in performance culture, 174-175
energy usage by streaming AI interfaces, 223
error messages in streaming AI interfaces, 223
event loop, 75
event loop ticks, 75

F

facades, 141-145
FCP (first contentful paint), 15
feedback loops, 55
feeds, infinite, 215
fetch streaming, 211
FID (first input delay), 16
field monitoring
  case study, 34
  CrUX (Chrome UX Report), 31
  defined, 13-14
  importance of, 64
  other uses, 31
  web-vitals.js library, 28-31
Financer.com case study, 195-196
financial site case studies, 194-196
first contentful paint (FCP), 15
first impressions, 5-8
first input delay (FID), 16
first interaction, loading third-party scripts after, 152-153
flow, 6
framework usage trade-offs, 94-95
framework-specific third-party script optimization, 158-162

G

garbage collection in JavaScript, 108
Gatsby, 162
Google Chrome case study, 198-199
graceful degradation, 11

H

hints, 84, 86, 135
hot functions, 106
HTTP/2, 84
HTTP/3, 84
hydration, 80-83

I

idle (in RAIL model), 10
idle until urgent (IUU) pattern, 153
iframes, 137-138, 156-157
image generation, 216
importing libraries, 52-54
incremental rendering, 68
infinite scrolls/feeds, 215
INP (interaction to next paint)
  AI-generated code and, 49-50
  AI-generated React components, 54-55
  defined, 16
  React component optimization, 61
  streaming AI interfaces, 219
interaction to next paint (see INP)
internationalization, 222
interpreting metrics reports, 18
IntersectionObserver API, 138-140
inventory of third-party scripts, 123
island hydration time, 213
IUU (idle until urgent) pattern, 153

J

JavaScript
  backend performance, 110-113
    monitoring, 113
    Node.js event loop, 110
    optimizing, 111-113
  constraints
    browser architecture, 104-105
    devices, 101-102
    network, 103-104
JavaScript engines
  JIT (just in time) compilation, 106-107
  limitations of, 109

moving off main thread, 108
JavaScript Profiler, 24
JIT (just in time) compilation, 106-107

L

lab testing
    Calibre, 26
    DebugBear, 26
    defined, 13-14
    DevTools Performance panel, 21-24
    JavaScript Profiler, 24
    Lighthouse, 19-20
    Puppeteer, 27
    SpeedCurve, 26
    third-party tools, 26-27
    WebPageTest, 24-26
    YellowLabTools, 26
largest contentful paint (see LCP)
latency, 103-104
layout instability (see CLS)
layout tree, 70
LayoutNG, 73-74
lazy loading third-party scripts, 137-141
lazy parsing, 108
LCP (largest contentful paint)
    AI-generated code and, 49-50
    AI-generated React components, 52-54
    defined, 15
    React component optimization, 61
    streaming AI interfaces, 219
libraries, importing, 52-54
Lighthouse
    performance auditing with, 13, 19-20
    third-party script metrics, 124-125
    WebPageTest comparison, 25-26
load (in RAIL model), 11
loading
    resources, 83-86
    third-party scripts
        conditional loading, 145-148
        facades, 141-145
        lazy loading, 137-141
        sequencing and prioritizing, 131-136

M

macrotasks, 75-76
main thread, 68
    JavaScript constraints, 104-105
    moving parsing and compiling off, 108
    network stack interaction, 85
    task scheduler, 78-80
main-thread bottlenecks, 54-55
maintainability versus micro-optimizations, 95
MCP (Model Context Protocol) server, 63-64
media content, streaming via AI, 215-216
memory usage, 32
metrics
    alerting, 33
    balancing, 91-92
    CLS (cumulative layout shift), 17
    CWVs (Core Web Vitals), 13
        capturing with web-vitals.js, 28-31
        types of, 14-17
    FID (first input delay), 16
    field monitoring
        case study, 34
        CrUX (Chrome UX Report), 31
        defined, 13-14
        other uses, 31
        web-vitals.js library, 28-31
    INP (interaction to next paint), 16
    interpreting report, 18
    lab testing
        Calibre, 26
        DebugBear, 26
        defined, 13-14
        DevTools Performance panel, 21-24
        JavaScript Profiler, 24
        Lighthouse, 19-20
        Puppeteer, 27
        SpeedCurve, 26
        third-party tools, 26-27
        WebPageTest, 24-26
        YellowLabTools, 26
    LCP (largest contentful paint), 15
    perception versus, 92
    performance budget setup, 33
    SI (speed index), 17
    TBT (total blocking time), 17
    text, streaming via AI, 209
    for third-party scripts
        AI-based scripts, 124
        inventory of scripts, 123
        with Lighthouse and DevTools, 124-125
        with WebPageTest, 125-127
    TTI (time to interactive), 17
    types of, 7-8
    UI components, streaming via AI, 213

micro-optimizations versus maintainability, 95
microtasks, 75-76
mobile devices
    constraints on, 101-102
    performance equity for, 8-9
Model Context Protocol (MCP) server, 63-64
monitoring
    backend performance, 113
    stall rates, 221
monkey-patching, 109
Moore's law, 102
MPAs (multipage applications), 162-164
multiplexing, 84
multiprocess architecture, 68

N

navigation process, 69
network
    constraints, 103-104
    resource loading and, 83-86
    streaming AI interfaces, 218-219
    streaming AI text, 211-212
Network Service process, 68, 83
network-aware loading, 147
news and media site case studies, 186-191
Next.js Script component, 158-161
Node.js event loop, 110
nonblocking scripts, 133-134
noncritical third-party scripts, 132

O

observability of streaming AI interfaces, 220-221
offloading (see sandboxing)
optimization
    AI limitations, 39
    AI-aided, 43, 61-64
    of AI-generated code, 42
        challenges in, 199-200
        React components, 56-61
    case studies (see case studies)
    of JavaScript backend, 111-113
    page loading timeline, 86-90
    testing, 64
    of third-party scripts
        AI and, 168-170
        ecommerce sites, 166-168
        framework-specific optimization, 158-162
    principles of, 127-129
    single-page versus multipage applications, 162-164
    tag managers, 164
    WordPress and CMS platforms, 164-166
trade-offs
    balancing metrics, 91-92
    in code splitting, 92-93
    framework usage, 94-95
    metrics versus perception, 92
    micro-optimizations versus maintainability, 95
    performance budget, 96
    with third-party scripts, 96
    when to stop, 97

P

page loading
    AI-generated React components
        optimizing, 56-61
        performance issues, 50-55
    blocking, 71
    event loop, 75
    loading third-party scripts after, 152
    network stack and, 83-86
    optimization timeline, 86-90
    preload scanner, 74
    RAIL model, 76-77
    rendering issues, 77-78
    rendering pipeline, 69-74
    server-side rendering, 80-83
    threads, types of, 68
painting, 70
parsing, 70
    JavaScript constraints on, 104-105
    moving off main thread, 108
partial hydration, 81
partial paint, 74
Partytown, 155-156
perceived speed of streaming AI text, 212
perception versus metrics, 92
performance
    AI-generated React components and, 50-55
    case studies (see case studies)
    optimizing (see optimization)
    rendering issues, 77-78
    third-party scripts, 119-121
    as user experience, 3
        equity in, 8-9

first impressions, 5-8
metrics (see metrics)
performance-first design, 10-12
performance budget
    defined, 11
    managing trade-offs, 96
    setup, 33
    text, streaming via AI, 210
    for third-party scripts, 128
performance culture
    AI and, 177-178
    champions of, 175-176
    performance as feature, 173-174
    team education, 174-175
    workflow integration, 176-177
performance marks, 220
performance profiling, 61-64
performance-first design, 10-12
positioning script tags, 132-133
preconnections, 135, 142
preload scanner, 74
prerendering, 86, 185-186, 198-199
prioritizing
    resources, 74, 85
    tasks, 78-80
    third-party scripts, 131-136
privacy and streaming AI interfaces, 222
profiling AI-generated code, 42
progressive enhancement, 11
progressive hydration, 82
psychology of waiting, 6
Puppeteer, 27

Q
Qwik, 82

R
rage clicks, 6
RAIL model, 10-11, 76-77
Rakuten 24 case study, 182-183
raster threads, 68, 74
Ray-Ban case study, 185-186
React, 161
React components (AI-generated)
    optimizing, 56-61
    performance issues, 50-55
real user monitoring (see RUM)
redBus case study, 192-193
rendering

backpressure, 218
incremental, 68
performance issues, 77-78
pipeline for, 69-74
prerendering, 86
server-side, 80-83
streaming AI text, 210-211
streaming UI components, 214-215
RenderingNG, 73-74
request blocking, 126
requestIdleCallback API, 151-152
resource hints, 84, 135
resources
    caching, 85
    loading, 83-86
    prioritizing, 74, 85
    scheduling, 85
response (in RAIL model), 10
response time, 3, 5-6
resumability, 82
route-based splitting, 53
RUM (real user monitoring), 14, 28, 31-33
    (see also field monitoring)

S
safety (of content) in streaming AI interfaces, 223
sandboxing third-party scripts
    defined, 155
    in iframes, 156-157
    server-side solutions, 157-158
    web workers and Partytown, 155-156
scheduling
    resources, 85
    streaming AI interfaces, 217
    tasks, 78-80
    third-party scripts
        after onload, 152
        breaking up tasks, 153-154
        on first interaction, 152-153
        idle until urgent pattern, 153
        requestIdleCallback API, 151-152
        setTimeout API, 154-155
Script component (Next.js), 158-161
script tags, positioning, 132-133
scripts and event loop, 75
scrolls, infinite, 215
selective hydration, 83
sequencing third-party scripts, 131-136

server-sent events (SSE), 211
server-side architecture
    streaming AI interfaces, 218-219
    third-party scripts, 157-158
server-side rendering (SSR), 80-83
service workers, 85, 158
setTimeout API, 154-155
Shopify Carpe case study, 184-185
Shopify case study, 200-201
Shopify Sunday Citizen case study, 184
SI (speed index), 17
single point of failure (SPOF) problem, 121, 127
single-page applications (SPAs), 162-164
slow loading, 52-54
slow start, 69
SPAs (single-page applications), 162-164
speculative loading, 86
speed (in user experience)
    first impressions and, 5-8
    perceived, 212
    psychology of waiting, 6
    response-time thresholds, 3, 5-6
speed index (SI), 17
SpeedCurve, 26
SPOF (single point of failure) problem, 121, 127
SSE (server-sent events), 211
SSR (server-side rendering), 80-83
stall rate, 209
stall rates, monitoring, 221
stream trace views, 221
streaming AI interfaces
    accessibility, 222
    antipatterns, 225
    checklist for production, 226-227
    CWVs and, 219-220
    design patterns, 224
    energy usage, 223
    internationalization, 222
    media content, 215-216
    network considerations, 218-219
    observability and debugging, 220-221
    privacy, 222
    responsiveness under load, 217
    safety and errors, 223
    text, 209-212
        metrics, 209
        network considerations, 211-212
        perceived speed, 212
        performance budgets, 210
        rendering, 210-211
    UI components, 213-215
        failure modes, 215
        metrics, 213
        rendering, 214, 215
    user experience and, 207-208
streaming compilation, 108
style calculation, 70
Sunday Citizen case study, 184
suspense reveal latency, 214

T

tag managers, 164
tasks
    breaking up, 153-154
    prioritizing, 78-80
    scheduling, 78-80
TBT (total blocking time), 17
team education in performance culture, 174-175
Telegraph Media Group case study, 186-187
testing
    AI-generated code, 42
    optimizations, 64
text, streaming via AI, 209-212
    metrics, 209
    network considerations, 211-212
    perceived speed, 212
    performance budgets, 210
    rendering, 210-211
text-to-speech (TTS), 216
thermal throttling, 102
third-party scripts
    defined, 117
    loading
        conditional loading, 145-148
        facades, 141-145
        lazy loading, 137-141
        sequencing and prioritizing, 131-136
    metrics
        AI-based scripts, 124
        inventory of scripts, 123
        with Lighthouse and DevTools, 124-125
        with WebPageTest, 125-127
    optimizing
        AI and, 168-170
        ecommerce sites, 166-168

framework-specific optimization, 158-162
principles of, 127-129
single-page versus multipage applications, 162-164
tag managers, 164
WordPress and CMS platforms, 164-166
performance issues, 119-121
sandboxing
   defined, 155
   in iframes, 156-157
   server-side solutions, 157-158
   web workers and Partytown, 155-156
scheduling
   after onload, 152
   breaking up tasks, 153-154
   on first interaction, 152-153
   idle until urgent pattern, 153
   requestIdleCallback API, 151-152
   setTimeout API, 154-155
trade-offs, 96
usage examples, 118
threads, types of, 68
time to first byte (TTFB), 209
time to first interactive island, 213
time to first meaningful component, 213
time to first token (TTFT), 209
time to interactive (TTI), 17
time to last token (TTLT), 209
time to useful token, 209
tokens per second (TPS), 209
total blocking time (TBT), 17
TPS (tokens per second), 209
trade-offs in optimization
   balancing metrics, 91-92
   in code splitting, 92-93
   framework usage, 94-95
   metrics versus perception, 92
   micro-optimizations versus maintainability, 95
   performance budget, 96
   with third-party scripts, 96
travel site case studies, 191-194
TTFB (time to first byte), 209
TTFT (time to first token), 209
TTI (time to interactive), 17
TTLT (time to last token), 209
TTS (text-to-speech), 216

U

UI commit latency, 209
UI components, streaming via AI, 213-215
   failure modes, 215
   metrics, 213
   rendering, 214-215
user experience (see UX)
UX (user experience)
   AI limitations, 40
   feedback loops, 55
   performance as, 3
      equity in, 8-9
      first impressions, 5-8
      metrics (see metrics)
      performance-first design, 10-12
   performance as feature, 173-174
   streaming AI interfaces and, 207-208

V

Vercel case study, 196-197
video generation, 216
Vodafone case study, 183
Vue, 161

W

waiting, psychology of, 6
Web Vitals JavaScript library, 14
web workers, 155-156
web-vitals.js library, 28-31
WebPageTest, 14, 24-26, 125-127
WebSockets, 212
WordPress, 164-166
worker threads, 68
workflow integration, performance in, 176-177
WPT (see WebPageTest)

Y

Yahoo! Japan News case study, 189-191
YellowLabTools, 26

About the Author

Addy Osmani is a longtime Googler and engineering leader at Google Cloud AI, focused on helping developers build high-impact, user-centric applications with Gemini, Vertex AI, and the broader AI platform. For nearly 14 years prior, he led performance, developer, and user-experience improvement efforts on the Chrome team, where his work helped influence how the web measures speed, prioritizes stability, and delivers responsive experiences at scale for billions of users worldwide.

Across both roles, Addy's work bridges deep platform insights with practical guidance for developers and technical leads. He's also the author of several O'Reilly titles, including *Leading Effective Engineering Teams* and *Beyond Vibe Coding*.

Colophon

The animal on the cover of *Web Performance Engineering in the Age of AI* is an English greyhound (*Canis lupus familiaris*).

The English greyhound, or simply greyhound, is a breed of domestic dog known for its remarkable speed, sleek build, and calm temperament. Originating thousands of years ago, with roots tracing back to ancient Egypt and later refined in England, the breed was historically used for hunting game such as deer and hare due to its exceptional sight and sprinting ability. Modern greyhounds are commonly associated with racing and lure coursing, but they are also beloved as gentle and affectionate companion animals.

Adults typically weigh between 60–70 pounds and can reach speeds of up to 45 miles per hour, making them one of the fastest land animals over short distances. Greyhounds are typically calm, quiet, and sociable with people and other dogs.

While the English greyhound is not an endangered breed, concerns have been raised over the welfare of racing these dogs, especially regarding treatment during and adoption after their racing careers. Many countries have enacted or proposed legislation to regulate or ban greyhound racing, and adoption programs have become instrumental in providing retired racers with loving homes.

Many of the animals on O'Reilly covers are endangered; all of them are important to the world.

The cover illustration is by José Marzan Jr., based on a black-and-white engraving from *Lydekker's Royal Natural History*. The series design is by Edie Freedman, Ellie Volckhausen, and Karen Montgomery. The cover fonts are Gilroy Semibold and Guardian Sans. The text font is Adobe Minion Pro; the heading font is Adobe Myriad Condensed; and the code font is Dalton Maag's Ubuntu Mono.

O'REILLY®

Learn from experts. Become one yourself.

60,000+ titles | Live events with experts | Role-based courses
Interactive learning | Certification preparation | Verifiable skills

Try the O'Reilly learning platform free for 10 days.

www.ingramcontent.com/pod-product-compliance
Lightning Source LLC
Chambersburg PA
CBHW062212220526
45471CB00009B/3176